Radicalism in Mediterranean France

RADICALISM
IN MEDITERRANEAN FRANCE

Its Rise and Decline, 1848-1914

by

Leo A. Loubère

STATE UNIVERSITY OF NEW YORK AT BUFFALO

State University of New York Press, Albany, 1974

Published with assistance from
the University Awards Committee
of State University of New York

Radicalism in Mediterranean France

First Edition

Published by State University of New York Press
99 Washington Avenue, Albany, New York 12210

Printed in the United States of America

Library of Congress Cataloging in Publication Data

Loubère, Leo A
    Radicalism in Mediterranean France: its rise and
decline, 1848-1914.

    Bibliography: p.
    1. Radicalism—Languedoc—History 2. Radicalism—
Provence—History 3. Radicalism—Roussillon, France
(Province)—History. I. Title.
HN440.R3L68   322.4'4'09448   73-171180
ISBN 0-87395-094-1

To my mother

CONTENTS

TABLES

MAPS

CHARTS

(Following page 132)

PREFACE

This book is an attempt to explain the transition of the lower South from domination by legitimists and Orleanists after 1815 to domination by Radicals and socialists after 1880. Some of the most dramatic episodes of this historical change occurred in mid-century, when it really had its beginnings. The 1848 revolution, which took most southerners by surprise, weakened for awhile the influence of conservative forces and made possible the emergence of a distinct left wing political movement. By 1849 it ran its own candidates in elections and won a few victories; in addition it mounted a determined opposition to the coup d'état of 1851 and won the prestige of a long list of martyrs. The left passed through a severe test, and although it emerged defeated, it had entered the political lists, found its leaders, won many converts, and now awaited future opportunities. These came in September 1870. The fall of Louis Napoleon hastened the transition by removing the governmental obstacles to its progress. Revolutions, then, were pivotal in this story, as they were in the national history of France, and they all began in Paris, not in the South.

However, these political upheavals, indispensable as they were to the process of change, are of less importance than the complex of local issues which provide a far superior explanation of change. One thesis of this book is that local rather than national issues were more important to the deep South. Revolutions in Paris changed governments, but local issues determined the nature and direction of the evolutionary process. Therefore the character and result of historical movements can best be examined and explained within the framework of the region.

The region here studied is the Mediterranean littoral. It consists of sections of three former provinces which were broken into departments during the 1790s: Roussillon (Pyrénées-Orientales), lower Languedoc (Aude, Hérault, Gard), and lower Provence (Bouches-du-Rhône, Var).[1] For purposes of analysis, I shall deal with the region on several levels. A broad geographic study reveals numerous subregions with distinct physical features that strongly conditioned and varied economic development and social structure. These features have nothing to do with arbitrarily drawn departmental boundaries; however, any description of political evolution must take these administrative units into account. On the other hand, no departmental voting population was a natural unit, and in order for regional history to be meaningful, it must penetrate into each department to examine the *arrondissements* and their constituent units, the cantons, and even the communes where feasible. The *arrondissement* became particularly important because its boundaries coincided with those of subprefectures, and many electoral battles turned upon the positions taken by local administrators who were all agents of the government in Paris. Of course, the department was usually the arena in which effective political organization was carried out; but again, departmental federations, especially those of the Radicals, were dependent on the willingness of cantonal and *arrondissement* notables to join forces. A regional study, therefore, can become more fruitful than a national one in that it can move among several levels of human activity within a geographic area and allow generalization about a population, smaller but more unified and uniform than the national one. Unified yet varied, the region is almost an ideal area in which to test long-accepted generalizations about national characteristics and to offer a few new ones.

Within the region, provided one enters deeply enough into the smaller areas, it is also possible to come closer to the true human experiences that make up the drama of history. This study does not concentrate on the hereditary leaders or elected rulers of the people, nor does it seek exclusively to generalize about large aggregates of men in their style of life and their habits of voting. Rather it attempts to explain

---

1. I have not included Alpes Maritimes because it was created only in 1860 and included a large Italian population.

those forces which strongly influenced the decision making and party preferences of large numbers of voters. To accomplish this end, I have found it necessary to bring into my narrative a large amount of detailed information. Perhaps some of my readers will complain of not seeing the forest for the trees, but I hope that my narrative and particularly my conclusions provide them with sufficiently large vistas and well-marked trails.

Detail, of course, can be frustrating in that an excess of it can obscure broad views. On the other hand, many small and seemingly unimportant local happenings had a greater influence on the lives of peasants and artisans than national and international events of which they were either unaware or only vaguely aware. The question is roughly this: should the historian look only at the crowds of the past as a faceless aggregate mass, or should he attempt a closer, more personal view. My method, I hope, falls somewhere in between generalization and particularization.

This study uses and attempts to combine four approaches to the study of man: history, electoral sociology, quantitative analysis, and human geography. It seeks to find those forces which induced voters to follow a particular tendency designated here as Radical. I use the capital "R" to distinguish this tendency and its adherents from other movements called radical because of the extremism of their doctrines. The Radicals formed the extreme nonsocialist left, if by socialism is meant the collective ownership of property rather than merely social reform. At mid-century the Radicals were the disciples of Jean-Jacques Rousseau and of the Jacobins of 1792-93. They formed part of a national movement that criticized laissez faire capitalism and high finance, defended the small producer, the artisan worker and the peasant, and favored political democracy, greater social equality, civil rights, and national liberation. Among the Radicals, whose typology is also part of this study, there were extremists and moderates, and the four approaches I use make it possible to examine types of politicians and types of electorates within their natural milieu over a given time span. The geographic, economic, social, and cultural influences on politics form the true material of this study. Therefore I have usually tended to emphasize impersonal factors such as topography, economic production, and social structure, and to define leadership in terms of these same factors.

On the other hand I have recognized the major role played by individuals in furthering or retarding the Radical movement, and I have willingly brought into my analyses the exceptions which disconcert system-makers.

This book does not offer a system to explain historical change. It attempts, rather, to bring out and analyze the kind of data that can provide insights into the dynamics of historical change. In particular it seeks to explain the rise and decline of the Radical movement by looking behind the external action of Radicals. In this way it hopes to discover the strange, often hidden nexus between politicians and voters and to explain both the style of the former and the behavior of the latter within a particular context. By and large my methods, even to the extensive use of detail, are those of several French scholars in the past two or three decades. The grandfather, or should I write the great-grandfather, of us all is André Siegfried. In addition, the numerous works written or edited by François Goguel have influenced my approach. However, I should state here that I do not consider myself a "Siegfriedian." I personally feel that Professor Siegfried as a pioneer was somewhat too deterministic in his explanations, that he did not sufficiently account for the accidental and the human element in collective political behavior.

To these historians and political scientists I owe a debt of gratitude for preparing the way. In particular I wish to thank Professors Robert Laurent of the University of Montpellier, Antoine Olivesi and Pierre Guiral of the University of Aix-Marseille, Ernest Labrousse and René Rémond for their advice and bibliographical suggestions. I wish also to express my gratitude to the directors of departmental archives: R. Debant (Aude), J. G. Gigot (Pyrénées-Orientales), M. Gouron (Hérault), J. -J. Letrait (Var), and M. Sablou (Gard), and to the directors of the municipal libraries in Perpignan, Carcassonne, Narbonne, Montpellier, Nîmes, Marseille, and Draguignan. To M. Jean Lecutiez of Arles, I owe a special acknowledgment for his assistance.

I also wish to acknowledge the contributions of students in my seminars over the past four years who have carried out research projects which provided data and insights for my own study: Paul Adams, Cornelia Dopkins, Laura Levine Frader, Anthony Novitsky, Wayne O'Sullivan, Linda and Sandra Perosa, Serafino Porcari, Chris Rounds, and Roy

Sandstrom. I owe a considerable debt of gratitude to Lawrence Glasco who introduced my students and me to the computer and to Paul Protzman, our pioneering programmer. I must admit, however, that my own reliance upon computer data is limited in this study. In part because I had already written the main outlines of the manuscript before embarking on the hectic career of a computerizer and most computerized results merely confirmed tabulations I had earlier made on my electric calculator; in part because my knowledge of computer science and of statistics is elementary, to say the least.

I am also indebted to Edmund Brown, James Graham, and Edward Fox who graciously read the manuscript in its early drafts and offered valuable counsel which enabled me to improve the final work. For the weaknesses and errors which still exist I alone am responsible.

I am also thankful to Mrs. Margaret A. Mirabelli who struggled with my awkward style in an heroic effort to improve it. But, alas, the days of miracles are over and I hope that the reader will find sufficient merit in the content of this book to pardon my shortcomings as a writer.

INTRODUCTION

A common expression in the lower Midi asserted that wine made the sun to shine and the clouds to rain. By "wine" was meant the producers' prices rather than the gastronomic quality of the beverage and, indeed, the skies looked bright when prices were high and gray when they were down.

And so it was with public opinion; in a remarkable alliance the fortunes of politics followed the graph line of wine prices. This correlation was inevitable in a wine culture. The deep South was a region in which both public and private life was dependent upon the flow of the fermented juice of grapes. In consequence, most of the important variables we can investigate in order to understand political evolution are dependent upon wine, or its opposite, nonwine.

Income, of course, was determined by the wine market, that of the growers and vineyard workers directly, that of the auxiliary population indirectly. Among the latter were the multitude of merchants and artisans who sold their wares to vintners, the professional men who provided services for them, the cafe and bar owners who created the convivial ambiance in which so much socializing took place, the transporters who carried wine to market, drinking much of it on the way, and the politicians and bureaucrats who made and administered the laws intended to foster viticulture.

Even farmers who did not produce marketable wine, and who provided fodder and food for the animals and people of the vineyard areas, were involved in the wine culture, and the volume of their sales depended also on the price of wine. Yet, the cereal producers and pasturalists, both confined to the high hills and mountains, were not truly

1

part of the wine culture as were other service people. They were, in a sense, outsiders whose way of life and temperament were distinct, the results of geographic isolation, a high degree of self-sufficiency, and the persistent attachment to cultural traditions, such as inherited religion and nobiliary authority, which winemen abandoned—or nearly abandoned—with unabashed rapidity.

Other variables deepened the division. Wine for the market was produced chiefly in the coastal plain and low hills. To this area it attracted upland population, especially the young, with the result that not only cultural values but also age separated uplanders and lowlanders. The latter, younger, more turbulent, more given to change, and open to new ideas about economic and social organization, displayed a left-wing temperament which intensified during and after each wine crisis. Wine production attracted also a sizable and fairly young foreign population, Italians in Provence, Spaniards in Roussillon and Languedoc. As many of these fellow Mediterraneans settled down and acquired citizenship, they added an additional youth group to the lowland population, and one that also revealed left-wing proclivities after a period of acclimation. They too were an uprooted people, furnished an important element of the vineyard labor force and almost naturally gravitated first toward Radicalism, later toward socialism. Population shifts, therefore, markedly influenced politics and provided a solid demographic base for the left. Cantons in which Radical candidates enjoyed a wide following were usually far more populous than highland cantons in which they did not.

Wine production also encouraged the urbanization of large numbers. Mediterranean departments were among the most urbanized in France outside of Paris and the Seine, and the ratio of urban to rural was highest in the vineyards. Now the voters of wine towns in particular, and of cities, showed a marked preference for the left. Radicalism as a movement found most of its leaders in coastal and valley towns, also many of its followers. It was less successful in the larger cities such as Montpellier and Nîmes which were under noble and bourgeois domination until the twentieth century, and in Marseille where the population turned to nationalist republicans or socialists. Marseille in this respect followed the lead of Paris which had been the major Radical stronghold until the 1890s. The Radical phenomenon as a form of social Jacobinism could hardly have found roots in the South had it not won a favorable reception among the small-town population of vineyard owners and workers, artisans and professional people.

Evidently the rise of the Radical movement was dependent upon another variable: the labor vote. Apart from several exceptions, vineyard workers and artisans tended to favor the left. What is notable is that the working classes, at least until the wine crisis of 1907, seemed to share relatively little of the class consciousness that developed rapidly among the industrial workers in France's textile and metallurgical centers. There were too many worker-owners in the rural labor force, and they, like most artisans, cooperated with middle-class groups to use politics in preference to labor unions to express their grievances.

The working class was complex in its composition, but so were all the classes mentioned above. Such descriptive general categories as middle class, wine-growers, or workers were not as highly unified or monolithic as they may appear. The details of the following chapters should make the reader aware of the highly varied social structure of the wine areas. Inevitably the response of many members of each class to the Radical movement differed. There were vineyard owners and their workers who were stoutly royalist or moderate republican, as were some artisans and professionals. The Radical movement itself stretched from moderates who called themselves Radicals to Radicals who insistently called themselves socialists.

All of these variables taken together created a particular situation which was favorable to change, and Radical politicians profited from it. While the success of several of them resulted as much from their ability and personality as from a favorable situation, it is hardly a cogent argument that the success of the Radical movement was somehow the creation of individual personality or that it was blindly secreted out by the pressures of environmental forces crushing upon one another. Large numbers of voters consciously chose Radicals and behind their choice was a catalyst which must be singled out. At this point wine production appears even more clearly. Like cotton in the southern United States, it was a monoculture and not only created a special form of society, it markedly conditioned the direction in which this society evolved. Unlike cotton, however, its direction was to the left.

Several social scientists have indicated that people living in wine-producing areas showed greater open-mindedness and receptivity to new ideals and change than those living under other forms of rural economy. Wine producers in the Vendée were more favorable to the Revolution of 1789 than other types of farmers.[1] In Ardèche and Côte d'Or departments, viticultural cantons were rapidly republicanized after 1870.[2] George Duveau also once made the observation that lowland wine-producing circumscriptions were more republican than highland cereal-producing ones. Unfortunately there does not exist a full-scale study of wine districts and politics, and therefore one hesitates to generalize about their relation. The data available—and it is very limited—does not indicate a high degree of positive correlation. The Southwest was not left wing either in the middle or later nineteenth century; the Radical party spread in some departments there, but only after 1900 when it occupied a more moderate place in the political spectrum. In Gironde, the truly great viticultural department of France, most wine producers, regardless of their status in the wine hierarchy, were conservative with a capital "C." In the regions of quality viticulture of the Loire Valley, Saumur and Vouvray, the small wine growers were consistently conservative. The same was true in Châteauneuf-du-Pape, a wine area in that most Radical of departments, Vaucluse. And so it was in the better growths of the Beaujolais. But then, the Mâconnais, just to the north, was radical since mid-nineteenth century. In Côte d'Or, moderate republicanism was as popular as Radicalism in wine cantons, and the Radicals were distressingly timid in the movement for social reform, In Marne, the center of the champagne district, moderates and conservatives won elections in the vine circumscriptions, Radicals elsewhere.[3] Perhaps the difference lies in the degree of quality. The vinegrowers of Gironde, Côte d'Or, and Champagne were of a different type from those of the lower Midi.

Vintners of the South were rather quick to bring their demands and frustrations into the arena of politics. The high rates of abstention notwithstanding, the southerner was a political man, passionately interested in politics and the art of electioneering. In fact, he was more skillful, more of an artisan, in politics than in the production of wine, and the connoisseur finds his politics more full bodied, of a deeper color, with a superior nose than his wine. But the two activities came together in the public mentality of the grower and worker because wine, regardless of its quality, was both a way and a source of life. The vintner produced for a market economy and was very heavily dependent on the condition of the market. Moreover, he differed from most other peasants in that he was generally not self-sustaining: vineyards became too valuable to be planted in other crops. He was heavily involved in a cash economy and therefore could not ignore governmental actions and laws affecting the two-way flow of cash, outward as tax payments and general costs, inward as profits and credit. Outward flow was fixed, but inward flow was determined by the wine market which depended on local, national, and international factors, tended to be unstable, and reacted profoundly to crises.

For these crises, the vintner blamed the government. He therefore politicized wine production, and did so less as a normal evolutionary process than in the form of sudden antigovernment tirades of a highly emotional nature. Since his whole way of life undermined tradition and his attachment to the status quo, he naturally turned to the left, to the movement advocating change, a "new deal" for the farmer and artisan in the shape of fiscal and credit reforms, of better market control, and cheaper transportation. After each major crisis, those of 1848–49, the 1870s–80s and 1901–7 came a notable shift to the left among large numbers of wine producers. Of course, many viticulturalists were not so inclined and supported moderate or conservative parties. They were found especially in areas not invaded by the vine-killing phylloxera until the 1880s or where viticulture was not the major crop but only a supplementary one. However, the great mass of them, and especially those with marginal enterprises immediately ruined by a crisis, revealed early the excitability in politics which characterized the lower Midi. Parisian mobs became tumultuous over Boulanger and Dreyfus; southern vintners, while certainly not immune to nationalism, went into the streets because of wine prices and glutted markets. And their demonstrations acquired a magnitude and vehemence which rivaled those of Parisian Boulangists.

This "situational interpretation," to use Berkhoffer's terminology, can be expanded.[4]   That is, the tendency toward the left can be seen as a by-product of the process of modernization in the wine industry. The first stage in the process occurred from the 1840s to the 1860s when production, simply by its rapid growth rather than by technical or organizational innovation, achieved unprecedented records. After the destruction of most vines by the phylloxera in the 1870s and 1880s came the second stage, which combined technical and capitalist innovation, but also the recovery of peasant production of a traditonally individualistic type. This phase coincided with the triumph of the Radical party. Then, after the crisis of 1900–7 when wine prices fell below costs came the third phase: capitalist production remained the same, but during this phase wine underwent the transition from peasant to cooperative production and marketing. Large numbers of peasants identified cooperation with socialism and were motivated to favor politicians of the newly organized SFIO or independent socialists. As before the South was in the forefront of France's political evolution.

The situation of the lower Midi of course was not so self-enclosed that the large movement of ideas in France was drowned in wine. The major planks of Radical electoral programs were drawn up by Parisian politicians—at least before their route in 1889—and firmly defended by southerners. The broad ideals of social reform meshed well with the legislative requirements of southern vintners and there is no reason to believe that they were more cynical or self-seeking than other pressure groups whose personal needs were identified with the progress of society. Winemen were neither heroes nor villains and their political movements must be understood as responses to their needs as they saw them.

These movements seemed extremist in the context of the rather sluggish economic and social evolution at the national level. Had voters in the West and western Center of France followed the example of the Midi, had these rural and small-town populations been as open-minded and market conscious as the southern vintners, France would probably have advanced ahead of England and Germany toward a welfare state. With the search for technical and organizational modernization in the wine economy came the desire for experiment in new forms of governmental and social relations. The move to socialism was the expression of a deep-felt desire to achieve that most modern of inventions: individual freedom and small ownership, on the one hand, and collective action and security, on the other.

Most southern socialists promised to bring this desire to fruition and in areas long dominated by Radicals they successfully identified with this rural form of modernism. They did not, of course, achieve collective ownership, and it is doubtful that most of them intended to do so. They were, for various reasons, "heated up" Radicals rather than revolutionaries, and this new type politician fitted in well with the southern temperament. The voting population demanded laws favoring wine interests and creating a social security system. These laws they eventually obtained, in piecemeal fashion. The Radicals had demanded as much, but they failed to retain their identity with reform as well as with the wine interests, which was necessary in viticultural districts. Their decline, therefore, resulted from their failure to master the latest wine crisis, and from the inability of their leaders, both at the local and national level, to exploit crises for the benefit of the Radical movement, as they had in the past. It was, finally, their misfortune to be part of the ruling party when the wine crisis attained its violent state in 1907, and they therefore were held responsible for the party's failures both to raise wine prices when general prices were on the rise and to carry through a program of general social reform which they had championed since the nineteenth century.

This book, then, is a study of the political evolution of the six Mediterranean departments of France, and its thesis holds that the major force behind this evolution is to be found in the economy and social structure of the region. To be sure, the existence of a "major force" does not exclude others. Historical evolution has rarely been so simplistic, save in historians' minds. Therefore, considerable space is devoted to the exceptional situations. In fact, one critic of this book when it was in manuscript accused its author of having prepared a short introduction consisting of grandiose generalizations, and then of having written a long book to display all the exceptions to them. The exceptions are numerous indeed and account for a good deal of the detailed analysis which can easily cause the reader to lose both the general trends and, alas, his interest in them. In the hope of avoiding this, it will be useful to offer the reader an overall view of the book's organization. The first three chapters deal with the society and economy of the lower South and with the origins of republican movements there. Chapters four and five explain the dynamics and instability of a predominantly viticultural economy, and chapter six seeks to correlate the impact of this economy on politics as displayed by the rise of Radicalism. The remaining chapters perform the same function, but for a later date, and probe for the causes of further evolution of the lower South away from Radicalism and toward socialism.

NOTES

1. See Charles Tilly, *The Vendée* (New York, 1967), chapters 1–3.
2. A. Siegfried, *Géographie électorale de l'Ardèche sous la IIIe République* (Paris, 1949); R. Long, *Les Elections législative en Côte d'Or* (Paris 1958) and R. Laurent, *Les Vignerons de la Côte d'Or au XIXe siècle* (Paris, 1958).
3. See J. Saillet and J. Girault, "Les Mouvements vignerons de champagne," *Le Mouvement social*, No. 67 (April–June 1969), 79–110.
4. See Robert F. Berkhoffer, Jr., *A Behavioral Approach to Historical Analysis* (N.Y., 1969), chapter 2.

CHAPTER ONE

THE SETTING, 1848

In 1815 the lower Midi was the scene of the White Terror and was dominated by legitimists; a century later it had made a full swing to the left and was dominated by Radicals and socialists. The dramatic beginning of this transformation came during mid-century when the Revolution of 1848 took most of provincial France by surprise. Among the political forces least prepared to take advantage of the situation created in Paris was the extreme left; yet within a year's time men calling themselves by the revolutionary name, *démocrates-socialistes,* won considerable support. Their activity initiated a new tradition that laid the basis of the broad transformation.

The Second Republic was the seed-time of the extreme left in the lower Midi. During the last decade of the July Monarchy, there had occured, chiefly in Paris, a division in the republican movement. The moderates gathered around the older journal, *Le National,* while the more advanced rallied to *La Réforme.* The latter found their leader in Alexandre Ledru-Rollin. There was not, either before or during 1848, a deep doctrinal difference between these factions. They stood for adult male suffrage, a unicameral legislature and weak executive, legal equality among all citizens, more social equality, and economic reform to be carried out through workers' cooperatives. The difference was one of emphasis rather than substance; the extreme left of *La Réforme* struck more heavily on social equality, cooperation, tax reform to relieve the lower classes, and easy credit for small peasants eager to own land. With a sense of militancy it referred to itself as *républicain et démocrate.* It was a late derivative of the Jacobin party of 1793, more specifically of the Mountain, and in this book it shall often be labeled as either Jacobin or Mountain.

The focal center of the entire left was Paris. There were also left wing

9

OPPOSITE:

LOWER SOUTH, TOPOGRAPHY

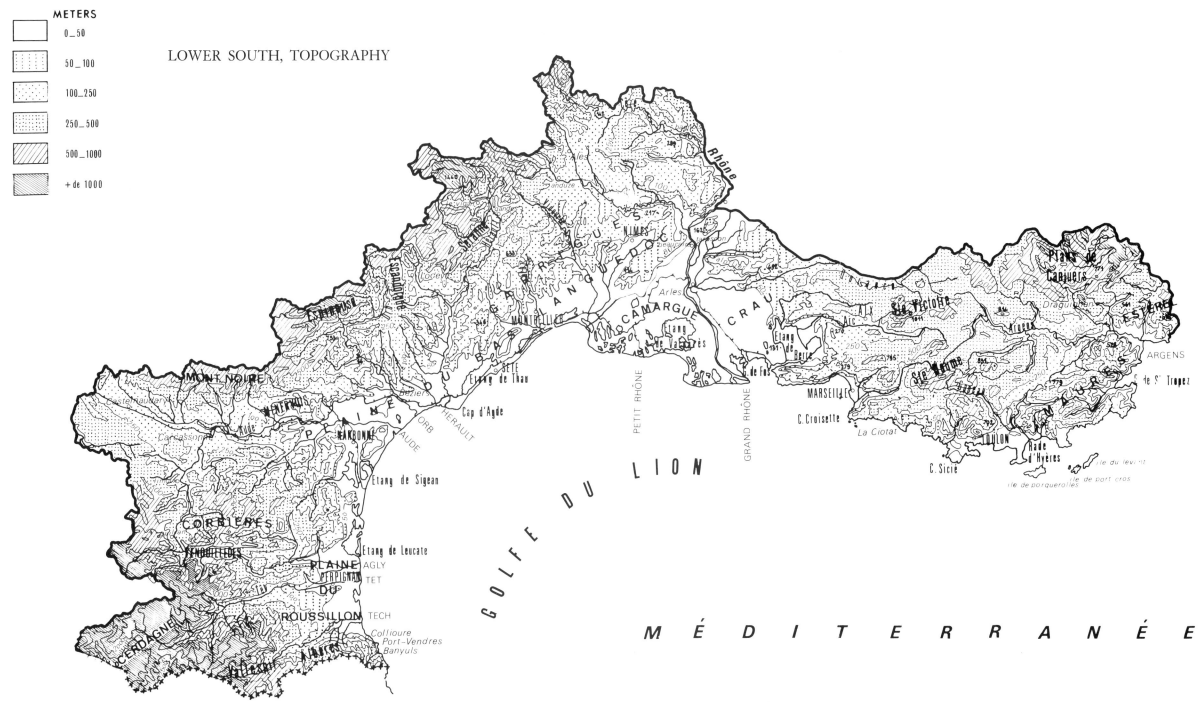

LOWER SOUTH, TOPOGRAPHY

METERS

0_50
50_100
100_250
250_500
500_1000
+ de 1000

GOLFE DU LION

MÉDITERRANÉE

MONT NOIRE
MINERVOIS
NARBONNE
CORBIERES
FENOUILLEDES
PLAINE DU ROUSSILLON
CERDAGNE
ALBERES
Etang de Sigean
Etang de Leucate
AGLY
TET
TECH
Collioure
Port-Vendres
Banyuls
Carcassonne
Castelnaudary
Aude

BAS LANGUEDOC
Espinouse
Escandorgue
Lodève
Béziers
ORB
HERAULT
AUDE
Cap d'Agde
SETE
Etang de Thau
MONTPELLIER

CEVENNES
GARRIGUES
NIMES
Anduze
Rhône

CAMARGUE
Arles
Etang de Vaccarès
PETIT RHÔNE
GRAND RHÔNE
G. de Fos

CRAU
AIX
Ste Victoire
Etang de Berre
MARSEILLE
C. Croisette
La Ciotat
C. Sicié
Ste Beaume
TOULON
Rade d'Hyères
île du levant
île de port cros
île de porquerolles

Plans de Canjuers
Draguignan
ESTEREL
ARGENS
G. de St Tropez
MAURES

Echelle 1/1250 000

oppositional forces in several provincial areas where opinion made their existence possible. That Paris was a center of discontent is not difficult to explain; rather, the major task for the historian is to discover why and how the extreme left gained followers outside of the capital. Everywhere in France there were militants during mid-century; their numerical strength, however, varied considerably. Clearly there existed forces and conditions, challenges if you will, which aided or frustrated their ambitions. This chapter and the next is an attempt to analyze the relation between men and their environment, that is, the interaction between the will of men and their background of economic, social, and cultural forces; my aim is to discover how this interplay led to the emergence of the extreme left in mid-nineteenth century.[1]

ROUSSILLON AND LOWER LANGUEDOC

The old provinces of Roussillon and lower Languedoc had been divided into four departments during the 1790s; Pyrénées-Orientales, Aude, Hérault, and Gard. These administrative divisions notwithstanding, the entire region formed a geographic and economic whole with sufficient uniformity and variety to allow of meaningful analysis and comparison. Uniformity resulted from the predominantly agricultural economy. The greater part of the population lived on the land and the conditions, needs, and produce of the soil largely determined political attitudes and social position. In consequence these latter varied rather closely with the topography. Since each department was formed around an important river, whence the names of three of them, they were both riparian and thalassic; river valleys and the sea coast conditioned life in them. So did the geographic and economic zones which, following the coastline, cut across administrative-political boundaries.

The coastal plain formed a belt from about two miles to twenty or more in width where it faded into the major river valleys. The lower portion of the plain consisted of white sandy beaches stretching from the Rhône estuary to the high cliffs of the Albères mountains. The blue sea and bright sand, today the delight of vacationers, gave way to pine scrub, greenish and burned by the salt-laden wind, to variegated bushes and weeds, and to marshes and ponds (étangs) cut off from the sea by narrow necks of sand. Such a place was sparsely populated and little used until mid-century when its soil, inhospitable to other crops, was planted in vines. This change to vineyards involved considerable investment and introduced capitalist agricultural techniques. That these changes came slowly was due to scarcity of investment capital and lack of adequate, cheap transport. The transformation, later hastened by the wine crisis of the 1870s, was really just beginning in the 1830s and 1840s. Yet it had already produced a notable modification of the social structure: the proportion of vineyard day laborers began to grow, outnumbering owners in some communes by four to one, and everywhere forming an important if not always numerically dominant segment of the adult population.[2] Certain river valleys were also areas of labor concentration because of the appearance of capitalist vineyards. Of course it is important not to exaggerate the size and force of this landless proletariat. Combined with it were many peasant laborers who owned land (albeit insufficient to live on), and many self-employed farmers who relied on the labor of their immediate families. Its compactness therefore varied from commune to commune and from canton to canton.

Small and medium farms were more numerous in the zone of green, gently rising hills which came after the plain. They served as a counterforce to the large estates owned by nobles who often lived in nearby towns and cities. Here, cereals usually occupied as much acreage as vines, sometimes more, and almost always the better land. The vineyards, considerably older, represented a vast amount of labor carried on by generations of land-owning peasant families who were as deep-rooted in the soil as the vines and whose whole outlook was dominated by daily and seasonal routines centuries old.[3] In the thin, rocky soil of this zone, especially in the eastern part of it called the Garrigues, the production of raw silk was the chief cash crop. In Gard silk was more profitable than wine.[4] In Hérault, polyculture was also the rule, but silk gave way to raw wool in the high hills which stretched westward into the Minervois of Aude. Raw wool was also an income-producing product in the upper Gard Valley and in the hills surrounding the Plain of Roussillon.

The division of land had been in process and many peasants either owned or sharecropped a small farm. They grew most of the things they required to fulfill their simple and extremely frugal lives. And, without doubt, they would have been quite cut off from the outer world had they not spent their winters producing silk and woolen goods which they sold for cash. In addition, they usually worked part time on the lands of wealthy owners who lived in the lowlands.

The part of the Cévennes lying in the northern extremity of Gard and Hérault and the Montagne Noire of Aude made up much of the mountain zone. These mountains, modest in height, were really high hills and plateaux cut by streams. Sharp, deep valleys made travel difficult and encouraged isolation. Here the peasants lived in high valleys, tenaciously terraced the steep slopes to grow cereals and chestnuts, cultivated silk worms in Gard and reared sheep in Hérault, and in off seasons found temporary employment as woodsmen in the spare forests or as stone cutters in quarries or as miners in local coal and iron mines. Cut off from the outside, uneducated, and traditionalistic, they were passive and submissive in outlook.[5] In the Corbières, the Mountain zone of Aude, whose barren peaks stretch into northeastern Pyrénées-Orientales where they meet the rugged Fenouillèdes, life resembled that of the Cévennes. And yet, peasant attitudes, as will be shown later, were markedly different: more republican, open to new ideas, *frondeur* even. The same was true of rural inhabitants in the Albères mountains and, to a lesser extent, the Pyrenees areas of Vallespir, Cerdagne, and Capcir in the upper Tet Valley. Perhaps the presence of a fairly large number of vineyard workers in the Corbières and the lower Fenouillèdes, and of woodsmen in the Pyrenees, contributed to the difference, for both suffered severely from the economic crisis of 1847-49. Their loss of purchase power seriously affected industry.

Historically, industry was a normal complement to agriculture since most of it was devoted to making wool and silk cloth, the distillation of wine into alcohol, the crushing of olives into oil, or the milling of grain. By mid-nineteenth century, however, textiles were already in a state of decline. Entrepreneurship and capital were turning to large-scale wine production, but as yet on a modest basis.

In mid-century various types of industrial productive centers were scattered widely.[6] By far, textiles were the chief employers of non-agricultural labor and the most lucrative. Woolen and some cotton textiles existed near the larger waterways: Limoux and Chalabre in Aude; Saint-Pons, Riols, Bédarieux, Lodève, Clermont, and Saint-Chinion in Hérault, and Sommières in Gard. Woolen textiles were located principally in the hills where water power was available. Since there were few steam engines, industry suffered during the summer when rivers became streamlets. Then many workers went off to labor in the fields. The reverse occurred in winter when unoccupied farmers and field-hands supplemented their incomes with domestic spinning and weaving. But this industry, which offered a livelihood to so many workers and peasants, suffered from another drawback: its dependency upon orders from the Ministry of War. After a brief period of prosperity in 1848–50, textiles withered and unemployment grew because the ministry turned to northern producers of military cloth.

The eastern sector of lower Languedoc was a leading center of silk textiles. Spinning and weaving were located in a zone stretching from Ganges and Le Vigan in the high hills, eastward to Alès (formerly Alais), then southward to Nîmes. Gard ranked third, after Paris and Lyon. There were more steam engines and a greater concentration of labor in the communes of Alès and Nîmes than elsewhere. In Nîmes there were 157 mills each employing more than twenty workers, and roughly two-thirds of this labor force was male.[7] Yet there, as nearly everywhere else, the domestic system prevailed. It was, of course, used in the many hamlets isolated in hills and mountains, where peasants spent their winter months spinning and weaving for money, the only money they would see until harvest time in the vineyards when they would flock to the low hills and plains to work as grape pickers.

Other industries were, as yet, less important. Shipping was largely confined to alcohol and wine carried in small boats using the little harbors of decayed ports. The influence of the sea was largely confined to the weather conditions which produced the climate favorable to wine production. In the only port of any consequence, Sète (formerly Cette), there were some small boat yards, a foundry employing about 400 workers, and numerous petty crafts dependent on the export of wine, such as cooperage. Only in the mountain districts of Camplong, in Hérault, and the northern Alès *arrondissement*, in Gard, were there sizable accumulations of non-textile labor. Here coal and iron mining were developing, and there was some metallurgy. Lack of adequate transport hindered their rapid growth until the Second Empire. But already the Alès basin was third largest in France, utilizing over 2,000 miners and several hundred iron workers in numerous communes north of the town of Alès. In the town itself, there were several hundred men employed in metallurgy.[8] There were small mining operations in scattered areas and some metal production using *forges catalanes*, in the Corbières, and in the Pyrenees from Ria, near Prades, southward to Arles-sur-Tech. These activities satisfied local needs, used wagons and muleback for transport, and hired local peasants for seasonal operations. The census of 1851 listed 452 miners for 21 employers and 125 metal workers for 26 employers in Pyrénées-Orientales.

The structure of society reflected this economy. A rural population constituted its base; however, this rural element consisted of several categories. *Propriétaires-cultivateurs* owned land sufficient in acreage to provide them a livelihood (six or more hectares of vineyards, and thirty or more hectares of cereals or pasturage). They were to be found everywhere. Tenants and sharecroppers, more than half of whom owned some land, made up only a small percentage of the social category with patronal rights. They were to be found chiefly in the hill and mountain zones. Most arable land in the lower Midi was farmed either by owners and their families or by hired laborers. *Journaliers* or day laborers either outnumbered their employers or equaled them in number in many communes of the plains. In the lower hill cantons, and especially in lower fertile river valleys, they formed a sizable minority. Their numbers diminished sharply in the upper hills and mountains where large estates were confined to a few communes devoted to cereals and pasturage.

In Gard, land was more divided, with the result that *journaliers* amounted to only one-half of the owners. In Pyrénées-Orientales, land division was also pronounced, largely as a result of rugged topography and the yet underdeveloped vineyards of the plain. If the 1851 census is more or less accurate, male *journaliers* equalled about 39 percent of the male farming population. Most were located in the Plain of Roussillon and the valleys of the Agly, Tet, and Tech. However, the ideal of proprietorship was dominant in the Midi and further reinforced by large numbers of *journaliers-propriétaires,* roughly one-third of all day laborers in Gard and one-half in Pyrénées-Orientales. They did not possess enough land for a livelihood and had to supplement their meagre incomes by hiring themselves out as fieldhands, chiefly in vineyards. Therefore, they were to be found predominantly in the plain and Rhône valley. Some lived also in the highlands of Gard where they cultivated a small plot of mulberry trees with the aid of which they produced raw silk which their women spun into thread. In Hérault, with its larger acreage devoted to vineyards, land was less divided, therefore *journaliers* outnumbered *propriétaires* by several thousand. Yet, at least one-third of them were part owners and often shared an outlook similar to that of full owners. This similarity would be particularly pronounced as regards fiscal policy, credit, irrigation, and transport. The social structure of Aude is more difficult to define because of the lacunae in its archives. On the basis of information scattered in police reports and the press, it is evident that there was a large rural proletariat in the plain, especially in Narbonne canton, and a predominance of small and medium-sized farms along the Aude Valley and in the Corbières.

In the Corbières and Pyrenees an important element of the labor force consisted of woodsmen, a social group of only minor size in the Cévennes which stand bare and stark, covered often with scrub and other bushes able to live in pockets of thin soil. The Corbières and to a lesser extent the Cévennes and Pyrenees included many small farmers who had traditionally made use of publicly owned pasturage and forests. The July Monarchy had encouraged either the sale or rental of this property to individuals, thereby excluding the marginal peasants from what they considered their historic rights. This situation aroused the anger of many peasants, and drove them to riot several times both before and shortly after the February Revolution.[9]

The owners of estates and the employers of most rural workers were nobles or well-to-do bourgeois, who were either legitimists or Orleanists. Active industrialists and merchants also inclined toward parliamentary monarchy and Protestantism. Some well-to-do bourgeois, however, were militant democrats who became leaders of the extreme left. Generally they were landlords or wine producers and economically independent.

Far more important for our study are the intermediate urban classes: the middling and petty bourgeois of tradesmen and professionals. It is essential to bear in mind that before modern communication appeared life was centered in cantonal capitals or larger communes, for the big city was impossibly far away (between Toulouse and Marseille there were no big cities). Even a small locality's social structure, therefore, was complex. Each town had a population of farmers, so there was rarely a sharp distinction between town and country. It also had its complement of medical doctor, pharmacist, notary, justice of the peace, small and medium merchants, clerks, artisans, and cafe owners who were numerous in the hills and plains.

Much of the daily activity and political interests involving local affairs were centered in the cafe. In nearly every cantonal center there were several, one for each political nuance. They were often the headquarters of political clubs and in several instances the owner was the organizer and head. Each cafe subscribed to newspapers desired by its clientele. Only in larger towns were there cafes which offered a variety of journals.[10] The cafe was, above all, a link between town and country; on market days peasants gathered there and listened to republican propaganda spread by a free thinking doctor or pharmacist, an ideological lawyer or notary who might or might not have political ambitions. Their activities made of the cafe the hostile counterpart of the parish church where the *curé* spread legitimist ideals.

The public house was the gathering place of another social group whose role in the growth of the extreme left was paramount: the artisans. Their role was particularly brought to light during the trials before mixed commissions after the coup d'état of 1851. Small town shoemakers, carpenters, masons, plasterers, stone cutters, tailors, locksmiths, coopers, and tanners usually made up the cadres of extreme democratic societies and were active propagandists among the peasants. In larger communes the directing heads were of the middle class, yet it was chiefly the artisans, allied with the local grocer, butcher, distiller, and other petty bourgeois who began the political education of the peasants. Many had traveled to learn their craft, were literate and open to new ideas. They were far more active than most of the industrial workers, who were native hill people, often illiterate and, in many cases, followed conservative leadership. Not all artisans, not even a large majority of them in every town, turned to extreme or even to moderate republicanism. Those who lived in towns of 1,000 to 3,000 in population went to work in the fields part of the year and were frequently under the tutelage of conservative rural authorities upon whom they were partly or wholly dependent.[11] This dependency, which the workers acknowledged by accepting charity from the upper classes, probably increased during periods of depression.

In 1847–49 the economy of lower Languedoc and Roussillon was in serious trouble, as was that of nearly all of France. Naturally public opinion, as best it can be discerned, reacted sharply to harsh times.[12] Without fail, local notables and workers complained of the depression. The petty industry widely dispersed over the area, especially in the zone of hills, was depressed by the collapse of local markets, its main outlet. The decline of wages, balanced by a serious decline of prices, was not a great calamity for the workers; they suffered rather from mass layoffs. Without wages they could not purchase the wares and services of other artisans who were equally distressed. Worse, they did not even have field labor to fall back on. Agriculture was crushed by bad weather and a shocking fall of prices; cereals could not be sold at a profit and were hurt by foreign competition.[13] Small wonder that the hill and mountain cereal growers clamored for tariff protection and condemned the extreme left, as well as economic liberals, who favored free trade. On the other hand, wine interests in the lower hills and plain clamored for free trade as the price of wine in 1849 fell to its lowest level in twenty years. Most Midi table wine was distilled into alcohol and exported to other parts of France and especially to foreign countries. The free access to foreign markets seemed essential.[14] Inferior wine not distilled was sold to the lower classes in the region. Local and foreign sales of quality wine and alcohol were difficult, however, because all alcoholic beverages were heavily taxed, both nationally and locally. Hence the importance of the fiscal issue in local politics. Silk, which rivaled wine in Gard, also suffered from the late freeze of 1848 which dried up mulberry leaves.[15] Finally, numerous small merchants were adversely affected, since they sold to the local population. Opinion was extremely pessimistic in 1848 and continued so into 1849. Such pessimism was also widespread in Provence.

LOWER LANGUEDOC

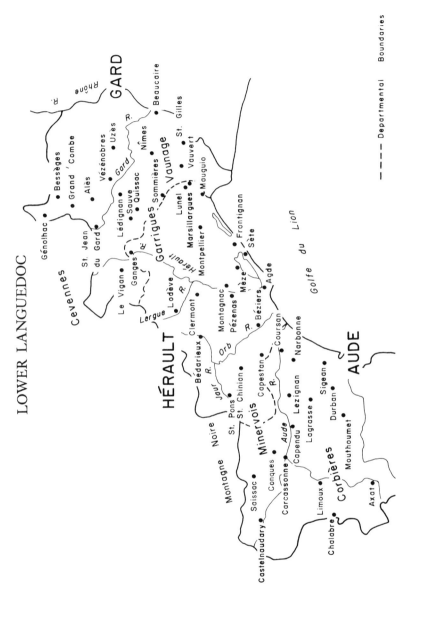

- - - - Departmental   Boundaries

LOWER PROVENCE

- - - - DEPARTMENTAL BOUNDARY

Rhône

Durance R.

Beaucaire
Tarascon
Châteaurenard
Alpilles
Organ
Fontvieille
Eyguières
Arles
Salon
CRAU
Lambesc
CAMARGUE
Istres
Fos
Pt. de Bouc
Golfe de Fos
Golfe du Lion
Etang de Berre
Barre
Martigues
Touloubre R.
Durance R.
Verdon R.
Artuby R.
Verdon R.
Plans de Canjuers
Camps
Fayance
ESTEREL
Fréjus
St. Raphaël
Le Muy
Draguignan
Aups
Salarnes
Argens R.
Massif des Maures
Grimaud
St. Tropez
Le Luc
Besse
VAR
Callobrières
Cuers
Solliès-Pont
Riens
Tavernes
Mgne. Ste. Victoire
Aix
Arc R.
Fuveau
Gréasque
Trets
Roquevaire
Allauch
Aubagne
Marseille
Ste. Bôme de la Chaîne
Huveaune R.
Brignois
Gapeau R.
Le Beausset
Ollioules
Toulon
Hyères
La Seyne
Bandol
La Clotat
BOUCHES-DU-RHÔNE
Mer Méditerranée

PROVENCE

Provence in its topography offers the historian the beauty of its landscape and the challenge of its variety. There are no long stretches of
coastal plain as in Languedoc and Roussillon. The *arrondissement* of Arles
forms a transition: it consists of the vast delta of the Rhône River as well
as the lower valley. (For the locations of *arrondissements,* see map 5.)
It is flat for miles, the bottom portion consisting of large swamplands
which are called the Camargue, and a vast stony area called the Crau.
Its flatness is broken only by the Chaine des Alpilles, arid hills rising to a
thousand feet at their highest. The southern part is so sparsely populated
that the canton of Arles is, in area, the largest in France. To escape the
uninviting Camargue, the bulk of the population settled northward
of the town of Arles, along the Rhône and Durance valleys. The rest
of lower Provence stretches east between the Alps and the Mediterranean.
Even a quick glance at a topographical map makes clear that the land is
more uneven: there are no definite zones as in Languedoc; lower Provence, east of Arles, is rather an area of hills, low mountains, and fertile
valleys. As might be expected, the population tended to crowd into
valleys and therefore was rather highly concentrated in towns and
villages. Only in the flat lands north and east of Arles was there a scattered population, often living in isolation on homesteads, a habitation
pattern that was exceptional. In Bouches-du-Rhône most people lived
in 106 communes, which were generally small; three-fourths of these
communes had under 2,000 people concentrated in a town or village,
hence were rural according to the census bureau. Larger centers of inland
population were located in valleys: around Aix, Brignoles, and Draguignan and in the long, narrow plain arching northward from Toulon,
through Cuers to the Argens estuary.

Outside of Arles *arrondissement,* the small rivers which had cut these
valleys were an important determinant of population locus, provided
that the valleys were wide enough for civilized life. Local rivers often
cut only narrow valleys useful for communication but not wide enough
to provide agricultural space for the highland population. So in
Provence, as in Languedoc, hillsides were laboriously terraced, especially
for the cultivation of olive trees. Life was hard and monotonous, and

land was too scarce for sizable families. Therefore younger persons began to move away, especially after the severe crisis of mid-century. Highland cantons west of the Rhône suffered a similar exodus; in Provence, however, the paths of emigration did not spread as widely over the coast; they centered rather on the road to Paris and especially on the roads to Marseille and Toulon. Both the departments of Bouches-du-Rhône and Var experienced the phenomenon of sizable coastal cities looming large over sparsely populated hinterlands.

The coast of Provence combined clusters of hills and low mountains, and flat stretches where towns grew at the expense of the rural hinterland. In addition to the larger municipalities mentioned above, there were industrial centers and ports: La Ciotat, La Seyne, and Hyères. These were rather medium-sized towns lying at the feet of high hills. Even more diminutive were centers of commercial fishing such as Saint Tropez and Saint Raphaël. Unlike the people of Languedoc and Roussillon, the coastal population of Provence in mid-nineteenth century was not spread out on large vineyards, but concentrated in relatively isolated communes; because of the rugged terrain, which reached into the sea as high cliffs, communication among them was easier by sea than by land. The seacoast in Provence resembled the mountains in Languedoc: it was populated, outside of the port cities, by a sturdy, rural folk, widely scattered; these people remained conservative and traditionalistic save in the area of Toulon and Saint Raphaël. In fact, the people of the mountains in the northern part of the departments were more receptive to republican ideas than those of the coast. Fishing was hardly a progressive factor in the life of the *méridional*.

The rural economy of lower Provence was somewhat more mixed than that of Languedoc. In both areas there was a strong desire to preserve the local food supply, therefore cereals were grown everywhere even in soils not suited to cereal production and without irrigation. Given the poor soil of much of Provence and the arid climate, agriculture offered not more than a moderate profit when limited to cereal production. Low yield was the fate of Aix *arrondissement* and most of Var north of the plain of Cuers. Yet Aix was, along with Arles, the granary for the southeast. Arles, more suitably located, had the lowest acreage and the highest productivity and produced three-fourths of Bouches-du-Rhône's total crop.[16] In Var, cereals were grown chiefly in the northern and northwestern cantons of Brignoles *arrondissement:* Brignoles, Saint-Maximin, Tavernes, etc. Save in Saint-Maximin with its large estates and their labor force, land was highly divided.

But throughout Provence the great land divider was wine, although this was less true in mid-nineteenth century than later. Until the improvement of transport by means of railroads, wine, like cereals, was produced chiefly for the local market. Most of it was of mediocre quality, similar to that of Languedoc, therefore the amount which could not be sold was distilled into alcohol for export. And once again as in Languedoc, wine was an important cash crop, along with olives. Marseille *arrondissement*, poor in cereals, was the chief producer of wine grapes before 1830. Steadily it gave ground to Aix, the major producer, and even to Arles in later years of the century. The focal point of wine was Aix whose acreage and total production equalled that of its two neighboring *arrondissements.* Vines were also widespread in Var. They were a fundamental part of the economy in the lower area of Brignoles and in the Toulonnais, and in the plain of Cuers.[17]

Of course, this description is based on the statistics available, and they reflect the general unwillingness of Provençals to rely heavily on one crop. Agriculture was literally mixed, that is, vines and olives were usually planted together on terraced hillsides, and rows of vines often alternated with rows of wheat or corn or barley. Under such a system the productivity of vines was quite limited (4 to 7 hectolitres per hectare) because olive or other fruit trees cut off the sunlight and absorbed much of the nutriment from the soil. Not until the phylloxera crisis of the 1870s was this multiple-planting system abandoned.[18] Given the lack of transport and the resulting production for small markets, there was not much incentive to change planting techniques in order to expand production. Moreover peasant growers were often illiterate and traditionalistic, especially in the northern cantons bordering on the Alps; they lacked capital and fertilizer, neglected fodder crops, and persisted in the use of the fallow-land system.[19] More advanced techniques and specialization were found chiefly near port cities. Here, truck gardening was encouraged as these cities grew, and better grades of wine were produced for export. Marseille, Toulon, and Bandol (Ollioules canton) were stimulants.

The highly mixed agriculture made for a more uniform and complicated social structure: uniform in that monoculture was somewhat less important and peasant farmers grew vines, cereals, olives, fruit and vegetables as a hedge against the failure of any one of these crops. The social structure was more complicated than that of Languedoc by the presence of many tenants and sharecroppers. In Bouches-du-Rhône the rural population was remarkably evenly divided between land owners (*propriétaires cultivateurs*), tenants and sharecroppers, and day laborers; each category had about 16,000 males.[20] This was an exceptionally large number of tenants and sharecroppers, however, those owning some land totaled about one-half the number of independent proprietors. These categories, of course, cannot be rigidly fixed, and the data of the 1851 census leave much to be desired. They provide an idea of general socio-economic groupings rather than precise totals. Moreover, many of the *journaliers* were land owners, as they often were west of the Rhône.

Property and ownership was even more widespread in Var. Quite similar to the department of Gard, it was an important area of silk production, and raw silk, accompanied by domestic spinning and some weaving, provided additional resources which peasants directed toward land purchase. In Var, peasant ownership was several centuries old, originating in the nobles' grant of freedom and land in return for several feudal dues. When the National Convention abolished these dues in 1793-94, the peasants acquired full proprietorship.[21] Undoubtedly the peasants of Var owed much to the Conventionals, and a republican tradition persisted in many rural cantons, as we shall see. These owners made up the bulk of the active rural population: there were 32,380 of them. In contrast there were only 14,049 *journaliers,* about one-third of whom were *journaliers-propriétaires.*[22] Full time workers were located chiefly in Brignoles and in the western sector of Toulon *arrondissments.* Here vineyards were large, capitalized, and in need of labor. Tenants were more than double the sharecroppers but a small minority in the total population. As in Languedoc, most land was farmed directly by the owner or under his supervision. This social structure, then, was that of an area whose people were devoted to wine production. Annually, mountain people came into lower Provence for the *vendange* or the grape harvest, but, as in Languedoc, they were not politically important until a decade or more later, when they came permanently. As in Languedoc, native wine growers scorned them for their crudeness, and assimilation had a long way to go.

Another social group, important in Var, were the *bûcherons,* (woodsmen and cork gatherers), who lived in the towns and villages of the Maures and Esterel mountains. Like their counterparts west of the Rhône those of Var were politically knowledgeable. The mountains were neither high nor isolated from propagandists, rather they were similar to the lower Corbières in Aude, and there was even a combination of forest and vineyards, which encouraged left-wing leanings. Woodsmen of Var also acquired a keener sense of class, perhaps as a result of deteriorating industrial relations; their employers were often former workers struggling to succeed and unsympathetic to social reform. Therefore *bûcherons* early turned to political radicalism, and later, when such activity was closed to them by the Second Empire, they resorted to strikes.[23]   Their pattern of life, the discipline imposed on them, the routine, led them to resemble industrial more than rural workers.

Full-time industrial workers were not numerous in lower Provence. As in Languedoc, industry of consequence was located near or on the coast, especially in ports: Marseille for soap, sugar refining, and chemicals, La Ciotat and La Seyne for metallurgy and shipbuilding, Toulon for its naval yards. Inland, there was a sizable concentration of textile and chemical workers at Aix and several hundred miners in and around the northern sector of Roquevaire canton. The census of 1851 listed 2,100 miners for Bouches-du-Rhône, only 96 for Var. As in Languedoc and Roussillon, manufacturing meant chiefly petty artisanal activity, and it was widespread.[24] In consequence, the pattern of life of artisans in Provence was quite similar to that west of the Rhône. The floating element of the population existed mainly along the coast. Not only artisans, but lignite miners as well, owned or rented land which they cultivated, possessed homes, were quite stable and devoted to family life.

This pattern of life was seriously affected by the economic crisis of mid-century. However, lower Provence was spared its full impact until 1849 when it proved to be especially severe.[25]   There appears to have been more hardship in Bouches-du-Rhône than in Var.   In the western sector of Provence much of the coastal industry, the cereals of Arles, and the wine of Aix were for export.   These producers depended on cash income to buy food.   Var, on the other hand, was like Aude: it was too backward to suffer severely in its standards because they were low.   However, it reacted quite differently in its politics from both Aude and Bouches-du-Rhône.   For the people of the latter departments, the crisis was temporary and patience was needed.   The form of government was not a primary factor in its functioning to aid both urban and rural producers.   For many people of Var, however, the crisis brought despair of the present and hope in the future.   Therefore decisive political action was needed to make fundamental changes, and only a republic could undertake such action.   These differences, quite marked in 1849, had already begun to emerge during the previous year.   Hence the different receptions of the February revolution.

NOTES

1. For the entire coast see, Paul Barrère and Raymond Dugrand, *La Région Méditerranéenne* (Paris, 1960).   For the lower Languedoc see Raymond Dugrand, *Villes et campagnes en Bas-Languedoc*, (Paris 1963).   Dugrand does not include all of Aude; however, I have included it because it constitutes a political unit, and given the prominence of the Aude Valley, an economic unit as well.   For Roussillon, see Bernard Alart, *Géographie historique des Pyrénées-Orientales* (Perpignan, 1859). For Provence, L. Pierrein and P. Guiral, *Les Bouches-du-Rhône* (Grenoble, 1945), and P. Masson, ed., *Les Bouches-du-Rhône, encyclopédie départementale* (Marseille, 1913–29), [C.] N. Noyon, *Statistique du département du Var* (Draguignan, 1846).

2. See the manuscript copies of *Recensement de* 1851, unclassified in Archives Départementales, Hérault and Pyrénées-Orientales; 1OM 138 in A.D. Gard; missing in Aude. The manuscript census is far more valuable than the published census returns which do not give statistics for communes, but only for the entire department, as regards the professions of the population.

3. Cereals were certainly important in the hills, as was pasturage in areas near textile centers.   However, wine was a major cash crop and even in cantons where vineyards occupied a relatively limited acreage, it made the difference between well-being and

scarcity. See the reports in France. Assemblée Constituante, 1848–49, *Enquête sur le travail agricole et industriel*...1848, in Archives Nationales, C946, 953, 954.

4. B. Chauzit, "Monographie agricole du...Gard," *Bulletin du Ministère de l'Agriculture*, 17 (1898), 1529 ff.; L. Destremx de St. Christol, *Agriculture Meridionnal : Le Gard et l'Ardèche* (Paris, 1867),), 37 ff.; Gustave Coste, "L'Etat de l'agriculture dans le départment du Gard vers 1835, *Mémoires de L'Académie de Nîmes*, VIIe série, 42 (1924–25) pp. xlv–li.

5. H. Martin, "Coup d'état dans l'Hérault, 1851", Unpublished *Diplôme d'Etudes Supérieurs*, University of Montpellier, n.d., 6–15. R. Bertrand, "L'Evolution économique et sociale d'une commune viticole de l'Hérault," (Law Thesis, University of Montpellier, 1950), 8–16.

6. Precise information about the location of industry is difficult to obtain. Some detailed statistics, not always reliable, can be found in the manuscript copies of *Recensement de 1851* and in, France. Bureau de la Statistique Générale, *Statistique de la France: Indu - trie:* (Paris, 1847–52), vol. II.

7. H. Rivoire, *Statistique du département du Gard* (Nîmes, 1842), II, 53; H. Reboul, *L'Industrie nîmoise du tissage au XIXe siècle* (Montpellier, 1914), 110 ff.; Pierre Gorlier, *Le Vigan* (Montpellier, 1955), 310–21.

8. France. Bureau de la Statistique Général, *Statistique de la France : Industrie,* vol. II, *passim,* and *Recensement de 1851*, A.D. Gard 1OM 138. For Hérault, the labor statistics of the census (1851) are of least value: Employers and workers are lumped together, and the totals are unreliable.

9. See A. Soboul, "La question paysanne en 1848," *La Pensée, revue du rationalisme moderne,* nos. 18, 19, 20 (1948), 55–66, 25–37, 48–56; "Des troubles agraires de 1848," 1848 *et les révolutions du XIXe siècle,* 39 (1949), 1–20, 39–61.

10. A.D. Hérault 39M 128. Numerous police reports complain that workers spent too much time and money in public houses. For the continuing importance of cafes see Michel Augé-Laribé, *Le Problème agraire du socialisme* (Paris, 1907), 266–67.

11. See Emile Appolis, "Lodève," *Cahiers d'histoire et d'archéologie,* (Nîmes, 1936), 22–24; F. Teisserenc, *Industrie lainière dans l'Hérault* (Paris, 1908), 31 ff.

12. The *Enquête* of 1848 leaves much to be desired as a document for narrowly defined economic history. But in this essay concerned with the relation between social structure and politics, the *Enquête* is most valuable, indeed, comparable to the *Cahiers des doléances* of 1789. The impact of the crisis on people's thinking can be measured in a general way by studying certain parts of the questionnaires filled out by local notables, and sometimes by workers.

13. In Aude, wheat prices between 1849–50 suffered their lowest decline since 1825–29. See G. Barbut, *Historique de la culture des céréales dans l'Aude de 1785 à 1900* (Carcassonne, 1900), 36–37.

14. The report from Béziers in the *Enquête* explained, "Les douanes sont au commerce ce que l'esclavage est à la civilisation." Until the improvement of transport, the Midi could more easily and cheaply export its alcohol to other parts of the world than to the north of France.

15. Destremx de St. Christol, *Agriculture méridionale,* 53.

16. P. Masson, ed., *Bouches-du-Rhône, encyclopédie départementale,* 7/435 ff. An important source for economic information.

17. A.D. Var 14M 29–1, "Statistiques agricoles."

18. Yves Masurel, *La Vigne dans la basse-provence orientale* (Gap, 1967), 19–20.

19. C. Noyon, 546; Y. Goirand, "Histoire économique et politique du Var, 1848–70," DES, Aix-Marseille, 1955, 10; *Bouches-du-Rhône, Encyclopédie départementale,* 7, 444–45.

20. A.D. Bouches-du-Rhône 10M 1–25, census of 1851.
21. Noyon, 193, 543–44.
22. A.D. Var 11M 2–1, Census of 1851.
23. E. Constant, "Les Conflits sociaux dans le Var sous le second Empire," *Actes du 83ème congrès national des Sociétés Savantes* (1958), 545–50. M. Agulhon, *La République au village* (Paris, 1970), chap.4.
24. A.D. Bouches-du-Rhône 10M 1–24; A.D. Var 11M 2–1; Noyon, 636. France. Bureau de la Statistique Générale, *Industrie*, II, *passim*.
25. See the chapters by P. Guiral and M. Agulhon in E. Labrousse, ed., *Aspects de la crise...de l'économie française...*1846–51 (La Roche-sur-Yon, 1956).

CHAPTER TWO

EMERGENCE OF THE EXTREME LEFT, 1848-1849

SECOND REPUBLIC IN THE SOUTH

The Second Republic provided the national context in which the republican movement came back to life. Almost dormant since 1841, republicans of all shades took up the cry for electoral and parliamentary reform during 1847 and organized a series of banquets where prominent leaders toasted the beauties of political freedom and legal equality. Some speech-makers, representing the extreme left, even called for economic reform and social equality, the extent of which remained obscure in their rhetoric. However it was not their rhetoric that brought about the February revolution, but a desperate government effort to prevent a banquet scheduled to be held in Paris. The overthrow of the July Monarchy was a Parisian affair, and news of it provoked varying reactions in the provinces.

The lower Midi was taken aback, if the local press truly reflected opinion; but no one sought to defend the fallen regime. Its southern opponents, both legitimists and republicans, were jubilant. Neither would have turned to violence to achieve their aims, but that had been done for them by the republicans of the capital. Suddenly everyone became "republican," a term so vague — and therefore so popular — that it was taken up by nearly all aspirants to political office. For the moment, however, moderate republicans dominated local political activity and the opposition press. The sobriquet "radical" had appeared earlier but was never used widely after February.[1] The April 1848 election turned into a marked victory for old-line republicans and for those monarchists who now asserted that they, too, favored a republic capable of preserving order and peace. These republicans were remarkably successful in economically backward departments: Pyrénées-Orientales,

29

Aude, and Var. Their success resulted from aggressive action by local men who immediately seized such centers of power as prefectures and subprefectures, and their take over was more easily accomplished in the smaller towns, Perpignan, Carcassonne, Limoux, Narbonne, Béziers, Draguignan, than in the larger ones, Montpellier, Nîmes, Toulon, and Marseille. These larger communes, albeit more decidedly urban in character and important centers of the left-wing press, did not play the dominant political role that one would expect. Moderate men captured control of them and moderation was the keynote of the commissaires sent out from Paris to govern the departments until new elections.

The department of Bouches-du-Rhône was hardly influenced by its capital, and the events in the city followed their own way. Neither were inclined toward republicanism, whether moderate or Radical, and Marseille had only one left-wing journal, *Le Progrès social,* directed by Antoine Agenon, who was in jail when the February revolution freed him. He immediately tried to take over the city government but failed.[2] Upon the arrival of the new commissaire, Emile Ollivier, *Le Progrès social* became his quasi-official organ. Indeed, it had the rather unpleasant task of urging the turbulent port workers not to beat up Italians who competed for jobs.[3] The journal lived up to its title, however, and was decidedly pro-worker, at least until May. It propagandized a theme that became axiomatic with the emerging extreme left: the "classes moyennes" had captured power and profited from the Revolution of 1789. Since then, they had excluded the people of lower classes from power and social betterment. Now the time had arrived for the people to end this monopoly of power and share in the benefits of social progress. The new revolution, in consequence, must have as its goal more than political change, it must actively seek economic and social reform.[4] In accord with all advanced republicans, Agenon insisted on the purging of both the administration and judiciary as a first step. He expected much from Emile Ollivier, his former pupil in political ideology, and organized a march on the prefecture in Marseille. Ollivier, however, not only rejected his demands, he charmed the crowd with oratory *à la Lamartine* and urged an alliance of all classes. The extreme left now grew distrustful of the new commissaire, especially after they did so poorly in the April elections.[5]   Agenon and his followers tightened the organization they had created for the elections; at its head was a Comité Central Républicain, presided over by Agenon; nearly all trades were represented in it.

The political situation in Marseille deteriorated. Workers complained of the public works program, a form of National Workshop, when their wage dropped from 2 francs 50 to 2 francs, and of the long work day, twelve hours. They assembled at the Prefecture to demand a ten-hour day, as in Paris. Ollivier was unable to appease them, and Agenon was noncommittal. Frustrated they resorted to barricades. This uprising of 22–23 June was brief and suppressed after but limited fighting. It ended at about the same time that the June Days began in Paris. But since it was quickly put down and brought about far fewer arrests, it did not stifle the left; rather, it had the effect of bringing into political action a good many artisans who now became the social base of the extreme left.[6]   In the size and energy of its labor force, Marseille was exceptional; the rest of the department remained tranquil, as did all of Provence. The June episode in Marseille marked an end of left-wing activism, not the beginning, in most communes.

The department of Var prior to 1848 was as conservative as its western neighbor. It had a deep-rooted monarchist tradition and the workers in the naval yards of Toulon, much like the dock workers in Marseille — or in Sète — were fairly conservative and Catholic.[7]   When they resorted to strikes the local clergy often served as mediators. Apparently the major radicalizing force came in with workers drawn to the naval base during its expansion after France's invasion of Algeria. With them came the ideal of modern trade unionism which conflicted with older ideals of compagnonnage and paternalism.[8]   However, these changes came slowly and most workers seemed little concerned with politics. Var as a department had remained loyal to the July Monarchy. There are not even traces in Provence of a Carlist-republican coalition to oppose Louis-Philippe, a fairly common phenomenon in several cities of Languedoc and Roussillon. Without doubt, a large part of Var's population showed early an enduring characteristic: indifference to politics. The subprefect of Toulon noted it on the eve of the February revolution.[9] We shall note it often in later decades.

Since abstention was more prevalent in towns, where the lower classes were not yet highly active in politics, the republican movement began as a moderate one. The early clubs which appeared in towns were favorable to Ollivier's program of class reconciliation. Only in Toulon were there left-wing clubs—at any rate, three placed the word "radical" in their title.[10]   Opinion, however, leaned toward "la République des honnêtes gens."[11]   Moderates won the April elections easily, and neither the insurgencies of 15 May in Paris or of June in Marseille and Paris disturbed the calm. The only note of alarm was the beginning of an economic crisis in the shipyards.[12]

Elsewhere in the Midi all these events led to the frustration of advanced republicans after the June Days. To emphasize their opposition to General Eugene Cavaignac, who crushed the revolt in Paris, they began to call themselves Montagnards. Their clubs, once open to the public, became secret societies to escape new laws aimed at repressing free assembly. Their contact with the broader public was carried out through their press. In Montpellier, an ardent journalist, Louis Auriol, founded *Le Montagnard du Midi* and set up Montagnard societies. In Carcassonne, the Jacobin *Fraternité*, edited by Theodore Marcou, replaced the moderate *Républicain de l'Aude* during September. Its program was typical of the Mountain: free, public secular education, economic co-operation which it called "solidarisme," the right to work, a progressive income tax, property for everyone, and the abolition of usury. It warned that if Louis Napoleon won the presidential elections and then threatened the Republic, "Insurrection would become the most sacred of duties."[13]

Jacobins now emerged as a distinct republican force. With them came a new style of campaign for the December presidential elections; it was fervent, even physically violent when street fighting became necessary, and centered in banquets where Robespierre and Saint-Just were toasted amidst shouts of "vive la guillotine."[14]   All this occurred in halls or fields decorated with red and tricolor flags and banners, phrygian caps and busts of Marianne. When the guests had exhausted their stock of food, wine, and words, they formed into a long cortege and marched through the streets with flags waving and drums beating.[15]   At times the police intervened and on several occasions mounted police charged with sabres drawn. Then the demonstrators let go a salvo of stones before taking to their heels. This oppositional impulse was uncompromising toward General Cavaignac "the butcher." In consequence, the moderate press distrusted and decided to ignore it.[16] However, the dynamic character of the extreme left must be underlined. The age of its most active militants was relatively low, in the twenties and thirties; and although a majority of them had families they sacrificed even their jobs for the cause. Often their wives and even their children participated in the more festive programs such as planting liberty trees and crowning them with phrygian caps, or serenading a local hero or dancing the farandole in long serpentine columns, or just plain mischief which police reports refer to as "tapage nocturne." This, the "human element," would play a decisive role in subsequent events.

For the presidential elections three candidates came forward representing three important political and social trends.[18] Ledru-Rollin stood for popular sovereignty and more social equality; Cavaignac led the moderate republicans who were strongly devoted to male suffrage, and just as strongly opposed to social reforms based on governmental action; Louis Napoleon Bonaparte was the favorite of conservatives who hoped to use him to effect a restoration of monarchy and of social order. In line with most of France, Languedoc and Roussillon preferred Louis Napoleon, but Roussillon differed in that it put Ledru-Rollin ahead of Cavaignac. Provence, on the other hand, preferred the general and wavered between Ledru-Rollin and Louis Napoleon. In the lower South the leader of the Mountain came out with an average of 14–15 percent of the registered voters, roughly 10 percent above his national average. He was weakest in Aude (10 percent) and in Var (12 percent), and, in reality, in Bouches-du-Rhône where some of his backing came from legitimists in Châteaurenard and Arles where Bonapartists were even more hated than in Marseille.[19]

The main rask of Radicals, especially in Aude and Provence, was to expand into rural areas. To be sure, the population of Provence was more urbanized than that of Languedoc, according to the definition of the census bureau: 2,000 or more persons *agglomérées* or concentrated in the town. But such a town, if relatively isolated as many were in the rugged terrain of Var and Bouches-du-Rhône, was less open to new ideas than were smaller communes, officially classed as rural, in the coastal plain west of the Rhône. In this sense, Provence in mid-nineteenth century, excluding Marseille and Toulon, was less truly urban than Languedoc. In Hérault, the twelve largest towns gave Ledru-Rollin 70 percent of his vote. Throughout eastern Languedoc and Roussillon his important urban vote was fairly spread out over each department because no one town overshadowed all the others. But Provence was dominated by cities. In Var, he received 25 percent of his vote from Toulon, and another quarter of it from the next ten largest towns, not all of which were urban in the strict sense. His support was even more concentrated in Bouches-du-Rhône where he received well over 50 percent of his votes from Marseille.

From February through December 1848 the extreme left had not yet made significant advances into the countryside. The peasant population continued to favor conservatives and, at best, moderate republicans, and followed, therefore, the general trend throughout France. Radicals, as yet, were unable to seize upon local issues or to come forward as local men, "fils du pays," even though most of them were southerners. In the eyes of southern peasants, any kind of extremist program appeared a "foreign" innovation, an import from the North, from Paris, not even written or verbally presented in the local dialect, the only language most of the rural folk could understand. The great need of the Radicals, therefore, was to find local recruits among the lower classes and to utilize issues that made sense to the rural and urban masses. That they went about this task seriously and with some success becomes apparent during 1849. They were aided by the worsening economic situation throughout the Midi.

Between April 1848 and May 1849, as the prices of wheat and wine dropped further, the republican press revealed a growing concern about fiscal and social reform. Especially after the June Days, it became more critical of the social conservatism of the government. A major complaint was the drink tax, another, even more pressing, was unemployment among vineyard workers. In early 1848, people in the Midi grew increasingly hostile to a fiscal system which, in their volatile opinion, drained the South to benefit the North. Violence occurred in some areas in the form of antifiscal riots. Local tax collectors were threatened with lynching and their offices set on fire to destroy records.[20] Chiefly after the election of Louis Napoleon, the republican press found it convenient to attack the government's tax system, and there was a marked swing toward Radicalism among all these journals which were published in distressed wine centers. In their columns the wine issue became inextricably bound up with the social question, because the low grade alcohol and wine of the Midi were consumed by the lower classes. Unfair levies deprived the poor of their *boisson hygiénique*. The nectar of Bacchus had already become a source of poetic inspiration to the extreme left: "La vigne est l'emblême cardinal d'amitié. C'est le plus pur produit des amours de la terre et du soleil. Le vin est le lait des vieillards, le consolateur des affligés, le soutien des faibles, le viatique des forts."[21] Not long before its end, the Constituent Assembly had voted the repeal of the drink tax, effective as of January 1850. However, when a consumers' tax replaced it wine producers complained that only middle men and winestore owners would benefit.

Of course, conservatives also represented wine interests and called for the abolition of the taxes which still weighed on alcohol: *droits réunis, droits d'entrée* and especially the *octrois*.[22] If only to compete, then, republicans took a more advanced position on taxes, and therefore, in the Midi, moderate republicanism was destroyed in 1849–50, not only by the rise of political reaction, which provoked extremism, but also by the violently fought out tax issue. As the republican press became Radical it came out in favor of a progressive income tax, the nightmare of moderates and conservatives. In addition, it called upon the men in power to recover the "milliard des émigrés" and to use this sum to reimburse all peasants who had paid the forty-five centime tax.[23] All Montagnard journals now initiated a petition to effect this return, a common tactic in Midi departments which reveals the level of unified action and planning achieved since 1848.[24]

The extreme left also recognized the need for a state more active in social and economic life. Since the economic crisis continued in 1849, they called for legislation on hours and insisted that the right to work be officially recognized. Since this right would necessitate additional expenditure in the form of public works, they demanded that the state nationalize certain monopolies such as railroads, insurance, and finance. Above all they demanded cheap credit for peasants' and workers' cooperatives. The *Fraternité* of Carcassonne was the most "socialisant" and revealed the influence of Barbès and Louis Blanc. However, it was really Jacobin and hoped to encourage land partitioning (*morcellement*) as a solution to the peasants' problem: land purchase would be fostered by cheap long-term credit. It even advocated the emission of paper money based on land, which was reminiscent of *assignats*. Whose land was not made clear; presumably the property still in church hands. Part of its general program was also the abolition of usury, as pointed out already. However, none of these latter-day Jacobins called for the abolition of debts, as had some of Louis Napoleon's electoral agents in 1848. Had they done so, the debt-burdened peasants might have reacted differently, since Louis Napoleon had not carried out his promises. Ideally, the journals wanted greater emphasis on equality and fraternity. Their inspiration, they claimed, was the social gospel of Christianity and the ideal of the family as a social unit whose members are bound together by love.[25] Finally the Radical left called for a broad extension of public education. In the questionnaires of the *Enquête,* local notables had shown some concern for education but surprisingly little for professional training, which was seriously lacking in the Midi, as it was in France. Radicals were emphatic on the need for free, secular schooling which would include greater emphasis on professional training, especially in agriculture.

This was the extreme left's program for the 1849 elections, and to emphasize its extremism it entered the contest referring to itself as "*démocrate-socialiste.*"

The elections of May 1849 marked the high point of the Mountain in France. In most departments, and especially in the Midi, the Rhône and Saône valleys, and the Parisian basin, extreme left militants consciously sought to profit from the political pressures and economic distress which crushed the middle republicans. Moderation no longer offered an effective defense against attacks on republican ideals; the government severely restricted freedom of speech and assembly, it repudiated social reform, and did nothing to relieve the suffering resulting from unemployment and low wages, and—most cynically—it abandoned the most cherished aim among left-wingers, national liberation. When Louis Napoleon prepared to send troops against the Roman Republic, moderate republicanism was doomed, as was its creation, the Second Republic. The May elections hastened the abandonment of the parliamentary middle as public opinion tended to back the president.

Consequently the elections of May 1849 marked a serious defeat for the socialist-democrats whose immediate future became sombre indeed. However, they made it possible for the extreme left to win an identity, distinct from that of mere republicanism, to discover its ideology and to win its eventual victory with the establishment of the Third Republic when the defeated leaders of 1848—51 reappeared and won power. Of course, in the short-run, division in republican ranks, where it occurred, contributed to electoral losses.

ELECTORAL SOCIOLOGY, 1849: ROUSSILLON AND LANGUEDOC

The elections of May 1849 offer a confusing picture of success and failure for the extreme left. Neither in France nor in the lower South is there a single factor which, by itself, explains the outcome. Even in the Mediterranean departments the electoral map reveals a lack of uniformity and a clearly discernible pattern. National issues did not sufficiently penetrate the coastal area to make for greater uniformity. Even though Ledru-Rollin, a national figure, ran in three departments (Hérault, Gard, and Var) and won in two of them, local issues predominated and well-known candidates carried the victories. Domocrats won only eight seats (Ledru-Rollin won twice) out of thirty-two for the Mediterranean departments. These eight could hardly make an impressive showing among some two hundred socialist-democrats in the Legislative Assembly, most of whom came from the bastions of the left: Paris, the Rhône and Saône valleys, and the Center. Of our six departments, merely three returned socialist-democrats. The observer living in 1849 was not likely to predict a brilliant future for the left, and yet, by the 1880s and 1890s Mediterranean France accounted for nearly a quarter of all Radicals and held first place in the list of their strongholds. Clearly then, the roots of the movement in the South must be sought in an earlier phase, the Second Republic, when it first emerged. What were the factors, already existing, that promoted its later triumph? Our study begins with a brief description of the electoral results in the six departments. In each the results were partly influenced by the ability of local politicians, first to preserve unity among reform forces, and secondly to campaign effectively under conditions seriously hindering unified support. There were also impersonal or environmental factors which bore upon politics and these deserve detailed investigation. Their importance, unlike that of individual politicians, was more enduring and will be weighed accordingly.

TABLE 1: ELECTORAL RESULTS MAY 1849 OF RADICALS

Department	Political color of the slate	% of Registered voters	% of Ballots	% of Abstention
Pyrénées-Orientales	Moderate and Radical	45	67	31
Aude	Radical	33	43	25
Hérault	Radical	27	30	33
Gard	6 Radicals only	13	18	26
	with 2 Moderates on Radical slate	15		
Bouches-Du-Rhône	Moderate and Radical	34	46	24
Var	Moderate and Radical	25	42	40
	5 Radicals only	26	43	

In Pyrénées-Orientales, division among republicans did not occur. Moderate and Radical republicans faded into each other, and differences were never brought up for discussion. Therefore, Pierre Lefranc, Jacobin, and Theodore Guiter, neo-Jacobin, ran on the slate with the Arago brothers, Emmanuel and François, moderates with left-wing pretentions. This list had been highly successful in 1848 and literally ran away with the election. They received more than double the votes of the monarchists and won every canton save Mont Louis, high in the Pyrenees, where Guiter received only a fraction of the ballots won by his list and pulled its average down.[26]   Guiter had not even left Paris to campaign! Clearly, Roussillon was strongly republican and would remain so. The success of Radicals, however, would depend on their continued support by the miraculous Aragos. Later, when division would occur, they would suffer decline.

The split in republican forces weakened the movement in Languedoc, where there were no candidates comparable to the Aragos. In Aude the

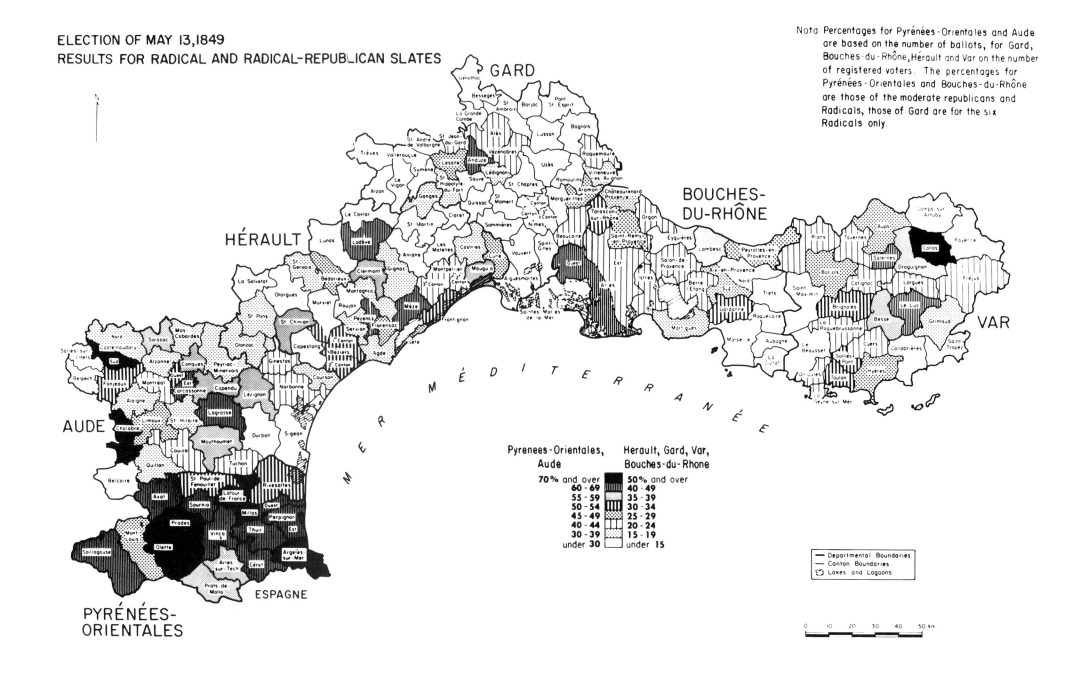

ELECTION OF MAY 13,1849
RESULTS FOR RADICAL AND RADICAL-REPUBLICAN SLATES

Nota: Percentages for Pyrénées-Orientales and Aude
are based on the number of ballots, for Gard,
Bouches-du-Rhône, Hérault and Var on the number
of registered voters. The percentages for
Pyrénées-Orientales and Bouches-du-Rhône
are those of the moderate republicans and
Radicals, those of Gard are for the six
Radicals only.

GARD

BOUCHES-
DU-RHÔNE

HÉRAULT

VAR

AUDE

MER MÉDITERRANÉE

PYRÉNÉES-
ORIENTALES

ESPAGNE

Pyrenees-Orientales, Aude	Herault, Gard, Var, Bouches-du-Rhone
70% and over	50% and over
60 - 69	40 - 49
55 - 59	35 - 39
50 - 54	30 - 34
45 - 49	25 - 29
40 - 44	20 - 24
30 - 39	15 - 19
under 30	under 15

Departmental Boundaries
Canton Boundaries
Lakes and Lagoons

0   10   20   30   40   50 km

Opposite:

Election of May 13, 1849
Results for Radical and Radical-Republican Slates

Radical slate, headed by the folk hero Armand Barbès and supported by the *Fraternité* suffered a decline since April 1848. The average vote for the entire 1849 list was 29,838; for the victorious conservatives, 36,000. Considering only averages, the loss was not disastrous. And, significantly, the voters in 1849 voted for the list rather than for individual candidates as they had done in 1848, when the range of the republican slate had extended from 53,308 to 11,029. The defeat, moreover, was promising for the future. On the basis of its program the Moutain won 43 percent of the ballots cast and 33 percent of the registered voters. Abstention equaled nearly 25 percent, an indication that many constitutionalists decided to support the right. Moderate republicanism was crushed; there was no moderate slate. The voters had chosen between red and black.

In Hérault, republicans were given a choice between moderates and socialist-democrats whose list was headed by Ledru-Rollin and Jacques Brives. They turned to the extreme left massively. In December 1848 Ledru-Rollin had received only 11,580 votes; he now won 31,202. The Radical slate now averaged 27,600 votes as compared to 31,700 for republicans of various colors in 1848. The combined averages for the Radicals and moderates in 1849 revealed that republicanism was able to hold its own since the previous year. More significant was the leftward shift of republican sentiment, despite extensive pressure by the administration in favor of conservatives. Radicals had campaigned militantly and both Brives and Ledru-Rollin won seats, despite the fact that their slate received only 30 percent of the ballots, and 27 percent of the registered voters. Since they were included on the moderate slate, they pulled ahead of fellow Jacobins to win. Abstention equaled 33 percent, a severe blow for moderates.

In Gard, the extreme left was weakened by internal feuds between Jules Cazot and the doctrinaire extremists of the Club Martin *cadet* headed by Pierre Encontre. While they all distinguished themselves from moderates, they nonetheless included on their list two of the best known ones: A. Bousquet and Jacques Favand. Ledru-Rollin was the only Radical with more than a local reputation, hence he was included on the moderate list as well. His prestige, which weighed heavily in Hérault, was far less valuable in Gard. The Radical slate, excluding

Bousquet and Favand, averaged only 16,323; including them, it averaged 19,000. No republican candidate was elected and even had all republicans united, their combined total was roughly 5,000 votes short of that of the conservatives. The eastern part of lower Languedoc had almost returned to its royalist tradition.

The emergence of the extreme left as a distinct political movement was a major result of the 1849 elections. This emergence was solidly based on the republican alliance in Pyrénées-Orientales, dramatic but limited in Aude and Hérault, weakened by divisions in Gard. Here was a curious situation because in 1851 and after 1870 this pattern reversed itself. Hérault remained pivotal, but initiative passed from Aude to Gard. An explanation of this phenomenon is essential to our understanding of a century-long process by which lower Languedoc (and the Mediterranean coast) passed from royalism to Radical-Socialism.

Several factors must be considered. First there was the environmental factor combining geography, economy, and social structure. Then, against this background came into play the human factor, the will of men to achieve political success. At times it overcame a hostile environment as in Saissac canton (Aude), at times it failed to exploit a friendly one, as in Vauvert canton (Gard). The human factor is a disturbing one in our analysis, not only because it is often unpredictable, but because it was influenced by the cultural factor combining religion and tradition. Since human actions were not always merely unconscious or automatic responses to physical environment, generalization is both difficult and hazardous. Nonetheless it is necessary if we are to understand the process of change.[27]

Let us begin our analysis with the topography of Languedoc and Roussillon and bring under scrutiny several feasible generalizations. First, people of the coastal plain were far more receptive to the extreme left than those of the high hills and mountains where ways of life were hostile to change. Even the peasants of the lowlands were almost a different breed, and certainly of a different culture, from their counterparts in the highlands. Of course, Soboul has ably demonstrated that peasant farmers in the mountains were not mere passive beasts, that they could protest and, indeed, did so with considerable violence.[28] However, the point to note is that their insurgency, which was sporadic, was directed usually against innovation, against the alienation of communal grazing and forest land on which they depended. They would or could not use the land efficiently nor would they allow others to do so. And this violence did not usually result in political innovation; rather, its perpetrators supported the conservative slate in 1848–49. They did not differ from the more passive peasants who had not resorted to violence earlier and who also supported either Carlists or, more rarely, moderate republicans. The former won in Hérault and in most of Gard, the moderates won in certain cantons where cultural factors, such as religion, acted upon the norm. Clearly the mountain people, although in worse poverty now than during the previous year, acted in a fashion conformable to the assertion that mountain people are more conservative than lowlanders. As yet the communication between highlands and plains was quite limited. Lack of roads or roads nearly impassable, illiteracy, rough terrain were conditions which prevailed. The vineyards of the low hills and plains were not yet extensive enough to influence life by introducing mobility.[29]   Highland peasants often spent a few weeks harvesting in the vineyards but returned home unaffected, speaking only their own dialect. They could, but only rarely, resort to violence against specific grievances; however, they had not yet reached a stage of awareness which allowed them to translate specific grievances into political action.[30] They sought to preserve rather than to change; they opposed capitalist innovation and accepted traditional social hierarchy and religion. Efforts at recruitment, carried on sporadically by Radicals from Bédarieux and Lodève hardly touched those isolated people.

Now the above generalizations are not universally applicable; there was variation. Religion became a major determinant by 1849 in some cantons. In Gard and Hérault, highland cantons with a large Protestant population voted generally for moderate republicans; only two of them, Saint-Jean-Du-Gard and Anduze (Gard), gave a substantial minority to the socialist-democrats, some of whom were native sons. Fear of Catholic-Carlist domination, not in any sense class or economic interests, determined this vote. There is a long history of bloody conflict between proud Huguenots and intolerant Catholics in the Cévennes. Since the late sixteenth century they had fought each other, and the revocation of the Edict of Nantes had reopened the conflict that led to violent revolt, such as that of the *camisards,* and to equally violent repression. Since the Revolution of 1789 most Calvinists in Gard strongly favored parliamentary government as opposed to legitimist divine right, and many had become republican during the 1840s. By 1848–49 parliamentary republicanism was the political expression of Calvinist Protestantism. Protestants from the plain to the mountains voted massively republican in 1849. The majority of them were landowners and ignored social democracy.

A situation more in accord with Soboul's thesis occurred in the Corbières mountains in Aude. Here some peasants had resisted the alienation of public forests, as in Axat and Quillan cantons, and large numbers of the lower class voted for the Barbès list, but not in greater numbers than those in Mouthoumet and Lagrasse cantons or even in Saissac canton in the Montagne Noire, where there are no reports of violent resistance. In all of these cantons, save Quillan, socialist-democrats won a majority, and usually a sizable majority, running over 50 percent of the ballots. Undoubtedly the peasants, because they depended heavily upon public forests for wood and grazing land, were hostile to a regime which kept open the door to private ownership of these resources. Also the woodsmen wanted state help in the form of roads and canals. They were united with the wine producers in the demand for an active public works policy financed by the rich, and Radicalism seemed to offer them a means to this goal. Since the lower classes here were as illiterate as those in the Cévennes, the extreme left carried on a good deal of missionary work. Recruiters came from the Aude Valley lying to the west and north, because local militants were extremely rare.[31]   Here human will overcame the obstacles imposed by geography.

However, human will did not function in a vacuum, and its influence was generally limited to short-term phenomena. In 1848–49 there was serious economic malaise and reformers were able to exploit it to their advantage. When conditions improved the peasant populations usually returned to the conservative or moderate views tightly woven into their traditions. Even where the personal factor was most notable, as in Pyrénées-Orientales, its long-term effect was unpredictable. Peasants in the Albères, the Fenouillèdes and the Pyrenees voted for the name of Arago, both in 1848 and 1849, and the name carried the Radicals on the list to victory. But while the Aragos could carry Jacobins as fellow travelers, they could not and did not try to make the left-wing into a viable force in the mountains. The Jacobins of Aude, in the long run, proved to be somewhat more successful with their highland missionary work than those of Pyrénées-Orientales.

Public opinion in the mountainous zone was clearly not uniform. Exceptional cases were numerous enough to make one wary of generalization. And yet, considering both short and long-term electoral performance, it is equally clear that most of the mountain people west of the Rhône River were either hostile or simply not favorable to the extreme left.

Even in the hill region, Jacobin victories were confined to important river valleys, usually where there was either some sort of petty industrial activity or important wine production or both. Where the extreme left did not win a majority, it often obtained over 40 percent of the ballots. The Aude Valley, which combined petty and medium property and a large number of independent wine and cereal producers, was and remained its chief stronghold. Here nature provided ease of communication and militants carried their program of cheap credit and public works to grape growers without capital or adequate roads. As wine production diminished westward of Carcassonne, so did left-wing influence. The canton of Castelnaudary-*Sud* was its unique western outpost in an area dominated by cereal production and large and medium landowners.[32] The upper valley, stretching southward toward the Pyrenees, was receptive but with the reserve of mountain folk before strangers. The valley of the Hérault was less clearly dominated; socialist-democrats won victories chiefly in cantons where textiles were concentrated and performed poorly elsewhere. The same was true of the Orb Valley in Hérault department and of the Gard Valley in Gard and the upper Tet Valley in Pyrénées-Orientales. In the Rhône Valley its strength was confined to the cantons of Aramon, Beaucaire, and Arles where there was a considerable landless agricultural proletariat, as well as some active organizers such as A. Tavernel in Aramon and J. Dufestel in Beaucaire. Despite these exceptions river valleys became important centers of the extreme left.

Where rivers met the sea the extreme left was supported by a majority or large minority of adult males, and if there was a large town at this juncture, it usually won a dominant position in political affairs. Here was to be found the combination of a petty middle class furnishing leadership, the urban class providing a cadre of organizers, and a vineyard proletariat making up an activist following. Here life was highly urbanized, open to new ideas, and tradition was more seriously challenged by a generally more volatile, mobile population. These areas played a major role in the political transformation of the Midi. Pivotal points were the mouths of the Tet, Aude, Orb, Hérault, and Vidourle rivers. Three of these junctures lay in Hérault department where towns were more numerous and where landless workers outnumbered landowners.

Thus far our analysis has concentrated on topography with economic activity and social structure as adjuncts. Equally revealing — and complicated — is the influence of social stratification on public opinion and politics. The success of Radicalism, both in 1849 and long after, depended less on class conflict than on class alliance. Its leadership came chiefly from middle class professionals and intellectuals and its strength depended on its leaders' ability to mobilize agrarian lower class support. This task was far easier in the coastal plains than in the highlands, in part because of the greater concentration of vineyard wage workers in the lowlands.

On the other hand, the electoral role of workers, however important, must not be exaggerated. In several communes of the plain of Languedoc lower class discontent had led to acts of insubordination before and after February 1848. In two instances this discontent clearly led to working class extremism in politics: in Mèze and in Lunel cantons. Equally in the cantons of Perpignan, Béziers, Frontignan, and Mauguio the socialist-democrats established, with the backing of vineyard laborers, bastions that became impregnable. They also had an extensive following in Florensac and Sète. However, the motivational forces which influenced elections and characterized opinion were not confined to one particular class. For while Radicals won majorities in cantons with heavy labor concentrations (Lunel, Mauguio, Mèze, Béziers, Perpignan) they also had a comfortable, albeit not quite as strong position, in cantons without a major labor force (Florensac, Frontignan). Finally in the cantons of Agde and Montpellier, response to the Radical program was disappointing and conservatives enjoyed greater success, precisely where workers outnumbered owners. This right wing strength resulted undoubtedly from activities by conservative leaders exploiting anti-Jacobin traditions, because the economy and social structure were essentially the same as in cantons favorable to the left.[33]

Conservative traditions were also deeper in the plains of Aude and Gard. Save for the flat land around the towns of Narbonne and Coursan, where the large working class became a bulwark of the extreme left, wealthy wine producers kept their labor force firmly in control. In the canton of Sigean, and even in those of Narbonne and Coursan, socialist-democrats formally accused employers of giving specially shaped ballots to workers and of standing near the ballot boxes to identify those workers refusing to use them.[34] The extreme left lost the election in Aude because it could not obtain all or most of the labor vote of the plain. In Gard, the *vignerons* (grape growers) of all classes favored the moderate list; that of Jules Cazot did not do well; neither did Ledru-Rollin who was on both lists. That there was a sizable class of small landowners hostile to the extreme left was undoubtedly a factor in this preference; however, the dominant Protestant population of the Vaunage southwest of Nîmes, regardless of class affiliation, was quite excitable and violently hostile to a central government which increasingly identified itself with conservative Catholic interests. Rather than to Montpellier these people looked to Nîmes which was their hope as a center of republican organization and their despair as the keypoint of Catholic power.

ELECTORAL SOCIOLOGY, 1849: PROVENCE

The electoral sociology of lower Provence has characteristics similar and dissimilar to those of lower Languedoc and Roussillon. As in Gard and Pyrénées-Orientales, moderate republicans had been stronger than Radicals in most cantons in 1848 and remained so into 1849. As in Roussillon, they were prepared to ally with the extreme left in the face of a common enemy and even to accept the provisional leadership of Ledru-Rollin. As a result of their doing so, the factions within the republican movement became obscured. It seemed that the socialist-democrats now emerged victorious, or at least enjoyed the advantages of leadership, and that the heavy vote for Cavaignac in the December election was to be annulled by the need of unity for the May elections. Frankly, such an interpretation does not carry us far. Given the great strength of the moderate vote in December, and the near-failure of republicans to rise up against the coup d'état of 1851, it is more likely that the ballots won by the combined slate in May were predominantly those of pro-Cavaignac groups who no longer enjoyed an alternative to coalition with the left.

Coalition was not a successful policy in Bouches-du-Rhône. Republicanism of every color suffered a setback in comparison to 1848. Undoubtedly the loss of legitimist support against Bonapartism was a crucial factor; the right, as in Gard, now had its own slate, dominated by legitimists, and it won by a majority of nearly 15,000 out of 77,382 ballots. Severe, brooding demoralization now settled over nearly all the left, inhibiting the growth of that pugnacious mood which took over in Var.

In Var there was an alliance of the moderate and extreme left, but the latter assumed leadership preparing for the May elections. They were more energetic than their fellow socialist-democrats of Bouches-du-Rhône, widely organized in secret societies, and they campaigned in cooperation with Solidarité Républicaine. Their ranks grew. In Saint-Maximin, for example, moderates reacted to legitimists success in local elections by joining the extreme left.[35] Of course these moderate leftists did not become revolutionaries but simply more ambivalent. They combined a demand for the right to work with a vigorous defense of private property, even property gotten by speculation and usury. They took up the program of low-cost public credit to aid the workers' access to property and to destroy usury. Apparently neither they nor true-blue socialist-democrats alarmed local civil and judicial officials who were unaware of this movement to the left.[36]

The electoral results undoubtedly took these officials by surprise. Of seven winning candidates for the department, five were on the list of "démocratie sociale," and of these five, three were or claimed to be of the extreme left. Henri Arnaud, Radical incumbent came out second, Ledru-Rollin third and Fulcran Suchet fifth. There were a peasant and a worker on the list; they ran last and lost. Because of the different social backgrounds of the candidates, there was a 5,000 vote spread between the highest and lowest totals. More so than elsewhere, the *Varois* tended to vote somewhat more for the men than for the slate. They also abstained in large numbers (40 percent). Most notable, however, was the success of Ledru-Rollin who, in December 1848, had received only 12 percent of all registered voters, and who now obtained 29 percent. D. Conte, a moderate on the same list, who would normally attract the pro-Cavaignac voters of December 1848, drew only 27 percent.

Here was a curious and unpredictable turn of events; the serious decline of the extreme left in Bouches-du-Rhône and its rise in Var. Paradoxically, the influence of Marseille as a left-wing center of propaganda and organization was greater in Vancluse, Drôme, Basse-Alpes, and Var than in Bouches-du-Rhône or even in Marseille itself. A simple economic explanation does not carry one far. In Bouches-du-Rhône republicanism of every shade, and especially the extreme left, suffered a setback in nearly every commune, regardless of economic and social conditions. The stronghold which Ledru-Rollin had captured during the presidential election, the low flat plain north and north-east of Arles, was partially lost, which seriously reduced the republican's electoral strength.

In Var, on the other hand, the socialist-democrats greatly enhanced their strength in the department and broadened their place in the republican spectrum by capturing the lovely plain of Cuers. The source of their strength was centered in Toulon, and from there it spread north through Soliès-Pont, Cuers, Besse, and Brignoles, and east to Le Luc, Draguignan, and Fréjus. Here was their fertile crescent, both politically and economically. From Toulon to about Le Luc it was an area of extensive vineyards, then the acreage devoted to grapes declined almost to the vanishing point in Fréjus.

The extent of vineyards in Var was only half that in Hérault, 60,000 hectares compared to 118,000. But it compared favorably to Gard (64,000), Aude (53,000), and Pyrénées-Orientales (36,000), and was more than double the acreage of Bouches-du-Rhône (25,000). In consequence, wine production was destined to play an important role in public life, and the generalizations bearing upon wine and politics west of the Rhône are equally valid for the department of Var. Bouches-du-Rhône, it is evident, was simply not in the same league and the extreme left's weakness there can partially be explained by the absence of a large wine-producing population. In Var, however, domocrats won solid victories in the wine communes from Toulon to Le Luc where agricultural workers, both part-owners and proletarians, were plentiful, and in Draguignan where they were not.

Of course, there are the ever-present exceptions to our generalizations and they are as disconcerting in Provence as they are in Languedoc. There were extensive vineyards centered around Le Beausset and Ollioules in the southwest and Saint Tropez and Collobrières in the southeast. The ratio of workers to employers averaged about one to one, just slightly lower than in the western plain of Cuers. Yet the Radical republican list suffered severe losses to conservatives, and there was a high negative correlation. This situation prevailed throughout the stretch of land between Marseille and Toulon. Undoubtedly, there was a situation here similar to that of Narbonne in Aude and Saint-Gilles in the Rhône estuary of Gard: a fairly sizable working class in the vineyards was closely controlled by employers. Yet, there were differences of topography. Probably the control was easier to establish in Var and so remarkably successful because many workers had recently immigrated from the mountains where they found life intolerable. Unlike newcomers in Languedoc and Roussillon who eventually turned leftward in their politics, those who moved into lower Provence did not enjoy the openness and ease of communication and urbanity so typical west of the Rhône. They moved into fairly rough terrain, low plateaux cut by streams, and fairly isolated villages. Moreover, wine in the Var cantons, the major cash crop, flowed toward the small port of Bandol in Ollioules canton rather than into Toulon or Marseille. The population must have been relatively cut off from two of the largest municipalities of the lower Midi.

Our generalizations about the influence of wine seem to hold true, even to the exceptions; however, the Alpine foothills of Var, unlike the highlands west of the Rhône, showed themselves to be far more receptive to Jacobins. The extreme left won solid victories in the northwest and in most of Fayence canton. There were practically no vineyards in the rugged, arid highlands and not much of a work force either. Yet the democratic-socialist list did remarkably well in the extreme northern highlands, that is, where its members did not win, they ran abreast of conservatives. The happy electoral outcome here was the result of several factors: severe economic distress throughout the Alpine area and a determined (and sometimes violent) resistance to the government's fiscal policies. There was also a considerable number of peasants who were highly dependent on upland forests and stubbornly opposed the encouragement the regime gave to private enclosure of vast stretches of trees both before and after the revolution. Deprived of rights of usage they felt to be theirs by tradition, they voted for the extreme left as a form of protest. Given the great importance of pine forests in Var, they exercised an influence at least the equal of that of wine. Combined with these objective factors was aggressive propaganda action by Jacobins emanating from the town of Manosque in the department of Basses-Alpes. Manosque was the only town of consequence in the area and Jacobins there were inspired by the press and emissaries of Marseille.[37] This missionary work was similar to that carried on in the Corbières Mountains of Aude and the upper Durance Valley in Bouches-du-Rhône. Police reports often refer to wandering republican agents who carried books, pamphlets, and newspapers to isolated villages and hamlets.[38] These men usually had at least one contact who put them up and provided an audience. Often, during the nocturnal meetings, a secret society came into existence. Not all the agents came from Paris, Lyon, or Marseille; there were local men, unemployed artisans, who went out from Toulon, Brignoles, Salernes, and Draguignan. Their activity was further aided by the conviviality of the Provençal population. Much like the Languedocians, they gathered in cafes and, especially, in the *chambrée*, that is, a small group of friends who met in a room to drink, gamble, and talk. (Not necessarily in this order.) The politically oriented *chambrées*, which were in the minority, might provide a newspaper such as *La Réforme* of Paris or *La Voix du Peuple* of Marseille, which was read in the evening by one of the literate frequenters. This energy was well spent. The northern cantons were not populous, but their support brought victory to the left. The election was close; the socialist-democratic list won by just under 2,000 votes.

URBAN VOTE

This slim margin provided by the voters of the high plateaux of the Plain de Canjuers was a happy boon, not a permanent conquest. The social and geographic forces which encouraged left-wing victories did not exist there. In particular, the urban factor was totally absent, and it was a major variable without which the Mountain was like a locomotive without steam. The permanent and major base of left-wing strength lay in the far more populous southeastern cantons where the population was more highly urbanized, thanks to Toulon shipyards and wine production. Throughout Provence, as throughout Languedoc and Roussillon, towns provided the extreme left with a major element of its mass following.

Ports were often strongholds. Arles was an important center of river traffic, and, much like Beaucaire in Gard, suffering from the decline brought about by railroad competition. Everyone from shipowners to stevedores felt the effects of it and united in their demand that the government initiate a public works program to deepen the estuary of the Rhône. There was a tendency to criticize the laissez-faire policy of the men in power, which facilitated the introduction of advanced notions brought in by sailors moving between Lyon and Marseille. However, there were already several hundred workers in the new railroad yards and locomotive factory. Undoubtedly they formed a sizable segment, in unity with dockers and sailors, who sided with the extreme left. The socialist-democratic list won in Arles *Ouest* on the right bank; Arles *Est* was legitimist.[39] These two forces were about evenly divided.

Marseille was also an important center of the republican left which, however, was still a minority in a traditionally royalist city. The financial and wholesale commercial classes sided with conservative forces and their stronghold were the districts north of the Old Port and in the suburbs. Republican strength was confined largely to the working class districts in the first canton and, with lesser support, to the second and third cantons *intra muros* where they lost but ran well with the backing of transport workers, artisans, and some professional men. In the hamlets of the suburbs and in the eastern cantons, as we noted already, the extreme left was seriously weak. Even La Ciotat with its rapidly growing shipyards and metallurgy gave a majority to the royalists. The ports of Var were generally more receptive to advanced programs: Toulon, and then Saint-Raphaël in Fréjus canton, were the two most important. La Seyne was both a port and, like La Ciotat, a shipbuilding center. It was already a major source of left-wing support and well ahead of La Ciotat in ideology. Bandol, on the other hand, voted hand in glove with its hinterland, that is, for the right.

Inland urban areas were equally divided. Tarascon was an agricultural market where the population, according to the *procureur général*, was "grossier, brutal, ignorant même le français." Here, as in other market towns, Châteaurenard for example, whites and reds hated each other bitterly by 1849, as bitterly as Protestants and Catholics in Nîmes and Montpellier. But there were few Protestants east of the Rhône, and the intense feeling was political in nature. But then, politics was a religion for the men committed to one or the other side. Aix, far more than Arles, was a conservative center. The animosities, which in Arles *arrondissement* bubbled and overflowed, were in Aix more constrained and decorous. Aix was an old administrative and judicial center and officialdom reigned. Republicans were numerous; they founded a short-lived journal, *Ere nouvelle,* and at least three clubs. But most *Aixois,* being prolegitimist, were hostile. They would not even give a majority to their moderate republican mayor because of his presence on the republican slate. He therefore resigned and was peremptorily replaced by a legitimist. The working class, similar to that of Montpellier and Nîmes, did not play an independent, class-oriented role in politics and would not do so until the 1870s. In this respect it epitomized the laboring population of Bouches-du-Rhône.

In the growing anthracite mining area in northern Roquevaire and southwestern Trets cantons, the extreme left was no more successful than in the Alès mining district of Gard. In both areas, where some rural communes were moving toward urban status, the miners as yet revealed the deep distrust of change common to the peasant folk from which they were recruited. Peypin commune, closest to Marseille in space and, presumably in influence, was the only exception. On the whole, the extreme left in Bouches-du-Rhône failed to penetrate effectively the political life of the urban centers.

In Var, on the other hand, its victory resulted in large measure from the support it acquired in Toulon, La Seyne, Draguignan, Le Luc, Brignoles, and Salernes. With heavy industry—the little that existed— located in towns, industrial workers tended to be left-wing, as in Toulon and La Seyne. In other towns, many artisans revealed a definite prefer- ence for the left, and after the Radicals improved their organization and propaganda, they won, with the aid of workers, the three adminis- trative centers: Toulon, Draguignan, and Brignoles. These three points form the ends of a triangle within which the Montagnards had concen- trated their strength. The base of it was the heavily populated plain of Cuers, which was comparable to the coastal plain of Hérault; within it was the greater part of the department's population; outside of it were mere satellite points of strength with a cantonal capital as nucleus. This triangle, as we shall see, was the focus of resistance to the coup d'état in 1851, a fact in itself which revealed how thoroughly the entire area had been converted to Radicalism.

The role of towns in politicizing rural folk was equally important west of the Rhône where the population was, at least numerically if not always temperamentally, more rural than in Provence. The strength of the Mountain there ultimately depended upon its success in winning a significant urban following and then in using its urban forces to sway the countryside. In Aude, Radicals won a high percentage of the ballots because they won all of the important towns, of which there were only four, the prefecture of Carcassonne and the subprefectures of Limoux, Castelnaudary, and Narbonne. They were also popular in many small textile towns often isolated in high hills or mountains, such as Chalabre whose mayor was an ardent Montagnard.[40] In Hérault, the Mountain placed two of its candidates among the winners because it won three *arrondissement* capitals: Lodève and its weavers with a sizable majority; Béziers with a respectable majority, and Montpellier with a minute majority and this thanks to the third or western canton which was partly rural and Protestant. Unlike Carcassonne which was predominantly Jacobin and not very rich, Montpellier was a seat of wealthy nobles and bourgeois who enjoyed considerable influence over the lower classes of shopkeepers, artisans, and unskilled workers (of whom there were very few). The truly urban element of the population was chiefly Catholic and conservative.[41]   More decidedly leftwing were the wool textile centers: Bédarieux, Lodève, Clermont, and Saint-Chinian, as well as the coastal wine centers: Sète, Mèze, and Frontignan. In nearly every instance, these towns carried the cantonal vote into the Radical camp. Hérault's silk textile center, Ganges, followed the pattern of the urban vote in Gard bacause of serious religious divisions.[42]

In Gard, the only administrative center which was markedly leftwing was Alès, with its western sector heavily Protestant and its many metallurgical workers. Le Vigan, like its neighbor Ganges, was moderate republican, Uzès was torn between moderates and Carlists, and Nîmes, the biggest textile center of the South, was predominantly Carlist. Even in the first canton, strongly Protestant, the Radical list could not surpass the moderate republican. Quite clearly the majority who had voted for republicans in 1848 turned back to monarchists in 1849.

In general, the extreme left profited more from the political role of small and medium-size towns than from that of large cities. The largest cities were Montpellier, Nîmes, Marseille, and Toulon, and only Marseille had over 100, 000 inhabitants, the remainder less than half of that. The first two were dominated by conservative notables who successfully restricted the proselytizing of the extreme left. Toulon, on the one hand, became an important center of the left with a veritable political hinterland stretching north and east. Marseille, on the other hand, had a fairly strong Jacobin contingent, which was unable effectively to swing the weight of its financial and intellectual leadership. It was completely surrounded by conservative populations living in semirural suburbs and villages. Its influence leapt over its environs and became apparent chiefly in the Durance Valley and in the lower Alpes. In consequence the political role of urbanization, favorable to the socialist-democrats, was centered in the small and medium towns under 10,000 in population and usually only half that figure. Unlike the cities these smaller communes had far more intimate contacts with the surrounding peasants and were far more aggressive in seeking to convert them. In this activity became manifest the influence of small-town professionals and, above all, of industrial workers.

There was a good deal of industrial activity in commonly designated rural departments, and in the lower Midi the extreme left was highly dependent upon industrial workers, if the term "industrial" is not limited to mean exclusively large-scale enterprise. There was a good deal of petty and medium industry in many communes and the ideal of the organization of labor attracted to the Mountain an important segment of the domestic and artisanal working class. Domestic industrial labor meant, by and large, textile labor, not spinning which was performed by females who could not vote, but weaving, washing, combing, dying, etc. Where textiles were centered in a town, even though the domestic system was common, workers tended to acquire a sense, if not of clearly defined class interests, at least of corporate interest. Male textile labor in Bédarieux, Lodève, and Clermont in Hérault displayed early development in strike organization and in trade formation, even hiding their unions behind the facade of mutual-aid societies. During the July Monarchy they were in advance of workers living in most other industrial areas.[43] However, their turn to the left in politics was of too recent origin to project them conspicuously into the Jacobin leadership which was artisan or middle class.[44] Rather they constituted a fairly active part of the rank and file. This role, of course, was not a passively narrow one; it was broadened by the fact that many of them enjoyed only seasonal employment. Although they generally lived in towns, they also worked in agriculture during two or three months of the year. They more easily carried their Jacobinism to the peasants in the surrounding countryside, thereby reinforcing the missionary work of many artisans. Given the seasonal nature of their work, they had the leisure to frequent cafes in nearby hamlets where peasants met "*pour tuer le ver.*" And of course, when peasants came to town on market days, they joined the local petty bourgeois and urban artisans who gathered in left-wing cafes to indoctrinate the rustics.

Due to their activity and to that of the artisans of Béziers, the territory comprised between Béziers, Bédarieux, Lodève, and Clermont constituted a "Radical square," comparable to the "Radical triangle" of Var. In both were to be found the most enterprising militants of the extreme left, the *vignerons,* and the industrial workers.

Apart from textiles the only other industries west of the Rhône employing large numbers of men were metallurgy and mining. Both were located in the high hills and mountains. In Alès *ville* the extreme left enjoyed considerable success among metal workers who had traveled, were open-minded, and in an urban milieu which protected them from patronal domination.[45]   Quite distinct from them were the rather large contingent of coal miners in the extreme northern cantons of Gard, who were usually hostile to the left. As in Bouches-du-Rhône most had been recruited from nearby mountain villages, were devoutly Catholic and easily controlled by the companies.[46]   Mining in Hérault was as yet confined to the commune of Camplong in Bédarieux canton and miners were only a few hundred in number. Unlike those in Gard many of them were Protestant. Unfortunately it is not possible to discover how they voted. About 40 percent of the registered voters abstained and perhaps miners found it convenient not to go to the polls. On the other hand, the conservatives defeated the Mountain by only a small majority, so it is possible that Jacobins from nearby Bédarieux had converted a sizable portion of the laboring class. However, if there was conversion it was not deep. Probably in the mining district of Hérault, as in those of Gard and Bouches-du-Rhône, Radicalism won followers less among miners than among artisans and petty bourgeois who usually displayed more defiance of the companies as well as of the government, and who, if they were Protestant or free-thinking, lent to their politics the fervor of religious militancy.[47]

RELIGION AND POLITICS

Certainly religion was a vital force in the lower Midi. Although the decay of the Christian Church was already underway, its gospel was still a source of general good will. At least it was just after the February revolution. But the halcyon days of brotherly love based on Christian belief and freedom of worship had largely disappeared between April and December when politics had acquired religious overtones. In the departments under study, the Catholic hierarchy was royalist at heart and in 1849 the archbishops actively took up that cause. The Roman policy of the government further divided Catholics from non-Catholics, with the result that political conflict was exacerbated by religious passion.

Both moderate republicans and Jacobins were or claimed to be Christian. Even in 1849 when Jacobins referred to themselves as socialists, they continued to preach a form of social gospel: "Le socialisme, ... c'est l'oeuvre pour laquelle Jésus-Christ est mort, c'est la bonne nouvelle annoncée par Saint-Paul."[48] In Roussillon, Aude, and Provence, where there was only a handful of Protestants, the Mountain became strongly anticlerical and prosecular. Its conflict with the church was largely a political one, since it sought to reduce the power of the clergy in government and education. It appealed to the lower class in its campaign against upper class clericals. In the eastern cantons of Hérault and even more so in Gard, the conflict was in great part a confessional one, between Catholics and Calvinists.[49]

Class feelings were obscured by religious alignments. Sometimes a common religion bound employer and employee in identical political views: the Catholic miners in Gard and Bouches-du-Rhône, many vineyard workers in Aude, the Protestant silk workers in Ganges and Le Vigan, many of the Catholic textile workers in the second and third cantons of Nîmes, as well as the common laborers in the city of Montpellier. Quite clearly the working class in Nîmes and the miners in Alès *arrondissement* were motivated by religious rather than economic or social considerations; they voted for conservatives who opposed the legislative bills which would have improved their living conditions. On the other hand, religious differences sometimes divided classes. In the textile center of Bédarieux workers tended to be free thinkers while employers were Protestant. In both local and national elections there the watchword of labor was "do not vote for Protestants!"[50] In the first canton of Nîmes, Catholic textile workers disliked their Protestant employers and voted for the right. In Nîmes as in Montpellier, violent conflicts broke out between the adherents of the two religions and each sought to control the National Guard so as to have an armed defense against its enemy. A similar style of visceral animosity broke out at times between red republicans and legitimists in Tarascon and Châteaurenard. Free thinkers reacted like Protestants to clerical-Carlist domination.

Not all Protestants, nor all Catholics, were united in two distinct political camps. Wealthy Calvinists, who lived in towns such as Nîmes, Montpellier, Ganges, Lunel, Bédarieux, Lodève, and Le Vigan, were generally Orleanists and they had been highly favored by the July Monarchy. When they accepted the Second Republic in 1848 they were constitutionalists; during 1849 many, probably most, became Bonapartists.[51] On the other hand, Protestantism provided the Mountain with some of its more ardent exponents: the agricultural laborers in Marsillargues and Mauguio in Hérault, and the workers and small farmers in Saint-Jean-du-Gard and Anduze in Gard. However, the bulk of the Protestant population in 1849 favored constitutional republicanism seasoned with a dash of Jacobin fervor — provided the fervor was not too intense and the Jacobins displaying it were native sons. Religious considerations therefore place serious limitations on an economic interpretation of voting behavior. The Catholic who had voted for republicans in 1848 out of hatred of the July Monarchy voted for royalists in 1849. The Calvinist who voted for moderates in 1848 and the spring of 1849 reacted accordingly by turning to the extreme left in the summer of 1849 and in 1850. In both cases the government's religious and educational policies rather than its economic or social policies brought about the change.

It is impossible to determine how extensive was the non-religious or non-church-going part of these voters. The censuses listed chiefly the number of Protestants and Jews, then classified the remainder of the population as Catholic. Yet the fact that religious practice declined sharply in the lower Midi later in the nineteenth century would indicate that it had begun to decline by the middle of that century. It is highly probable, then, that an indeterminate number of voters, located chiefly in larger towns and along the seacoast, were only nominal Christians or non-Christians. Given the increasingly pro-Catholic policy of the central government, they would logically join the extreme left to oppose it.

CONCLUSION

The extreme left emerged and grew as the end product of several forces. One of them was economic, and wine production made a multiple contribution. It was a perturbing element in southern life, bringing mobility and movement and a volatile population, less rooted, less traditionalistic. It was also instrumental in reshaping the social hierarchy by greatly expanding the base. It brought into existence a large rural proletariat that constituted the mass following of Radical leaders. Finally, it abetted urban ways of life and attitudes, even where there were no large cities, by increasing the commerce and industry serving its needs, and therefore population and voter density. Industrial and commercial activity not related to viticulture, textiles especially, certainly provided many of the voters whose ballots swelled the totals of the left. However, the present and the future belonged to the vine, not to the loom, even less so to the village forge. Woolen production had passed its peak in 1849 and capital was already turning to vineyards. The needs of viticulture and viniculture therefore, had begun to acquire the paramount position they would enjoy by the 1860s. And the democrats were certainly well on the way toward identifying the wine interests with their own cause. The location of their leaders and cadre in towns must not blind us to this important change . The extreme left had its head in the town, but its feet were in the low-lying countryside.

The town contained its most active organizational force: craftsmen and members of the middle class. They were in fairly close contact with rural workers and indoctrinated them. There was no sharp division between town and countryside; there was, on the contrary, exchange between the two in the wine districts. Even the command leadership, made up chiefly of men from the educated middle class, harangued peasants in the fields and visited small communes. Therefore a favorable social structure, in certain areas, was another force.

Geography was still another influence because socialist-democracy had its following predominantly in areas where communication and transport were easy, the coastal plain and larger river valleys. As a new movement it did not enjoy a favorable human response conditioned by centuries of propaganda. Its success required a radical change of human response; consequently a topography encouraging the spread of new ideas and a mobile population less bound by tradition were essential factors. Geography and the economy went hand in hand and the phenomenal growth of wine production attracted people to the lowlands where, eventually, they proved to be more receptive to novelty.

Ideology became a major force. Weak in 1848, it took more definite shape during the next few years as its roots went deeper into the populace.

Where this phenomenon did not occur, Radical democracy did not endure the governmental oppression of 1850–51. In Aude many peasants had voted for the extreme left out of economic despair; they did not become committed in their minds or their hearts. The same was true among some peasant communities in the highlands of Pyrénées-Orientales and Var. People who became committed ideologically came chiefly from the lowlands where, in time, Radical ideas would constitute a new tradition that would displace the old. Here the obstacle to innovation was not so difficult that it discouraged human effort. On the contrary, ideological transformation was generally not an independent factor; it was furthered by the continuous expansion of viticulture which produced a new civilization, more changeable in its thought as a result of the instability of its source of wealth, the wine market. With each generation (the 1840s, the 1870s, and the early 1900s) came a wine crisis, and each crisis furthered the growth of increasingly left-wing ideas. The eventual demise of conservatism, however, did not bring about a permanent victory for the Radical party after 1870. The relentless expansion of viticulture and the massive problems it created provoked more extremist demands for new solutions and evernew ideologies to rationalize them.

To be sure, ideology in mid-century was not everywhere so dependent on economic conditions that were still taking shape. Protestantism was, and would remain, remarkably free of such conditioning. It did not, for example, lead ineluctably to social democracy; its leftward inclination occurred chiefly where Calvinists were numerous and distrustful of their Catholic persecutors after mid-1849. This "drive to the left" became a fixed phenomenon in the Vaunage and upper Gard Valley, two regions with different economies and social structures, and yet a common mind.

The above factors, the economy, demography, geography, religion, and human effort leading to effective political organization, were long-term determinants and were as yet in their early stage of development. In the short run, the drive to the left during 1848–49 did not occur automatically or spontaneously as a result of objective environmental forces. It was not a notable phenomenon until the drive to the right in 1848–51 induced many moderate republicans to resort to extreme decisions in their defense of the Second Republic and to accept the leadership of the Mountain. Environmental factors conditioned the intensity and nature of this republican drive by limiting or fostering the propagandistic and organizational work of its leadership. In consequence, the extreme left was reinforced chiefly in the period from May 1849 to December 1851 by the political decisions emanating from the government in Paris.

NOTES

1. On 5 December 1847, during a reform banquet in Montpellier, the main speaker, Louis Garnier-Pagès, introduced the "radical" program which called for "guerre à l'exploitation des masses par quelques privilégiés." See *Banquet réformiste à Montpellier* (Montpellier, 1847), 19–27. At this time the word "radical" was used because the word "republican" had been outlawed by the July Monarchy. Borrowed from the English, it was used by French republicans to emphasize their intransigent opposition to the government. When the government was overthrown, the word lost its reason for being and practically disappeared. See Gil C. Alroy, "Les Radicaux après la Révolution de 1848," *Le Contrat social*, 10 (1966), 290–94. On the origins of the word see Jacques Kayser, *Les Grandes batailles du Radicalisme,* 1820–1901 (Paris, 1962), 7–14. In the present essay, Radical means the extreme left which in 1848 was commonly called "Montagnard," and in 1849 "démocrate socialiste," and at any time, *"républicain démocrate."* In the lower Languedoc there was no clear line of demarcation between an advanced democrat and a socialist. The extreme left studied here, however, tended to be more Jacobin than socialist, Rousseauist than Babeuvian, and it became the basis of the Radical movement of the Third Republic. I capitalize the "R" to distinguish the Radicals who followed Alexandre Ledru-Rollin in 1848–49 and Georges Clemenceau after 1871 from the term "radical" commonly used to designate any extremist.

   By these terms I mean that Radicals looked forward to an economy based squarely on small producers, that is, self-employed peasant farmers who owned their land, and independent artisans, either owners of their shops or provided with the financial means of acquiring a shop. They saw in Jean-Jacques Rousseau the champion of small property, and glorified him. They were neither ignorant nor scornful of Noel Babeuf, and appropriated the rather new word, socialist. As will be explained later, they tended to favor co-operative artisan industry, but were generally vague when defining social goals and became hostile to Louis Blanc's brand of Jacobin socialism.

2. A.N. BB[18] 1468, dr. 5272, report of procureur-général, 3 March 1848. See Thomas R. Christofferson, "The Revolution of 1848 in Marseille" (Ph.D. thesis, Tulane University, 1968).

3. See numbers of 21 March 1848 and *passim.*

4. *Le Progrès social,* 6 April 1848.

5. See P. Dubosc, *Quatre mois de République* (Marseille, 1848), 20–26.

6. For dossiers of men arrested see A.N. BB[30] 358. Some details are in *Bouches-du-Rhône, Encyclo. depart'le*, V. 168 ff, X 34; Christofferson, 171-75, has studied 150 out of 153 men arrested. Most were artisans, especially in the building and clothing trades, and two-thirds were under thirty years of age.

7. On the workers see M. Agulhon, "Apercus sur le mouvement ouvrier à Toulon," *Provence historique*, 7 (1957), 132–40; Charles Ribbe, *La Société des portefaix de Marseille* (Marseille, 1865).

8. A.N. BB[18] 1319, dr. 8877, report of *procureur général*, 1 August 1833; BB[18] 1443a, dr. 7050, report of 18, July 1846. Marseille had a large immigrant labor force, but stevedoring was closed to them, and most of them were artisans or unskilled laborers from neighboring departments.

9. A.D. Var 4M 16, report of 21 February 1848. Particularly valuable for the history of Toulon is Maurice Agulhon, *Une Ville ouvrière au temps du socialisme utopique* (Paris, 1970).

10. A.D. B-du-R 12U-1, police report of Toulon, 7 April 1848.

11. A.D. Var 4J 78, program of Marcelin Maurel.

12. A.D. Var 4M 16, report of 25 June 1848.

13. 4 November 1848.

14. A.N. BB[18] 1469, dr. 6579a.

15. A.D. Gard 6M 613, police reports, October to December; *Républicain du Gard*, October-December.

16. A.N. BB[18] 1474b, reports of the *procureur général*, October-November. The *Républicain du Gard* would have preferred to support Lamartine or even Ledru-Rollin but concluded that only Cavaignac could successfully compete with Louis Napoleon. Republican defense, therefore, demanded support of him. See 26, 29 November.

17. See A.D. Aude 5M 32; A.D. Hérault 39M 132.

18. For the elections see Andre Tudesq, *L'Election présidentielle de Louis Napoléon Bonaparte* (Paris, 1965).

19. A.D. B.-du-R. 2 M 1–2, report of December; 12U 1, report of the *procureur général*, 16 August 1848.

20. A.D. Hérault 39M 127, police reports of March 1848. On the issue of taxation see R. Schnerb, "Les Hommes de 1848 et l'impôt," *1848 et les révolutions du XIXe siècle*, 38 (1948), 5–51. A.N.BB[18] 1488, dr. 5272, reports of *proc. généraux*. Also Agulhon, *République au village*, chap. 3.

21. *Républicain du Gard*, 9 March 1849. See also *Voix du peuple* [Marseille], 12 August 1849, and *Journal du peuple* [Arles], 28 January, 17 February 1849 for attacks on the drink tax which was equally hated in Provence.

22. These were all regressive indirect taxes which made up a sizable part of the prices of consumable goods. The first two had been established by Napoleon I to pay his wars, the *octrois* was a levy collected by towns on all goods entering their toll gates. Unlike most wine producers, legislators considered wine a luxury and consequently taxed it more heavily than cereals; they also made no distinction between expensive quality wines consumed by the upper classes and the cheap table wines of the urban workers. The latter paid proportionately more in taxes than the former. Hence the lament of peasant growers.

23. The noble emigrés who returned to France in 1814–15 received compensation amounting to about a billion (*milliard*) francs for properties confiscated and sold during the Terror of 1792–95. The forty five centime tax was a land tax imposed on owners by the ruling moderate republicans in 1848.

24. *Fraternité*, 30 September 1848, 17 February, 10 March 1849; *Républicain du Gard*, 15, 28 February, 10 March 1849; *Indépendant*, 6 April 1849; *Journal du peuple*, 24 March 1849, p. 2; *Voix du peuple*, 1 April 1849; *Le Démocrate du Var* was vague.

25. *Fraternité*, 9 September, 18, 28 October 1848; *Indépendant*, 2, 6 April 1849; *Républicain du Gard*, 15 March 1849. The last named was far less committed to nationalization; however, it still favored social reform in a vague way. *Journal du peuple*, 21 April, 1849; *Voix du peuple*, 1 April 1849. Many peasants were more attracted by cheap credit than ideology; they had bought land on credit before the fall of agricultural prices in 1848–49 and now found the interest burden intolerable. More peasants turned to the left as the years passed and conditions worsened. A.N. BB³⁰ 382, dr. 9567a, reports of *procureur-général*, July-August 1851.

26. See returns in A.D. P.-O. 2M 1–66 and A.N. C1333. There was usually a 200 or 300 vote difference between the local hero François Arago and the Jacobins. In Saint Paul, however, Lefranc trailed by nearly 700 votes. H. Chauvet, *Histoire du parti républicain dans les Pyrénées-Orientales de 1830 à 1877* (Perpignan, 1909), 71, is in error about some of the returns.

27. Detailed electoral statistics for 1848–49 are deplorably scanty in local archives and non-existent in the National Archives. I found totals for communes only in A.D. Hérault 15M 9; cantonal totals are available in the local press and departmental archives.

28. Soboul, *op.cit.* Soboul states that peasants voted for Louis Napolean in December 1848 because moderates did not bring forth an economic program favorable to their aspirations. In 1849, disenchanted with Louis Napoleon, they voted for democratic-socialists. This thesis, I feel, is too rigid and schematic; peasant reactions were far more complex.

29. In the *Enquete* there was very little mention of migration from the highlands toward the lowlands. Apparently military service was an important displacer of young men. As yet, the population was growing everywhere, so that the lowland vineyards obtained much of their labor force from nearby communities. Full time work in vineyards required certain skills and finesse which the crude mountain people did not possess.

30. Their action still resembled that of eighteenth century peasants. On the latter see George Rudé, *The Crowd in History* (New York, 1964), chap. 1.

31. A few Jacobins were arrested after the coup d'etat of 1851; but only in one town, appropriately named Villerouge, was there a concentration of them: ten, more than in Narbonne, were seized. See A.D. Aude 5M 37–42.

32. A.N. BB³⁰ 362, 148, 177.

33. Agde was a declining port living from wine trade and fishing. Monarchism was a strong tradition there, and the first Radical-Socialist victory in municipal elections came only in 1898. See J. Picheire, *Histoire d'Agde* (Lyon, [1960]), 81–91. On the other hand, the extreme left won in the neighboring communes of Marseillan and Besson.

34. A.N. FIC III Aude⁴; see also *Fraternité*, 14–16 May 1849.

35. A.N. BB¹⁸ 1474a, report of *proc. général*, 27 April 1849.

36. A.N. BB¹⁸ 1471–73, *proc. général* reports of February-April 1849; A.D. Bouches-du-Rhône 12U 2, reports of March-April 1849.

37. See Philippe Vigier, *La Seconde République dans la région alpine* (Paris, 1963), I, 241, 247, 319; II, 148.

38. A.N. BB¹⁸ 1474a; A.D. Var 4M 16; A.D. B-du-R 12U 1, 12U 2.

39. A.N. BB³⁰ 370, report of *proc. général*, 14 February 1850; A.D. B-du-R. 2M 3–22.

40. See A.D. Aude 5M 32, ff. 100–80.

41. L. Thomas, "Montpellier en 1851, le coup d'état du 2 décember 1851," *Monspeliensia,* I, 11–12.
42. For Ganges, see A.D. Hérault 39M 142. It is noteworthy that textile laborers in Lodève, although employed at fairly good wages thanks to government contracts, supported the extreme left. This was an ideological commitment.
43. P. Stearns, "Patterns of Industrial Strike Activity in France during the July Monarchy," *American Historical Review,* 70 (1965), 371–94. Information on labor relations is most scarce for the Midi. A large scale strike occurred in Lodève and Clermont during 1845, directed against the introduction of machinery, as well as to improve wages. See Frank Manuel, "Introduction des machines en France et les ouvriers: La grève des tisserands de Lodève," *Revue d'histoire moderne,* n.s. 4 (1935), 209–25, 352–72. This was, to our knowledge, the last strike before the February Revolution; disputes in 1847 were conciliated by local *Conseils de Pru'hommes.* See A.N.F[12] 4476c.
44. Apparently they leaned toward the legitimists until 1848 when they were converted to democracy by the *sous-commissaire* Marcel Atger. See E. Appolis, "Un démocrate sociale sous la seconde République, Marcel Atger," *Actes du 87e Congrès National des Sociétés Savantes* (1962), 63–75.
45. There were between 1,500 and 2,000 metal workers centralized in two mills. Rivoire, *Statisque...du Gard,* II, 186, and census of 1851.
46. A.D. Gard 6M 613. In the decades to follow, Bessèges became a center of revolutionary syndicalism while Grand'Combe remained a center of royalism and Catholicism until the twentieth century. After 1870 many miners in Bouches-du-Rhône joined the extreme left.
47. It has not been possible to obtain a reasonably precise knowledge of petty bourgeois attitudes in the coal basins. Interesting to note, however, was the prolabor position of numerous local merchants in the mining districts during the 1880s and 1890s. They hated company stores and therefore the companies. They were the chief creditors of miners during strikes.
48. See *Independant,* 20 May 1849, also 17 June.
49. For statistics on the Protestant population see A.N. F[19] 10031[1]. Particularly important is G. Cholvy, "Les Protestants de l'Hérault: essai d'évaluation numerique, "*Annales du Midi,* 77 (1965), 319–32; Rivoire, *Statisque...du Gard,* II, 439–43; S.R. Schram, *Protestantism and Politics in France* (Alençon, 1954) is useful, although it concentrates on the later nineteenth and twentieth centuries.
50. E. Appolis, "La Résistance au coup d'état du 2 décembre 1851 dans l'Hérault", *Actes du 77e Congrès National des Sociétés Savantes* (1952), 497.
51. See A.D. Hérault 39M 142, police reports of 15 May 1852.

CHAPTER THREE

THE MARTYRDOM, 1849-1851

The election of May 1849 was certainly not a victorious one for the extreme left and no amount of rationalization could alter that poignant fact. It was a great blow because leaders of the extreme left, being ardent democrats, imagined their own movement as one involving the masses. But the masses had not become involved. The period from the election to the end of 1851 saw the extreme left minimize its role as a mass movement. Of course its leaders did not abandon their hope and their efforts to win over large numbers of voters; they kept in sight the by-elections of 1849–50 and the general election scheduled for 1852. But rather the socialist-democrats now turned consciously either to revolutionary tactics at most or to conspiratorial tactics at least in order to save French democracy from its enemies within the government. As the extreme left emerged into the chief opposition force in the Midi, as well as in France, its relation to economic, social, and geographic influence grew more restricted, especially as its following became increasingly confined to its 1849 strongholds. Its strengths and weaknesses were now somewhat less a function of environment and more of personal commitment and leadership at all levels. Although diminished in numbers, the hard core of the left displayed more firmly the determination and devotion of which martyrs are made. This chapter, in consequence, is devoted to a study of the men involved in the movement, whereas the two earlier chapters were concerned mainly with the physical and social environment within which these men acted.

65

ORGANIZATION OF THE LEFT

By the summer of 1849 democrats captured control of the republican press as well as the remainder of the party organization in the South. Their bid for leadership was facilitated by the government in Paris, for as it moved steadily toward the right, republicans of all shades moved rapidly toward the left. Louis Napoleon's Roman policy, his repressive laws against the press, assembly, and speech destroyed the reason for moderate strategy and reinforced the tendency toward revolutionary tactics. Ledru-Rollin, elected in Hérault and Var, encouraged this tendency when he led an abortive uprising in Paris against the use of French troops to suppress the Roman republic of Joseph Mazzini. Because he and several of his fellow deputies had to flee into exile, and because of other causes, a series of by-elections became necessary in 1849–50. Radicals now took the lead in choosing candidates and preparing programs. In Montpellier during July a "Comité Républicain Démocratique de 93" chose Ferdinand Flocon, editor of La Réforme of Paris, to run for the seat vacated by Ledru-Rollin. In Gard, during January 1850, Favand ran as a Jacobin and, like Flocon, took up the program of the extreme left, especially its fiscal planks.

It is doubtful whether this leftward shift was influenced in any decisive way by economic or social factors. Although the economic crisis continued to affect most voters, there was massive abstention in both elections. In consequence both candidates drew their support from a hard core of the republican left. Flocon received 10,000 fewer votes than Ledru-Rollin, who had won in May, but he did not even leave Paris to campaign. His votes came chiefly from the plain and valleys. Favand won because Catholic royalists split. He received 30 percent of the registered voters, roughly the percentage of the Protestant population in the department. His backing came precisely from where it had come in 1849, the Protestant belt stretching from Vauvert in the plain to Saint-Jean-du-Gard in the mountains. Clearly Protestant republicanism was becoming red.[1] And the Roman expedition plus the Falloux education bill were certainly more important causes of this shift than economic distress.[2] When the Falloux bill was debated, Protestants were talking of insurrection and had already organized a large number of secret societies.[3]

A similar situation, minus the Protestant factor, prevailed in Var during by-elections to replace Ledru-Rollin and Fulcran Suchet who was also involved in the Paris uprising against the Roman expedition. *Le Démocrat du Var,* which had moved leftward, hammered away at the flagrant violation of the 1849 constitution. Although the naval part of this expedition was economically beneficial to Toulon, agriculture, and especially the wine industry, were in serious difficulty. There were some violent attacks on fiscal bureaus and personnel by enraged crowds.[4] The election proved that the population was still almost evenly divided. A moderate and a conservative won, and the Jacobin candidate just barely lost; if workers in the arsenal and naval yards of Toulon had been allowed to vote in their home districts instead of in the arsenal where they could be watched, the extreme left might have won. Chances were diminished not only in Toulon but also in La Seyne and Hyères where the same procedures and pressures were applied.[5] In Bouches-du-Rhône, Jacobins played a minor role in the by-election. Moderates posed the candidacy of the venerable Dupont de l'Eure who did not even campaign. He was soundly defeated. By early 1850 republicans of all colors had already expanded their secret societies and began arming.

The geographic distribution of these societies coincides, generally, with the areas where Radicals either won elections or a sizable percentage of the vote. In the Cévennes there were few of them: one at Saint-Jean-du-Gard where the Mountain was strong; others at Ganges, Le Vigan, Génolhac, and Barjac where it was not. The republicans in the high zone did not resort to violence or to secrecy. Wherever Protestants were dominant in the highlands however, republicans became militant and every cantonal capital, as well as several small towns, had at least one society, some had two. In Alès, Anduze, Vézenobres, and Lédignan in the upper Gard Valley, there was open defiance of authority. Even in isolated cantons such as Lassalle, lying across the mountain and hill zones, there was a spirit of rebellion. For example, one young man, when called for military service in 1850, came dressed completely in red; others came with red flags bearing inscriptions such as "*la liberté ou la mort.*" Similar demonstrations occurred in all the departments. Wives sometimes dressed in red as goddesses of liberty; sometimes, according to the police, the local *fille de joie* so attired herself.

The existence of these *frondeurs* was an important factor in the rise of the extreme left. Although a minority, they were the local organizers who indoctrinated their neighbors, who read the press in cafes, who got out the voters, and who became martyrs in December 1851. They were Protestant in Gard and freethinking elsewhere and their Radicalism was a form of anti-Catholicism and therefore of anti-royalism. In the highlands of Gard they were active in an area dominated by small and medium farmers, with only a small landless working class—save in industrialized Alès. In the hill zone of Hérault, societies were also located chiefly in river valleys where Radicals were numerous. Limited in number, the locations of these left-wing centers form a crescent stretching from Lodève, through Bédarieux, along the Hérault Valley down to Béziers in the plain. This north-south belt, incidentally, was roughly the western extremity of really militant Radicalism, more accurately, of revolutionary Radicalism in Languedoc. In Aude, the extreme left had declined after 1849. Only in Carcassonne, Narbonne, and a few other communes were there societies and they were hardly active.

Aude is an interesting model which can serve to test the thesis that the rise of the extreme left was dependent upon several types of leadership functioning within a generally favorable economic and social structure. There was no lack of upper echelon Jacobin chiefs; Theodore Marcou in Carcassonne, Joseph Bess in Castelnaudary, and Theophile Raynal in Narbonne were as active and skillful as their counterparts elsewhere in lower Languedoc. What Aude lacked, in sufficient measure, was a petty bourgeois and artisan class to serve as a cadre of lower leadership, that is, as local organizers and militants. It also did not have the extensive textile labor force characteristic of its neighbors to the east. And, excepting several communes in the Narbonnais, it lacked a large rural proletariat. The Aude was the most economically backward department in the lower Languedoc and wages were in the lowest category for all of France. Possibly its very backwardness deadened the full blow of agricultural and industrial depression; without much manufacturing or a large active working class, its peasants could at least live off of their small holdings and wait. By 1850 they abandoned the perilous effort of translating their economic malaise into political action. In December 1851 many would vote against the coup d'état, but that must have been the last quiver of a dying reflex. The department did not fully participate in what might be called a political takeoff toward the left which came after 1849.

Of course, economic backwardness alone cannot explain the political direction a department would take. It is interesting to contrast Aude and Var, both of which had much in common. In Var, the Jacobin movement seems to have lost ground, especially in Toulon where police repression had become more effective during 1849–50. Yet, *Le Démocrate du Var* continued publishing until March 1851, and when it was suppressed, there followed *La Démocratie du Var* which held out until 2 December, 1851. In the first number *La Démocratie* wrote, with bitter jocularity, "Le Démocrate est mort, vive la Démocratie."[6] One finds here a state of mind which, in the last period of the Second Republic, decided the survival of the Mountain. Local leadership was remarkably tough; as moderates moved to the left, they brought their personal following, their clientele, with them, and they displayed the determination of new converts. In Draguignan, Pastoret was a most energetic leader; local police were determined to put him in jail, but juries were as determined to acquit him. Equally influential was Emile Ollivier who now sided with the extreme left. He traveled extensively in the department, was tried in court there, and was acquitted there. He was particularly influential because of his prestige among the peasants in the central and central-eastern areas. During his trial Jacobins from many communes came dressed with red vests, caps, ties, and kerchiefs. They formed a long cortege in his honor and sang "La Marseillaise" and "Le Chant du départ."[7] Clearly the ideals and attitudes of the extreme left cut more deeply into society in Var than in Aude. Equally important were the two left-wing deputies, Louis Clavier and Henri Arnaud, and even the moderate Dominique Conte, who travelled extensively during parliamentary vacations in hope of keeping up the determination of the people. Even many Toulonnais workers, although under close surveillance, wore red ribbons around their hats and violently resisted efforts of policemen to remove them.[8] The extreme left had taken root now in numerous small towns and villages in the geographic triangle described above.

Indeed, the role of larger towns and cities, more easily controlled by the police and army, steadily diminished as centers of left-wing activity. There were no serious uprisings in the cities in December 1851. That Jacobin forces were grouped in given geographic areas made organization and communication easier. Aude, however, was too highly disorganized with over 400 communes, and perhaps too divided sectionally, and certainly by local rivalry and village dissension. There were small communes separated by age-old hatreds, and the young people of each could not meet without resorting to violence. However, this condition was more prevalent in the isolated villages of the highlands. A more important factor was that the government, exploiting municipal rivalries, succeeded in separating the Narbonnais from the Carcassonnais and therefore it separated the two poles of left-wing organization. Divided, each center proved too weak to stand alone. Political repression, combined with promises of official economic aid, separated these areas naturally joined by the Aude Valley. Thereafter Carcassonne became the center of the extreme left. Its effectiveness, however, was severely limited in that it was too far removed from the coast and blocked on the west by traditionally conservative communes.

The department of Pyrénées-Orientales also became divided: the plain of Roussillon proved to be the most fertile area for the extreme left as it sought a separate identity during 1850-51, and the high hills and mountains were the least receptive. Political unity in the department, however, was achieved by the spread of moderate republicanism. This accomplishment was the legacy of the Arago dynasty. It was a firm bulwark against the spread of both royalism and Bonapartism. There was not a strong Orleanist movement, in part because there was not an extensive, wealthy upper middle class to foster it, in part because the Aragos' prestige brought professional and business classes into the moderate republican camp; an important agricultural middle class, which was fairly extensive in the plains, also entered the moderate camp. Below it was a fairly sizable agricultural working class centered in the plain west and south of Perpignan and in some communes north of the city from Rivesaltes to the coast. As in Hérault, the extreme left found its followers in the coastal plain and lower river valleys. Here were most of the secret societies, the artisans who were recruiters and activists, the professional men who provided top level leadership and financial backing, and the rural laborers and disgruntled peasantry.[9] It is possible that the artisan class played a larger role in Pyrénées-Orientales than in Hérault or Gard. The quality and style of life in coastal towns and villages was quite similar, but in the subsistence economy of the area, there was less demand for professional and business men, especially outside of Perpignan. In an assembly of left-wing representatives from many coastal communes, meeting on 19 April 1851, there were among the arrested seventeen artisans, three day laborers, two farm tenants and only four merchants. Unable to attract local notables, the extreme left flourished for a brief while, then declined and fused again with moderate republicanism, as a subordinate partner.

This same pattern characterized Bouches-du-Rhône. Here was a situation similar to Aude, with highly qualified leadership, with lawyers, journalists, and merchants who played key roles, but with more worker followers drawn in by 1850 as a result of the worsening economic situation. Public works were not sufficient to provide adequate relief. Consequently jobless workers either drifted into rural communes to get jobs or were used by the Montagnards as missionaries to spread the word. Propaganda by live voice was continued throughout the Republic. Some unemployed teachers were zealous in this thankless task, as were some wandering minstrels.[10] The press also continued active. The *Voix du Peuple* gave way to *Le Peuple* which had correspondents in small towns. Its influence was admitted and condemned by the mixed commissions of 1852.[11] However, the extreme left in Bouches-du-Rhône became excessively dependent on Marseille and during the so-called *complot du Midi* important chiefs were arrested, the leadership was severely handicapped in so large a city with the police omnipresent, and the city itself was not friendly. Numerous artisans and many dockers remained indifferent or hostile.

Yet, the artisan class in all the Midi became quite political-minded and among those who turned to the left, for whatever reasons, their commitment became increasingly ideological. This commitment must have been reinforced by the fact that by 1850–51 they were confronted with a moderately rising level of costs and a stable level of wages. Indeed, their wages remained at the low point to which they had fallen in 1847–

48.[12] However, it is doubtful that this economic factor was decisive. There is good reason to believe that most members of the extreme left, by 1850, were ideologically motivated and this was especially true of the working class. Now in Aude, and the highlands of Pyrénées-Orientales, where the working class was limited in size, the Mountain was more dependent on peasants, but peasants were turning to Bonapartism, lured by promises of government-supported public works to improve roads and conditions generally. Both the Radicals and the government promised these improvements, but every peasant knew that the government had money. Here is, perhaps, the real cause of peasant support for the coup d'état. A similar phenomenon occurred in Gard in Catholic areas; only ideological commitment and the Protestant religion reinforced the drive to the left in the western cantons. This ideological factor was decisive throughout the Midi and was made clear during the coup d'état.

PROFILE OF THE EXTREME LEFT

By December 1851 the extreme left consisted of a hard core of devoted men and an indeterminate number of followers, many of whom resorted to armed resistance against the coup d'état. Hérault and Var provided the largest contingents of resisters: 2,840 and 3,147 respectively, Gard and Aude the smallest, 380 and 251. Considering its size, Bouches-du-Rhône did not contribute significantly, 777 resisters, while Pyrénées-Orientales, the least populated department of the coast, offered 692. Over half of these resisters were freed or placed under surveillance by decision of mixed commissions. These commissions were determined to eradicate the left without excessively disrupting social and family life. Their so-called indulgence emanated from the belief that once the leaders of the hard core were removed the remainder would settle down. Therefore they released men who had been members and even chiefs of secret societies, and who had taken part in open resistance. They assumed that these men were égarés (led astray), of good background and family, and therefore not dangerous. Many of these judgments were rendered after these prisoners, who came from all classes, had written letters in which they deplored their conduct, denounced the reds who had led them astray and promised to be loyal subjects. In contrast the most active and conspicuous Radicals, chiefly professionals and artisans, were dealt with severely. It is this group which we shall study in order to observe the social composition of true Radicalism at mid-century. The vast majority, about 615 in Pyrénées-Orientales, 1,700 in Hérault, 215 in Gard, just under 100 in Aude, about 400 in Bouches-du-Rhône, and 1,900 in Var, were deported to penal colonies in North Africa, or, more rarely, in the tropics. A small number were jailed in France or sent into exile.[13] (See Appendix VIII)

In Aude, large numbers of rural folk had voted for the extreme left but would not join secret societies or rise up to save the Republic. In Gard roughly one-third of the peasants tried were deported, two-thirds released or placed under surveillance. The very large contingent sent to Algeria from Hérault resulted from the fact that Jacobinism had penetrated more deeply into the peasant class there than elsewhere. With its much larger contingent of rural vineyard labor, the number of peasants deported or jailed was nearly double the number of those released. Moreover the greater majority of this rural population lived in the plains and low hills, indicating a larger landed proletariat than in Gard or Aude where peasant support consisted in large measure of part owners and small owners. Unfortunately, we cannot state precisely how many proletarians there were in relation to land owners. Nearly all farmers were classed as *cultivateurs*; the only other significant classification of them was that of *propriétaires*. In Gard, the number of *propriétaires* was just under one-half the number of *cultivateurs*; in Hérault, it was only one-sixth. This tends to confirm the proletarian character of rural Radicalism in Hérault. Among the farmers deported a considerable majority belonged to secret societies and they formed about half of the leadership in them; they were active as decurions. In Gard and Aude, men classed as proprietors constituted roughly half of the agrarian leadership, whereas in Hérault proprietors accounted for less than one-third of it. The extreme left in Hérault, then, as it spread to rural areas, acquired more of a working-class character. Probably here is the explanation for the violence it resorted to when resisting the coup. In Roussillon, as in Hérault, armed resistance came out of the small towns and villages of the coastal plain and low hills, and it was primarily working class; 221 *journaliers,* 90 *propriétaires*, and 57 farmers of various sorts were arrested.[14] An important factor, however, was that most local leaders were either artisans or landowners. The roots of Radicalism were in the expanding vineyards.

In Provence, there were differences between Bouches-du-Rhône and Var. In the former the agricultural population provided about one-fourth of the resisters, in Var nearly one-half. The city of Marseille furnished just over one-half the men arrested, which explains the large number of artisans and petty bourgeois. The effective use of the army where so many Jacobin chiefs were concentrated stifled resistance before it became serious; there was really no uprising in Bouches-du-Rhône. In Var, Toulon was filled with troops so that the uprising broke out in the radicalized rural areas away from the coast. In fact, the leaders such as Duteil, who fled from Marseille to lead in Var, looked to the mountain people of the Basses-Alpes and led his troops northward rather than southward toward the quiescent coastal cities. Therefore it picked up large, wandering bands of peasants and rural artisans during its tragic march toward the Alpes where it was crushed. In Provence, *journaliers* as a social category were a negligible force in the resistance; at least, the term does not appear frequently in the documents. *Cultivateurs* comprised the immense majority of agricultural resisters. Of course the term *cultivateurs* subsumed several groups from wealthy farmers to worker-owners with barely enough income for subsistence, and undoubtedly some day laborers.

One *cultivateur* in Hérault was listed as having 18,000 francs in land and buildings, another as having 40,000 francs, others with 15,000 to 20,000, and several others with 3,000 to 10,000 francs in money real estate. These, of course, were exceptional cases, amounting to less than one percent of the total. On the other hand, proprietors usually possessed over 10,000 francs in money or land; one in Villeneuve (Hérault) enjoyed 70,000 francs, another 80,000 francs. Both were heads of secret societies and enjoyed considerable influence. In Gard the richest Radical was G. Caumel of Lassalle commune, who had a fortune of 120,000 francs. According to the police he spent it among the poor to buy flattery. Those others whose financial situation was elucidated had only a few thousand francs. Undoubtedly these reports are incomplete; however, they suggest why the extreme left in Gard and in backward Aude could not adequately support a press: the lack of really wealthy individuals to finance it. Radicalism in Hérault, then, had attracted, more so than its neighbors, the two extremes of the economic classes.

A similar situation existed in Pyrénées-Orientales. The Arago family was not wealthy, but it could count on the personal wealth of several devoted followers. In fact, Pyrénées-Orientales had the largest contingent of well-to-do: two at 25,000 francs, nine with 30,000–39,000 francs, eleven with 40,000–60,000 francs, seven with 80,000–100,000, one with 150,000, and 7 classified as *riche*. For the entire Midi there was a unique case: one prisoner with a fortune of 1,200,000 francs.

With supporters enjoying income from this wealth, it seems incredible that there was no Radical newspaper to succeed the *Indépendent* after its demise in the autumn of 1848. Even many less wealthy Radicals possessed sufficient income to help maintain a journal. There were some men listed as *journalier* whose wealth came to 5,000–10,000 francs, and although most had no visible wealth or only small bits of land, the resistance movement was not lacking in men who were financially sound and who had more to lose than their chains. In every department, *rentiers* made up from 1 to 5 percent of those tragic little bands opposed to Louis Napoleon.

The same extremes existed in non-agricultural professions. The gamut ran from the wage-workers of Bédarieux, earning about 1 franc 50 or 2 francs per day to the Montpellier lawyer Alphonse Coulandre whose personal wealth amounted to nearly 800,000 francs. There was Joseph Fabre, friend and supporter of the Aragos, and a banker whose wealth was evaluated at 200,000 francs; like most of the well-to-do (i.e., with 25,000 francs or more), he was expelled provisionally from France. The penal colonies were usually reserved for many low and middle-income prisoners. As with Coulandre, who was a lawyer, Fabre was an exception, and, without doubt, much of his wealth came from the land, as was undoubtedly true of most large fortunes. The major source of wealth in the Midi was agriculture and the wine trade. And most wealthy persons were strongly opposed to the extreme left. Nonetheless, the extreme left had a fairly solid economic base composed of some butchers, ovenkeepers, merchants, industrialists, and enterprising artisans who possessed modest fortunes or property valued from 2,000 to 20,000 francs. There was a wigmaker with 15,000 francs, a draughtsman with 35,000, a hotel keeper with 8,000, a day laborer with 20,000, a blacksmith with 40,000, a porter or carrier, called *"col de fer"* with 6,000, and a few blacksmiths with 4,000 to 40,000 francs. The well-off men, with several thousands in revenue or capital, were often local and departmental leaders, and the mixed commissions expended upon them the wrath which civil and military officialdom felt toward the extreme left. They were deported in large numbers. Altogether, in Hérault, they constituted about one-twentieth of the Montagnards involved in uprisings and about one-fifteenth of the deported.

Sharing leadership and constituting, with peasants and landowners, the true body of the left were men in the crafts, petty commerce, and the liberal professions. Particularly in Aude, Gard, and Bouches-du-Rhône, where peasant response was relatively weak, the middling and petty middle class displayed the strength and weakness of the left: strength in that they sacrificed wealth and freedom; weakness in that they could not unite in the face of a deadly threat. The industries most actively represented were artisanal. When the cry "to arms" was spread abroad, shoemakers responded with remarkable vigor. They and tailors made the clothing trade one of the most active. Equally active were men in the building trade: carpenters and cabinet makers, masons, plasterers, and locksmiths. Then came barrel-makers from the wine areas, tanners, and smiths. In Var with its forests, *bûcherons* constituted the largest non-farming group.

Where there were large concentrations of industrial wage labor, opposition to the coup was weak. Chalabre, Saint-Chinion, and Bédarieux were the only textile centers where labor acted vigorously. In Bédarioux the leaders condemned to death for killing police agents were, save for two, non-textile workers, and, among the rank and file, artisans were as numerous as weavers and spinners, although considerably less numerous in the total active population. The same observation applies to Saint-Chinion. In Lodève textile workers were organized in a Club des Cinq and in the Centurie Benoît and the Centurie Pioch. But they did not join the opposition, perhaps because of the presence of troops and because of economic prosperity. Neither was there any significant response from two important silk textile centers: Ganges and Le Vigan in the high hills. Not even the numerous Protestants took up arms. Miners in the large coal basin in Gard were organized in a militia to oppose the left, and the few Montagnards despatched there to stir up the miners encountered mute resistance.[15] The response was also weak in the small mining districts of Hérault and Bouches-du-Rhône.

In commerce and services butchers, bakers, petty merchants, and cafe owners predominated, followed by some salesmen, clerks, and barbers. The liberal professions supplied lawyers and notaries, as well as medical doctors and students. The arts provided a few writers, sculptors, and lithographers. Only Montpellier, Nîmes, Marseille, and Toulon could support intellectuals but they, like teachers and students, were closely controlled by the government. By no means was this a revolution of the intellectuals even though there were journalists who were often ex-teachers or lawyers or landowners. Notable were the two bankers, one from Perpignan, the other from Montpellier, and the one stock broker from Nîmes.

Practically all of these men were honest, law-abiding citizens. With few exceptions they had been born and lived in the same commune. If not, they came from a nearby commune where they had been born. Only a minority came from another department. Radical ideals, then, took root in the native, not the transient population. There were, as yet, few foreigners, and most of them were Spaniards or Italians working in the vineyards and disinterested in politics. Of the natives who were deported about 5 percent had criminal records: most of them had been prosecuted for insulting the police or local judges, for inciting to resistance, for *tapage nocturne,* all of which were political offenses. About an equal percentage had previously been found guilty of violating hunting laws. Poaching was as common among Languedocians and Provençals as smuggling was among Basques and was as tolerated by local opinion. To be sure, the insurrectionary movements gathered up all sorts of persons. There were a few convicted murderers, there were some thieves, chiefly men who had filched their neighbor's crops; there were some who beat their wives and abandoned their children; there were at least two pimps. But these elements accounted for less than one percent of the deported and for even less of the larger number who acted to oppose the coup.

In several instances in Hérault violence was extreme. In Bédarieux men with and without prison records invaded the police headquarters and shot several officers; however, they did so only after two officers had killed a seventy-year-old man and wounded his young companion, apparently without serious provocation. The official reports state that the bloodthirsty mob, after invading the headquarters, even cut off the testicles of one dead officer, an accusation that was not adequately proved and that was later denied by Tenot.[16]   The *révoltés* of Bédarieux were severely aggrieved and surely because the government had granted cloth contracts to Lodève, yet they were not more brutal than the commanding general, de Rostolon. Once in power they preserved order, threatened thieves with death, and did not molest conservatives. Their two most influential leaders, the rich proprietor Paul Belugou and the clockmaker Pierre Bonnel, opposed excesses. The same policy was followed in other communes where the lower classes seized power.[17]   There were, of course, acts of irrational brutality committed by excited crowds; the butchering by error of two republicans in Béziers after troops had shot down over seventy demonstrators and the murder of the local priest by the people of his commun were isolated incidents.

There was usually more threat to commit violence than actual commission, and in some textile centers, acts of disorder had little to do with politics. At Saint-Chinion, Saint Pons, and Riols (Hérault), weaver-peasants sought more to break machines than to save the Republic. Worker and peasant aggression sometimes took the form of stone throwing and isolated shooting at police officers and forest guards who sought to prevent poaching or the cutting of trees. The lower classes had to hunt to supplement their meagre diets, especially since agricultural prices were just beginning to rise after years of depression. But their acts, compared to the brutality of the soldiery and the veritable terror exercised by legitimists in Montpellier, seems rather restrained. Legitimists more so than imperialists, of whom there were few, took leading Radicals, attached them to bars of iron, chained them together, and marched them through the streets. It was they who put political prisoners into minute and filthy cells with only humid straw to sleep on, and kept them there until their hearings, two or three months later.[18]   There were acts of cruelty and bitterness on both sides; it is surprising that there were not worse excesses.

Undoubtedly a greater sense of responsibility existed among the resisters because about 60 percent of them were married. Over 85 percent of the married were fathers and among fathers, the vast majority had one or two children, with roughly 25 percent having three or more.[19]   Quite clearly it was not with a light heart that these family men took up arms. Since they constituted the bulk of the leadership, their ideological commitment was strong and to their children they left a republican heritage that survived them. Of course about a third of resistors were celibates, a situation explained by the relative youth of most Jacobins. Slightly under one-half were in their twenties. Hérault and Var had the largest contingents of young men under thirty. The Montagnards did not marry early, hardly at all until twenty-five years of age. Three-fifths of the bachelors were under thirty and over one-fifth in their thirties. Likewise most of the married men and fathers were in their late twenties and thirties.

Here was the Radical generation of the Second Republic who lived on to educate their children in the ideas of Jacobinism and who, with their aid, helped to found the Third Republic.[20]   Quite frequently Radical commitment was a family matter; fathers and sons, uncles and brothers were active together in local secret societies and joined together in the bands marching to save the Republic. That repression could not efface the memory of them was revealed in the plebiscite of 20 December 1851; Pyrénées-Orientales, Aude, Hérault, Gard, Bouches-du-Rhône, and Var, through a *non* or an abstention, ranked among the departments with the highest oppositional vote to Louis Napoleon's "crime." The remembrance of it lay dormant for nineteen years among the peasants and artisans of the plains and valleys and among the Protestants and woodsmen of the high hills and mountains.

NOTES

1. The verb "was becoming" for January 1850 is more suitable than "had become" because Favand's turn to the left was not, according to the prefect, clearly understood by all his supporters. See A.N. F[1c] III Gard[5], reports of January 1850.

2. See *Républicain du Gard*, 18 July 1850 for the republican and Protestant position on the Falloux bill. Also A.N. BB[30] 382, dr. 9567a, report of proc.-général of Nîmes, 9 June 1850. The Falloux bill offered the Catholic clergy extensive control over secondary education in public schools. It passed easily.

3. For lists of known societies and their organization, see the police reports in A.D. Gard 6M 613; A.D. Hérault 39M 132, 139, 144; A.N. BB[18] 1469 dr. 6579; BB[18] 1474B, dr. 6933a; BB[30] 391, 392a, 394.

4. A.N. BB[18] 1468, dr. 6356a.

5. See *Le Démocrate du Var*, 26 February, 12-13 March 1850, also A.N. FIC III Var[4], perfect's letter of 20 May 1850, in which he complains that abstention of the men of order had narrowed the margin of victory. In fact, about 1,971 arsenal workers abstained. And the abstention rate in Var was persistently high.

6. 24 April 1851.

7. A.N. BB[18] 1468, dr. 2756, report of proc. général, 15 March 1850; BB[18] 1474a, report of 3 March 1850; A.D. Var 4M 17, undated report.

8. A.D. Var 4M 17, subprefect's report of 26 June 1851. The eastern *arrondissement* of Cannes, attached to Nice after 1860 to form the new department of Alpes Maritimes, was far less prone to Jacobinism than the western *arrondissements*.

9. For clubs and political organization, see A.N. BB[18] 1474b, BB[30], 380, dr. 8167a. Also H. Chauvet, *Hist. parti républ'n,* 69–99.

10. A.D. B-du-R 6M 344, subprefect report, Aix, 7 October 1851.

11. Ibid., 6M 100.

12. See A.N. F[20] 712, 797, 798; tables in F. Convert, *Les Ouvriers agricoles et les salaires en présence du phylloxera* (Montpellier, 1878), 25.

13. Most of this information has been found in the local archives which contain extensive records often giving for each accused both vital statistics and information about the role played during the revolt. See A.D. Aude 5M 36–42; Hérault 39M 143, 161, 194; Gard 6M 461, 594–600, 3U 5 1–3; Pyrénées Orientales 3M 1–89; Var 4M 24–2 and 3; Bouches-du-Rhône 6M 36, 100; A.N. BB[30] 424; F[7] 12651, report of 13 December 1851. Useful information on the coup d'état can be found in A. Pieyre, *Histoire de la ville de Nîmes* (Nîmes, 1886–87), vol. II; Y. Goirand, *Histoire politique et économique du Var, 1848 à 1870,* Diplome d'Etudes Supérieures, Univ. of Aix-Marseille, 1955; Victor Fournier, *Le Coup d'état de 1851 dans le Var,* (Draguignan, 1928); E. Appolis, "La Résistance au coup d'état ... dans l'Hérault," *Actes du 77e Congrès National des Sociétés Savantes* (1952), 487–504. Louis J. Thomas *Montpellier en 1851;* Eugene Tenot, *La Province en décembre 1851* (Paris, 1868); J.F. Jeanjean, *Le Coup d'état du 2 Décembre 1851 dans ... l'Aude* (Paris, 1924); Martin, "Coup d'état dans l'Hérault," *op.cit.*

14. See A.D. Pyrénées-Orientales 3M 1–81. A.N. BB[30] 424 listed only 37 "cultivateurs," clearly an error.

15. A.D. Gard 6M 461, reports of subprefects, December 1851.

16. Tenot, *Province en ... 1851,* 114–17. See A.D. Hérault 39M 142, report of 4 December 1851, and Roger Allaire, *Histoire de la ville de Bédarieux* (Bédarieux, 1911), 189–204.

17. Tenot, *Province en ... 1851,* 102–3; Appolis, "Résistance au coup d'état," 492–97; Martin, "Coup d'état," 75–79. When resisters broke into town halls and country houses they took whatever arms and munitions were available, not valuables or money.

18. See the lurid accounts in *La Liberté* [Montpellier], 10 December 1869, p. 3, also Andre Minet, "La Bourgeoisie montpellieraine et le second Empire," Diplome d'Etudes Supérieures, University of Montpellier, 1963, 29.

19. These figures are rough estimates based on incomplete data, and apply chiefly to lower Languedoc.

20. By the law of 30 July 1881, the third Republic provided pensions for victims of the coup d'état or their heirs.

CHAPTER FOUR

THE VITICULTURAL EXPANSION
AND POLITICAL QUIESCENCE, 1852-1869

GOLDEN AGE OF WINE

The period of the Second Empire was one of meditation and moderation in the field of politics, and the Radical movement was not an exception. However, there were changes underway in the economy and social structure of the lower Midi which prepared the way for the rebirth and triumph of Radicalism after 1870.

The viticultural expansion was a phenomenon which occurred in several areas of France, but it left its most permanent impress on the lower Midi. Particularly in the wine sectors of Languedoc it could be referred to as a continuing revolution, accompanied by the periodic crises which are integral parts of revolutionary movements. Now southern France from 1850 to 1870 did not experience an equivalent of the eighteenth-century agricultural revolution of Britain or of northern France. On the contrary, land ownership assumed a complex pattern. As had earlier occurred in England and the north there was some concentration, but in contrast, there was a considerable expansion of small property, often at the expense of medium property. In addition, the rural population did not decline markedly; rather people shifted from one type of farming, polyculture, to another, monoculture. Also the great change did not involve basic crops such as cereals and fodder but exclusively the wine grape. Finally, there were no significant innovations in technique until long after the expansion had gotten under way. Increased production of wine grapes and of wine resulted chiefly from expanded acreage rather than new methods. Productivity went up because vineyards took over the better lands customarily planted in cereals, fodder, olives, and fruit. Formely vines had been relegated to the poorer, dryer, lighter soil of the hillsides. Or, as was often the case in Provence, rows of vines alternated with rows of other crops. But now the vine became king in the same sense that cotton was king in the American South.

Of course, not all areas in the lower Midi went over to a monoculture. The phenomenon was largely limited to the coast and low hills west of the Rhône where wine producers were tempted into speculative practices. East of the mighty river they were less inclined toward monoculture on such a large scale. Nonetheless, wine production in certain areas dominated agriculture without excluding other crops by the simple fact that wine prices were high. These generalizations, as well as exceptions to them, need further explanation.

First, grape production early showed signs of instability, especially in areas of its domination. The initial stage of a dramatic advance in grape production was checked by a disease called *oïdium* that attacked vines nearly everywhere from about 1852 to about 1856–57. The discovery of sulfur as a cure ended this momentary setback. And, indeed, this brief recession was not all evil. Having restricted wine production without wiping it out, the *oïdium* provoked an enormous jump of prices: from 5 to 10 francs in 1848–49 up to 40 francs in 1857–58. Thus did the golden age of viticulture make its entry.

In Pyrénées-Orientales, vineyards were rapidly expanded, thanks to profits augmented by high prices. They soon covered the plain of Roussillon, the valleys of the Agly, Tet, and Tech rivers, and the lower hillsides of the Corbières, Fenouillèdes, and Albères. Acreage rose precipitously: from 38,391 hectares in 1836 to 70,000 in 1875. Two-thirds of the increase came in the 1860s. Roughly three-fourths of the vineyards were in the *arrondissement* of Perpignan which produced about four-fifths of the department's wine.[1] In the lowlands vintners produced either a cheap table wine or the sweet dessert wines of reputation. In the hills they produced a palatable but not remarkable table wine.

The transition to monoculture was even more decisive in lower Languedoc. From Sigean Canton to the lower Rhône River the grape vine took over the medium and lower hills and particularly the coastal plain down to the highly sandy soil close to the sea. The richer lands, formerly reserved for cereals and pasturage, gave way more rapidly than in Roussillon. The Minervois is a good example of this change. Before 1853 its best land was covered with magnificent cereal crops, and vines were relegated to the shallow soils of hillsides. But within twenty years vines descended and covered nearly all the arable; even olives disappeared[2] (See Appendix IV). Since Hérault had the longest coast it led the way. J. E. Coste, departmental professor of agriculture, referred to it as "une sorte de vigne sans fin." By 1862 it produced only one-fourth the grain its population required, and this production was reserved for those ill-fated lands that nature had not endowed for vines: the uplands of Saint-Pons, Lodève, and Montpellier *arrondissements*. By necessity and bad luck these areas sought to maintain the ideal of self-sufficiency. However many young people repudiated such an ideal and as quickly as possible they set off for the lowlands where wages were higher and opportunities greater.

Increased employment resulted from the transition to mass production of wine. The *vigneron,* a new social type who shall be studied in more detail later on, came to look upon wine from the quantitative rather than the qualitative point of view. This was undoubtedly a natural out-growth of the viticole revolution, because most areas of the lower Midi had never brought forth a quality wine. Most wine, hardly drinkable, had been distilled into alcohol. However, with the coming of railroads which opened the rest of France to Languedoc, wine could be shipped northward and sold as wine rather than distilled for alcohol.[3] Another factor encouraging quantity as against quality was the rising cost of production. However, costs were still moderate as compared to the post-1870s; the decisive factor, therefore, was simply the desire to produce a massive amount of wine as a means of raising one's profits. Roussillon and lower Languedoc in 1875 produced about 20 percent of France's total. Of course, there were exceptions. The muscats of Banyuls, Rive-saltes, Frontignan, and Lunel, as some of the table wines of the Rhône Valley in Gard, maintained their quality.

Bouches-du-Rhône and Var followed the general pattern but with more hesitation, or perhaps, simply, with more skepticism. They were also at a disadvantage, because their terrain was less adaptable to mass production. Nonetheless wine became a dominant cash crop in the flat lands south and east of Arles, in the valleys of Aix *arrondissement,* around Brignoles, the plain of Cuers, and most of Toulon *arrondissement.* Acreage around Marseille declined steadily so that it ceased to be an important producer; here peasants found truck gardening and fruit more profitable for the urban market. Only the southwestern sector of Var really approached monoculture, but it was the exception. With the 1860s there was probably a decline of acreage devoted to vines in Provence. Vineyards there were not quite as productive as those west of the Rhône, yet their product remained the chief money crop and had an effect similar to that of the Languedocian vineyards. The six Mediterranean departments in 1875, the last good year before the phylloxera crisis, produced 17,231,000 hectolitres of wine, enough to provoke a serious fall in prices.

Silk production could no longer compete with wine as a major cash crop save in those areas ill-suited to grapes. But even the highlands were invaded as farmers pushed outward the natural frontiers of vineyards. This expansion was the result of efforts to fill the vacuum left by declining silk production. A disease called *pebrine* was to silk what *oïdium* was to wine. However, the results were different for each product. Wine, after its setback, surged ahead to profit from a privileged position in the national and European market; silk, after the *pebrine* was conquered by Louis Pasteur, faced a market that had been invaded by oriental producers and by synthetics. Both competitors forced prices down.

The southern agricultural economies, then, fared differently during the Second Empire. Yet, much of the literature considered the period a golden age of rural prosperity—undoubtedly because this literature reflected or was concerned with the wine interests. There were several factors which led to its optimism. Wine was the product which profited most from the building of railroads and the general improvement of transport. Great reductions in the cost of shipping opened the French and European market to it, so it successfully competed with other regional beverages and encouraged the decline of wine production in northern terrain unsuited to the grape. Given such opportunities, Midi vintners now grew particularly concerned about railroad rates, an issue that became an integral part of southern politics. Also the trade treaty of 1860 and the general lowering of tariffs that followed encouraged the export of wine to several foreign markets. In another sense tariff reduction was a particular boon; southern grape growers could buy foreign cereals more cheaply and therefore devote even more of their land to vines. Of course, domestic cereal growers were hurt, but they were looked upon as anachronistic. In the *Enquête agricole* of 1866, nearly all respondents affirmed that southern soil was not suited to cereals because the climate was too dry.[4] Local agricultural societies joined chambers of commerce, especially in Var, to urge peasants to concentrate on vines. This advice was followed; cereal growers had no choice, given the fall of their prices. Where adaptation was not feasible, the population declined as young persons drifted toward the lowlands and the larger cities. Among those who remained, high tariffs and irrigation canals were viewed as panaceas for all economic ills.

The population and social structure were naturally affected by economic change. The 1850s and 1860s marked a general population decline in highland cantons. The only important exception was Alès because of labor-attractive operations. In an age of rising expectations in coastal cantons, life appeared, and indeed was, hard and dreary elsewhere. The vineyards with their relatively high wages, rising demand for labor, and easy land purchase opened opportunities formerly undreamed of among the hill people.

Vineyards were gold and peasants rushed to get it, somewhat like the forty-niners had rushed to the fields of California. Yet, there was a difference. Peasants undoubtedly bought land in the hope of getting rich; but land to a peasant was far different from a gold vein to a prospector. The prospector took out all the wealth and departed; the peasant put into his holding his very being, sought to sink roots and to follow a way of life conformable to his existence as a farmer. Often this meant a conservative, austere way of life; in the southern vineyards, however, customs and expectations were transformed by the availability of capital and easy credit. Land purchase was remarkably easy. Land prices naturally rose in a dizzying fashion, but wine prices were so high that mortgages were often paid off in three or four years. Profits were such that a family could live well on five hectares of vineyards; ten hectares opened the way to an undreamed quality of life. The only dark spot was the crisis of 1866–67 when a glutted market caused prices to fall; the panic was of brief duration and ignored as a warning. The urban population of France was still growing and prosperous. It wanted wine and paid dearly for it. Therefore, producers of wine, from peasants to nobles, enjoyed a marked rise in living standards. Viticulture, rather than polyculture and industry, was the means to riches and change.[5]

Mobility, break from tradition, belief in progress, and rapid improvement became more commonly accepted in growing coastal towns. Béziers was fairly typical of them; from a small commune it became the major wine market of the Midi. To it, to Narbonne, Perpignan, Montpellier, Nîmes, Arles, and Brignoles, a new glitter was added: cabarets, casinos, red light districts, and town houses. Peasants bought pianos and peasants' daughters, ribbons in hair, learned how to play them—more or less.

These peasants were hardly in a mood to oppose the government. They favored its tariff policy, hoping to win foreign markets, and not until the last years of the Empire did they complain that their wine was not selling abroad. As in 1848, they also complained about the *octrois* and the drink tax. But they were not prepared for serious opposition. There were other reasons for contentment. Mountain people who came to the plain came as laborers, looking for higher wages—and found them, double those of their homelands. The lowland peasants, because of their skills and the general shortage of workers in viticulture, became a kind of labor aristocracy. Their wages reached unprecedented heights and it was they more so than immigrant peasants who bought land and became either *propriétaires* or *ouvriers propriétaires*. The sea coast and low hills, where small ownership had already begun to spread, was well on the way to becoming a land of peasant owners, save in Arles *arrondissement* and lower Hérault. In this optimistic climate, indifference or approval of the Empire was widespread among the lower classes.

The structure of society assumed more modern forms. A large *journalier* class emerged, chiefly along the coast and in river valleys where land concentration was appearing. But among these *journaliers* were numerous *propriétaires*. At least it seems so. Census returns are rarely precise and electoral lists are no better. People in agriculture are listed as "propriétaires" and "cultivateurs" or as "agriculteurs," rarely as "journaliers." This perhaps reveals a psychological state: a desire not to be classed as workers since there was upward mobility made possible by vineyard ownership, and an identification with property. Therefore increasing access to property became an important factor in all the Midi, at least among the natives who could more easily acquire it.

Expanding opportunities strongly influenced the way of life along the coast. Traditionalism gave way more and more to innovation; higher levels of living led to the optimism and speculation that deepened the division between the interior and the coast. Religious values declined and would continue to do so, clearing the way for dechristianization and the anticlericalism of the Third Republic. More than ever society became fluid. The idea of a lower class as the flat base of a triangular social structure gave way to a more diamond shaped one with the mass of *cultivateurs* in the middle and at a moderately pointed bottom the ignorant immigrants from the highlands and, especially, the numerous Italians and Spaniards who began to flood in as cheap laborers.

DECLINE OF TRADITIONAL INDUSTRY

The situation in industry and commerce was, in certain areas, more conducive to widespread discontent; however, the discontented became either sullen and quiescent or abandoned industry for agriculture. It was particularly during the Second Empire that an important option was made: in lower Languedoc, viticulture was chosen over industry as the main source of wealth. In the *Enquête Agricole* of 1866 there was constant complaint that capital was flowing away from agriculture and into industry and government bonds. This is doubtful, given the sums invested in the wine revolution. Investments in agriculture steadily took precedence over those in industry. Of course, the choice was partly forced by nature and by the government. Even after a cure for the *pebrine* was found and raw silk production made some recovery, silk textiles were confronted with competition from the Orient as well as with synthetics from Germany. Major centers such as Nîmes, Ganges, and Le Vigan were less affected, but large numbers of the small spinning and weaving plants and domestic shops were put out of business. From these areas there was emigration which increased in the nineteenth century, for textiles had provided the natives with either a complete income or one complementary to that of agriculture. But not only did work decrease, wages remained low relative to those of vineyards.[6] The farmers who did not leave witnessed unemployment and demoralization. The post-1870 recovery brought a shift of silk production from Nîmes to its source of raw materials, the mountainous northern part of the department, Le Vigan and Alès *arrondissements*.[7] Silk in Bouches-du-Rhône and Var suffered a similar decline.

Woolen textiles suffered a worse fate. The Chevalier-Cobden free trade treaty of 1860 dealt it a decisive blow; as devastating was the central government's decision to reduce the size and frequency of its orders for military cloth (*draps*) from Lodève, Bédarieux, Clermont, and Saint-Pons in Hérault, as well as from Carcassonne in Aude. Unlike the major silk centers, these woolen textile towns had notorious left-wing traditions; this situation might or might not have influenced the army's contract policies.

Undoubtedly the attitude of workers toward mechanization also had an effect. Politically radical, they were technologically conservative. They had resisted innovation before 1848, and they continued to do so under the Empire. The workers were also stubbornly individualistic. The result was that machinery required to fulfill government orders could not be used to produce cloth for civilian use, nor could new machinery be introduced. In addition, the treaty of 1860 forced the larger producers to consolidate and to absorb or to destroy the smaller ones.[8] From this practice came unemployment and underemployment rather than technological innovation as a means of reducing costs to meet British competition. During 1896 there were in Lodève 1,000 operatives unemployed and 2,300 on a three-day week. In Aude, left-wing politics were also fairly typical of woolen weavers in the Carcas-sonnais, Limoux and Chalabre. In the latter, textiles declined when the owners, fearful of their employees, moved to conservative communes nearby, or into Ariège department. As in Hérault, textiles elsewhere in Aude suffered a decrease in orders, lost their foreign markets to England, and declined. The labor force, slowly at first and then more rapidly, moved to the coast in search of better-paying jobs.[9]

Neither in Roussillon nor in lower Provence were textiles significant.

In the former, many small forges were put out of business by the treaty of 1860. In Arles locomotive construction and repair shops expanded. With an enlarged railroad labor force added to the dockers and artisans, left-wing politics were reinforced. This development was typical of Provence: vineyards, while not negligible, had less effect on the economy and demography than industry. Population movement was toward urban centers with an active industrial and commercial growth; Marseille with its great port and industry; La Ciotat with metallurgy; Toulon and La Seyne with naval yards and ship construction.

Another important industrial activity was coal mining. The active economy and rising standards of the Second Empire encouraged the use of local coal in place of charcoal. As with wine, railroad building opened markets to the pits of Hérault, Gard, and Bouches-du-Rhône, and even small ones in Pyrénées-Orientales. A sizable element was added to the labor force as more peasants were attracted away from the soil's surface in order to dig deep under it. Mining offered about the only inducement to the retention of population in highland, isolated cantons. To numerous economically deprived peasants, jobs in the mines represented not only an advance in life but the chance to remain close to the land. Many natives in nearby communes owned land, and immigrants from the mountains north of Hérault and Gard earned enough to buy small garden plots. The miners, therefore, were considerably more stable and submissive than the laboring class growing up in the vineyards and would remain so long after the fall of Napoleon III.

REPUBLICAN AWAKENING

The 1850s in the Midi, as in France, were not years of political activism. In the reports of prefects attorneys-general, the key words were "calme" and "tranquille." Curiously, the two departments where republicanism, even Jacobinism, had been most aggressive in 1848–49 became most devoted to the Empire in the 1850s: Pyrénées-Orientales and Aude. Save for the Perpignonnais and Carcassonnais, a political style took root there based on the willingness to favor the government in power. They were imperialist during the Empire, opportunist or moderate republican from 1876 to 1898, and Radical thereafter.

The form of politics which favored moderate republicanism after 1871 was incipient during the Empire. Republicans of all sorts united their forces in opposition to the common enemy, and Jacobinism faded or blended into the republican movement seeking political freedom. And since it was no longer menacing, national leaders of the left took up the word "radical" to underscore their absolute opposition to the authoritarian regime. In the writings of Jules Simon, the word radical became part of the general oppositional vocabulary, extremist in its detestation of the Empire and clericalism, moderate in its notions of a republican society for the future.

Movements against the establishment, then, were simply republican whatever they might be called. This result was inevitable, given the fact that leaders of the extreme left were dead, in penal colonies, or in exile. And yet, there was a determined effort on the part of local republicans to preserve their ideals and their identity. In these purely local manifestations of the will to freedom was preserved the spirit of mid-century Jacobinism, and they were most common precisely in those areas where that spirit emerged again later.[10]   Forms of opposition varied. They were individual: scribbling on walls of "Vive la République!" solitary cries in the night of "à bas la tyrannie!" They were also collective: secret societies. Local police during the 1850s insisted that democrats were still organized, that they retained their cafes in Languedoc and their *chambrées* in Provence. Most of the men arrested for clandestine activity were in their late thirties or older, which meant that the generation of 1848 was still active, the younger generation far less so. When an aging republican died, his funeral became a political act. When a man smoked a pipe with a bowl made in the image of Ledru-Rollin or Barbès, that was also a political act.

Such acts were isolated and often repressed. In the 1850s the bulk of the population was chiefly concerned with overcoming the maladies which struck vines and mulberry trees and silk worms. Farmers were in need of governmental aid, not only in their fight against nature but also to get improvements. Here was a compelling hold that prefects vigorously exercised upon the population: local public works programs depended on electoral results. Prefects willingly promised a railroad, an irrigation canal, better roads, subsidies, to influence voters. For example, Sète, a left-wing port in Hérault, was threatened with the loss of its railroad connection if its voters opposed the official candidate.[11] Despite oppression there remained several pockets of red identification: Perpignan, Béziers, and the stretch of communes between Brignoles and Draguignan. Most people, however, were indifferent or hostile toward the left.

The situation did not greatly change in the 1860s. The return of most exiles after the 1859 amnesty was offset by the leap forward of the wine economy following the *oïdium*; indeed the relation between politics and economic conditions was curious, even paradoxical. The highland people, as noted earlier, suffered most from the economic, especially the tariff, policies of Napoleon. Yet they remained strongly attached to his regime. Not because the peasants of the Pyrenees, the Cévennes and lower Alps were imbued with Bonapartism as a system; rather, they were attached to authoritarian tradition, order, and religion, and they associated these ideas with the Empire.

In the towns and cities of the coast and valleys appeared the first signs of serious political opposition. Since 1859 numerous penal colony prisoners and exiles had returned to France and by 1869 they resumed leadership. The continuity between the second and third republics became clear. In Pyrénées-Orientales, the old Jacobin Pierre Lefranc founded the *Indépendant* in Perpignan (1868). He was assisted by the son of Theodôre Guiter. In Carcassonne, Marcou established the *Fraternité* and Raynal became active in Narbonne. Not only the men, even the titles of the journals were the same. This conscious effort to maintain continuity with the past was apparent elsewhere; in Hérault and Gard the leading figures of the revived republican movement were the same as those in 1848, A. Laissac, Eugene Lisbonne, and A. Castelnau in the former, and Jules Cazot, J.L. Laget, Bousquet, and Favand in the latter. In Marseille, Gustave Naquet founded *Le Peuple* to continue the 1850–51 tradition. Alphonse Esquiros, ex-editor of *Voix du peuple* (1848–50), returned to organize the left and was eulogized for his intransigency toward the Empire.[12] Var was of course attached to its memory of the bloody coup d'état and, earliest among the departments, turned both to men who were heroes of that event and to new men nurtured on stories about it.

With the elections of 1869 came an occasion to act. Earlier elections

NOTES

1. André Vigo, *Evolution économique récente des Pyrénées-Orientales.* (Montpellier, 1936), 44–46.
2. Passama, *Condition des ouvriers,* 24–25.
3. See A.D. Hérault 11M unclassified, "Culture de la vigne."
4. France. Ministère de l'Agriculture, du Commerce et des Travaux Publics, *Enquête agricole* [1866] (Paris, 1867). Deuxième série.
5. Useful information about the rise of wine can be found in Augé-Laribé, *Problème agraire,* 44 ff.; G.F. Galtier, "Essai sur l'économie montpelliéraine" *Bulletin de la Société Languedocienne de Géographie,* 2em s., V (1933), 23–42; M. Tudez, *Dévelopement de la vigne dans la région de Montpellier* (Montpellier, 1934), 240 and *passim;* Degrully, *Production du vin,* 323 ff.; A.D. Hérault, 11M unclassified "Culture de la vigne," numerous reports; Barbut, *Etude sur le vignoble de l'Aude* (Carcassonne, 1912), 78 ff.; R. Plande, *Géographie et histoire ... Aude.* (n.p., 1942), 210 ff.; A. Vigo, *Evolution économique ... Pyrénées-Orientates,* 44–79; A.D. P-O 3M-163, numerous reports; Chauzit, "Monographie agricole du ... Gard," *Bulletin du Ministère de l'Agricylture,* 17 (1898), 1529–65; L. Destremx de St. Christol. *Agriculture méridionnalle* (Paris [1867]), 37–41; A.N. BB³⁰ 389, dr. 8167a, report of *procureur-général* of Nîmes, 18 January 1869; Y. Goirand, "Histoire économique et politique du Var de 1848 à 1870" Diplôme d'Etudes Supérieures, Univ. of Aix-Marseille, 1955–56; A.D. Var 14M 19, 29, numerous reports; *Bouches-du-Rhône, encyclopédie départementale,* Vol. VII, *Agriculture.*
6. Data are available in A.D. Gard 14M 133, 14M 212; A.N. BB³⁰ 382, 389.
7. H. Reboul, *Industrie nîmoise du tissage au XIXe siècle* (Montpellier, 1914), 21–23.
8. C. Saint-Pierre, *L'Industrie dans ... l'Hérault* (Montpellier, 1865), 186–200, 275; BB³⁰ dr. 8167a, reports on economic situation. See reports in A.D. Hérault 39M 227, 244.
9. A.D. Aude 14M 15–19; A.N. F²⁰ 501 Aude; Claude Fohlen argued that Languedoc deliberately chose to foster wine at the expense of textiles by shifting its pattern of investment from the latter to the former. "En Languedoc: vigne contre draperie," *Annales, économie, sociétés, civilisations,* 4 (July-September 1949), 290;97.
10. Information on local opponents comes mainly from their enemies: prefects in their reports (A.N. F¹C III series), and regional attorneys-general (BB³⁰ series).
11. A.D. Hérault 39M 227, 240; Louis Puech, *Essai sur la candidature officielle en France depuis 1851* (Mende, 1922), chap. II.
12. Jacques P. van der Linden, *Alphonse Esquiros* (Paris, 1948), 40–90.
13. For the election see A. Olivesi, "Marseille," in L. Girard, ed., *Les Elections de 1869* (Paris, 1960), pp. 77–123.
14. Marseille was singled out because of the large public works program there. See Raoul Bousquet, *Histoire de Marseille* (Paris, 1945).

CHAPTER FIVE

ADVENT OF AN ERA OF CRISES:
THE PHYLLOXERA, 1869-1881

etween 1869 and 1875 France passed through a period of intense change. The Empire was overthrown and the struggle for a new government lasted five years. Meanwhile she suffered a military defeat that was unexpected and therefore more demoralizing, especially since it was followed by diplomatic isolation for an entire generation. France also lost precious territory and had to pay an unusually heavy indemnity. The lower Midi naturally experienced these catastrophies, and yet the people there were remote from frontier problems affecting primarily the northeast. There were other regional problems emerging which, although part of the national scene, attained a particular intensity in the lower Midi and had a more lasting effect on its way of life.

At about the time that France gave herself a definitive form of government, the mid-1870s, the *vignerons* of the Midi entered a period of acute suffering. Roughly two decades after the *oïdium,* their vines were struck by a new blight. The cause of the malady was a plant louse called phylloxera which attacked the roots of vines and in distressingly short time killed the plant. According to most authorities, it had been carried to France from the United States on some experimental vine varieties and first appeared in the lower Rhône Valley in the late 1860s. Slowly it began its awful offensive simultaneously to the east and west, and eventually it appeared in nearly all the vineyards of France where it brought ruin.[1]   Given the great dependence of the Midi on wine, it was particularly disastrous there.

ECONOMIC DECLINE

Wherever the phylloxera appeared, the vines, whether in long rows or in clusters rapidly withered and perished. Without leaves the dead branches came to resemble knarled bare fingers reaching out of the earth. The summer green and the autumn reds and yellows of their leaves no longer decorated the landscape, and in all directions the dry and rocky soil that had given them life recovered its bleak, winter look. Neither the tender care of the vine men nor the sun and rain could overcome the silent, senseless invader. And the vine men, as though unable to believe the scenes of destruction they witnessed, refused to act at once. Each convinced himself that only his neighbors' plants would fall victim, not his own; how could a man believe what he saw when the scene before him was the relentless withering of his life's work. Vine growers, to be sure, were accustomed to natural disaster. Since the time when vines were first grown commercially, *vignerons* had witnessed periodically the destruction by insects, by frost, by hail, by storms and rain, and by war. But the loss had been that of a year's crop at worse. And before the advent of monoculture there had been other crops to fall back on. But the phylloxera loomed as the ultimate destroyer, for it not only wiped out a year's crop, it killed the vine itself and all hope of recovery. This terrifying fact was incredible to the generation of the golden age of viticulture, who had almost forgotten the low wine prices of the forties and the *oïdium* of the fifties.

Their refusal to believe could not make the new malady disappear. Unmindful, it struck first in the low Rhône Valley and then spread in all directions.

In Bouches-du-Rhône it followed the lower Durance Valley and then descended southward into the *arrondissement* of Aix and ultimately into that of Marseille. It killed about 90 percent of the vines. Curiously, it was less destructive in the vineyards of Arles, which were of lesser economic importance. Partly because of this discrimination, partly because of the safety afforded vines by sandy soils, Arles now emerged as an important wine area, comparable to the highly productive vineyards on the western bank of the Rhône River.[2] The immediate and long-term result was a dramatic uprooting of vines in the central and earstern sectors of the department, especially in the Marseille region bordering on Var.

The malady spread into Var after 1875 and struck the two major vine-yard areas: Brignoles and Toulon. Draguignan *arrondissement,* farthest

TABLE 2 VAR :   AREA PLANTED IN PRODUCTIVE VINES (HECTARES)

Arrondissement	1874	1881
Brignoles	30,000	6 000
Toulon	26,000	8,000
Draguignan	20,000	9,500

to the east, was least affected, sheltered undoubtedly by rough terrain which, dispersing the plantation of vines, made difficult the spread of the root louse. Subsequently Draguignan followed the same pattern as Arles and became, until the 1890s, the leading producer of wine, with larger acreage and higher productivity than the other two *arrondissements*.

Both lower Provençal departments suffered a severe cutback in their cash incomes. Yet having never resorted to monoculture, they had other resources to fall back on: cereals, truck gardens, fruit trees, and olives, and silk production which had partially recovered, and an active lumber and cork industry in the Maures and Esterel mountains. Moreover, if one excludes corks, most industry in lower Provence was less dependent on wine than in Languedoc.

The loss of income from wine was nonetheless serious. Even with its periodic bad years, wine had been the major cash crop. This explains why it made such a comeback, why replanting was carried out so vigorously in Arles, Aix, Toulon, Brignoles, and Draguignan. However, Provençal vintners never restored the acreage of the 1860s or even came near it. They rather concentrated on a somewhat better quality of wine less subject to extreme fluctuations in quantity and in price. They differed therefore, from their counterparts in Languedoc.

The tragic phylloxera crisis had its greatest impact west of the Rhône where it spread like an economic bubonic plague. It nearly wiped out the chief source of livelihood. In Gard it first struck cantons along the Rhône and then spread to those of the coast and central hills. It was

TABLE 3 GARD : AREA PLANTED IN PRODUCTIVE VINES (HECTARES)

Arrondissement	Before Phylloxera	1880
Nîmes	58,866	3,780
Uzès	21,322	1,238
Alès	16,278	1,296
Le Vigan	7,945	923

devastating.[4] The figures in Table 3 make clear that productive vines practically disappeared in Gard, that replanting would be a tremendous operation. Gard, much like Var, was doubly hurt because silk production, ruined by the *pebrine,* never recovered its earlier money income. However, it did recapture its former dominance in the high cantons of Le Vigan and Alès *arrondissements* where vines were not replanted and by the 1880s Gard became the largest producer of raw silk in France.[5] Silk, coal mining, cereals, and pasturage again became the chief sources of livelihood of the highlands. This was a step backward economically because some highland cantons had found a complementary income in the production of wine: in Alès canton, 20–29 percent of the available land had been devoted to vines, in Anduze 28 percent, in Saint-Hippolyte 35 percent, Saint Ambroix 19 percent, and Barjac 11 percent. In contrast, wine provided a major part of the income in the lower cantons. In the Rhône area Marguerites had 45 percent and Beaucaire 46 percent of their land planted in vines most of which were lost. In the coastal plain came Saint-Gilles with 50 percent, Vauvert with 69 percent, in the low hills Sommières 66 percent and Saint Mamert 53 percent. Farther up the Rhône Valley were Roquemaure with 44 percent and Pont St. Esprit 40 percent. Only the vineyards in the sandy soils near the sea escaped the pest, a situation similar to that in the lower portion of Arles. But in 1880 even the vines capable of resisting were affected by another malady as the result of flooding.[6]

Without doubt the department which suffered most was Hérault. Its long coastal plain and the lovely low hills just above it had overcome every scruple against monoculture. In 1875, the year of France's largest wine harvest, 83,000,000 hectolitres, Hérault alone produced 15,000,000 hectolitres, over 18 percent of the total. In 1869 vines grew on 226,000 hectares. But by 1883 her vineyards had fallen to 92,000 hectares, of of which only 47,000 could be called productive. Their output of wine was a mere trickle compared to earlier years.[7] Hérault was ruined; her population, especially the immigrants, began to drift southward toward Aude, or across the sea to Algeria. (See table 4).

TABLE 4: PERCENTAGE OF FRECHMAN BORN IN ANOTHER DEPARTMENT

Department	1861	1876	1886
Bouches-du-Rhône	18.0	22	28.4
Var	15.5	17	19.3
Hérault	11	17	3.5
Gard	9	13	5.3
Aude	6	10	15.6
Pyrénées-Orientales	4	5	3.3
France (mean)	12	14	16

Far more fortunate were the departments of Aude and Pyrénées-Orientales; the phylloxera did not ravage them until the 1880s. Not only were they saved the adverse effects of a glutted market which would have resulted from the high production of 1874 and 1875, they suddenly found the French and foreign markets suffering a shortage and wide open to their wines. For them the golden age of high prices, expanding sales, and quick profits continued for several more years. The Narbonnais singled itself out from the remainder of Aude department by becoming a nearly complete monoculture; cereals disappeared, along with most other crops save vegetables and some fruit for Narbonne and nearby towns. The lower Corbières just beyond the coast, and the Aude Valley up to Carcassonne also expanded their area of vineyards. In 1873 productive vines occupied 142,000 hectares; in 1882 they reached 162,700. Decline came soon after when the total fell to 91,000 which, when compared to Gard and Hérault, was not catastrophic because wine prices had risen. Aude, once a major cereal producer for neighboring wine departments, had now joined their ranks. Cereals for the market were grown chiefly in the plateaux of the western sector: in Castelnaudary and parts of Limoux.[8] Castelnaudary remained the bread basket of the department. Limoux *arrondissement* retained its traditional polyculture; it also produced a better wine in vineyards relatively safe from the phylloxera.

Pyrénées-Orientales enjoyed the same prosperity, at least along the sea coast and in its rich valleys. It differed from Aude in that its vineyard area was more restricted to the plain of Roussillon and the low hills of the Corbières and the Albères. Also it produced a better wine which enjoyed high prices and, with a significant export market, suffered less from price fluctuations. Moreover, when the phylloxera came—its arrival was as sure as death—it was less destructive in both Aude and Pyrénées-Orientales. It did not spare the vines; simply its duration was cut short by correctives.

The only corrective that was practical was the grafting of French vines onto American roots. Certain species of American root stock were able to live with the phylloxera. A less feasible measure, submersion of vines for a part of the year, was too costly and limited by the need for extensive irrigation projects. Only medium and large estates could undertake it. The use of sandy soil near the sea proved beneficial; the louse could not tunnel from one vine to another in the sand. The result was a steady displacement of vineyards from the hills to the sea's edge. The plains had earlier been fully planted; it was now the turn of once barren land situated between the railway line and the beaches and which stretched from the Camargue to the Albères. Once more real estate values were completely upset. Around Aigues-Mortes, for example, land which had once rented for 4 or 5 francs per hectare now rented for 500 francs.[9]

SOCIAL CHANGE

This migration of vineyards was not merely an economic phenomenon, it was also a social one of major importance. Vines required workers to cultivate them. Indeed, the labor supply was crucial because this migration involved heavy investments, and therefore most of the sandy soil was organized into large domains. The origins of the new labor force were complex. Much of the older agricultural working class which had appeared in the plains in the mid-century had, during the 1860s, steadily entered the category of *ouvriers propriétaires*.[10] But a large number of these peasants were adversely affected by the phylloxera. Heavily in debt or unable to pay taxes, they lost their land which was either repossessed or abandoned, and, beaten men, they either became full-time laborers or migrated. Even more hard hit was the self-employed small owner with five to twenty hectares of vines. This type had formerly been an important element of social stability; politically he was often either a moderate or a conservative. In mid-century he had practiced polyculture as a guarantee against crisis and famine. But now, fully dependent on wine, heavily in debt, menaced by merchants and wholesalers, he was faced with declining income and loss of land. The more enterprising, such as those around Béziers and in Vauvert, borrowed more to install pumping devices to flood their vineyards. Some survived. Others were crushed. They emigrated to Aude or to Algeria. They sold their land at terribly deflated prices or abandoned it. Much of it eventually came on the market as smaller parcels which, after the crisis, workers purchased. But long before that, many small owners sank down into the working class.

Particularly in the viticultural zones of Hérault, Aude, and Pyrénées-Orientales, and to a lesser extend in Arles and southern Var, there occurred a simplification of social structure comparable to that of countries rapidly industrializing. For about two decades, society was more sharply divided between an agricultural bourgeoisie of sizable landowners and an expanding labor force with some characteristics of a true proletariat, that is, landless, without security, and fully dependent on wages. This situation was inevitable because replanting the vineyards was a major operation requiring large amounts of capital which in turn reinforced the already existing capitalistic features of southern wine production. More so than before, wine became an industry like any other and tended toward consolidation and rationalization, without, however, attaining such goals in the highest degree. As replanting required a larger labor force, new immigrants descended from the Pyrenees, Corbières, Cévennes, and Alps, adding to the native working class. They had been doing so for two decades, but in small numbers. By the 1880s the stream swelled. During the initial stage of the crisis their movement was temporarily deflected toward Aude, Pyrénées-Orientales, and some larger cities, chiefly ports, that grew rapidly on trade with North Africa. As replanting progressed, labor was needed everywhere and migration increased. Added to it, and giving it a more decisively proletarian character, were Spaniards west of the Rhône and Italians east of it.

French immigrants, unlike many foreigners, abandoned their mountain homelands permanently. Behind them they left an aging people, old traditions, and gaps in the population sufficiently large to create a shortage of labor in cereals. But even with a labor shortage, wages were too low to hold them. Those who remained behind continued for a generation or two in the old ways of life; they married late and suffered a declining birth rate. They clung to their religion and to their rural culture.

The demography of the lowlands was quite different. The population was younger, more dynamic in its growth, and far more concentrated. However, one must beware of exaggeration. Marseille was the only *arrondissement* which literally jumped ahead in size; most other coastal areas grew steadily rather than dramatically during the century, and their population was different from that of the highlands as much by style of life or quality as by quantity. Only the areas of monoculture doubled their inhabitants after 1800, which occurred in the communes around Perpignan, Narbonne, Béziers, Montpellier, Nîmes, and Toulon. Where viticulture declined, even relatively, in importance, rural population declined: Arles, Aix, Brignoles, and Draguignan. Inland *arrondissements* lost population; exceptional were Alès because of mining and metallurgy, and Carcassonne because of vineyards and its role as an administrative and judicial center. Charts I and II point out the distinction. The lines of Chart I would rise more abruptly if the inland cantons were excluded, especially as regards Céret, Perpignan, Béziers, and Draguignan, all of which combined coastal and highland cantons (see Appendix VI). The coastal cantons of each *arrondissement* experienced a steady rise to 1876 or 1881, depending on when the vine malady arrived in Languedoc and Roussillon. Population along the Provençal coast followed a different path, partly influenced by the cities of Marseille and Toulon which sucked in peasants, or by the decision to reduce the size of vineyards, or by the development of the tourist industry. Vineyards, therefore, were much less of a controlling factor over population. Where they exercised such control, from Arles westward, there were usually two population peaks: 1876 (or 1881), and 1901. The drop after 1876–1881 resulted from the phylloxera, that after 1901 from overproduction of wine and falling prices. The ability of wine production to attract population was of course limited. The major gains were achieved before the phylloxera; afterward there was either a moderate decline, or sluggish growth unless there was a large commercial or industrial town nearby. Yet even slow growth led to the rise of importance of viticultural cantons because voters there could — and often did — outnumber those in the distant hills and mountains. Chiefly the high level of abstention in coastal cantons saved the uplands from nearly complete electoral impotency.

In the lowlands west of the Rhône the population remained thick along the coast and even villages retained an urban quality as a result of continuous intercourse with neighboring towns. Most newcomers, however, gathered in or around urban and semi-urban centers where there were large domains just beyond the suburbs. Narbonne and Béziers retained a high level of persons born in another department. So did Toulon, Montpellier, Nîmes as well as the ports and industrial cities on the coast.[11] Perpignan was exceptional as regards wine centers; it attracted chiefly peasants from Prades *arrondissement*. Its population born in another department came to only 17 percent, and that of the department of Pyrénées-Orientales came to only 5 percent, well below the national average in 1876. (See Table 5).

TABLE 5: NATIVE AND IMMIGRANT POPULATION, 1876

National Ranking	Department	% Born in Dept.	% Born in Other Dept.	% Foreign Born
4	Bouches-du-Rhône	66	22	12
5	Var	75	17	7.6
12	Hérault	81	17	1.4
26	Gard	86	13	0.6
44	Aude	89	10	1
60	Pyrénées-Orientales	91	5	3.8
Average France		83.7	14	2.3

Source : *Résultat Statistique, 1876*

Pyrénées-Orientales remained predominantly rural in its population. (See Table 6). This trait markedly influenced its politics, as will be shown. The same was true of Aude, the most rural of all the departments under study. Gard was almost evenly balanced by 1886, while predominantly urban were Hérault, Bouches-du-Rhône, and Var.

TABLE 6: PERCENTAGE OF URBAN AND RURAL POPULATION

Department	Urban			Rural		
	1856	1876	1886	1856	1876	1886
Bouches-du-Rhône.	76.0	81.4	83.5	23.8	18.6	16.5
Var	53.2	57.2	56.2	46.7	42.7	43.7
Hérault	50.4	56.3	56.7	49.5	43.7	43.2
Gard	44.4	47.9	49.0	55.6	52.1	51.0
Aude	24.6	26.8	33.0	75.3	73.2	67.0
Pyrénées-Orientales	29.8	39.4	40.7	70.1	60.6	59.2

It was not by accident, then, that these latter three departments became the most left-wing. Urbanism lay at the base of the new wine industry and of the new *vigneron* types who emerged during the 1880s and after. Like their predecessors of the 1860s vine producers sought upward mobility, therefore they favored the fluid society of urban communes, had a parvenu attitude toward wealth and material things, and became increasingly interventionist in their socio-political outlook in order to protect their economic position.

Traditionally the *vignerons* were individualists, true artisans whose wine, although it left much to be desired, was a personal creation often brought to a moderately good quality with equipment as deficient as their scientific knowledge. For most of the small producers who survived the phylloxera, this state of things did not change. What began to change was the *vigneron's* notions about the marketing of wine. He became increasingly market conscious. It was in relation to demand that there was an excess or a shortage of wine. Periodic crises played an important role: within memory of the phylloxera generation there had been the price collapse of 1846–49, then a sharp rise in price but little wine to sell because of the *oïdium*. The 1860s raised men's hopes until another terrible calamity, the phylloxera, worse and longer lasting than any other. Many of these same vintners, and their offspring, were later beset by the disastrous collapse of prices and the market from 1901 to 1907. In desperation they finally resorted to violence against the government.

The stages leading up to the bloody summer of 1907 involved the alteration of the *vigneron's* outlook. As already mentioned, he was a firm individualist by tradition. Of course his social life had a collective character; he lived in a village or town with a highly integrated life, his dancing, singing, cafe drinking were all group manifestations. His relations with the government were not intense; he had certain desiderata which affected his role as a wine producer, but during the Empire he was more or less content with limited gains such as lower tariffs. There was hardly a demand for an interventionist state, merely one that performed a few services. His rising expectations were based on his own individual initiative and skill as a wine maker; he trusted in nature more than in bureaucracy. He privately financed his land purchases, ignored the inadequately financed *crédit foncier* (land banks), and when he cultivated his land he put his personality into it. To sell his wine he treated with the local *négociant* or wholesaler whom he hated as any artisan hates middlemen. He did not resort to cooperatives to buy fertilizer or tools or to make and sell his wine, nor to mutual aid societies to insure him against accidents and sickness. In the midst of his highly integrated town society he stood alone against nature and a distant market which he hardly understood.

Not until the catastrophe of the phylloxera did his individualism begin to break down. There is a direct connection between the crisis and this alteration. Where the crisis was less severe, as in the vineyards of Aude, the transformation was slower to come, did not really appear until the collapse of prices in 1901. The same hesitation characterized vintners north of Perpignan and in the Albères.

During the period of transition, the 1880s and 1890s, the political ideal most in conformity with the outlook of vintners, traditional individualism and rising group consciousness, was Radicalism. The Radicals, representing the extreme left, provided that combination of individual property rights and social reform brought about by the state, which appealed to a transitional generation in the Midi.[12] The fall of prices after 1901 turned the *vigneron* more definitely toward socialism.

The shift to the left was spurred by the greater need for governmental intervention: to provide cheaper transport, to make tariff arrangements, to offer cheap credit, while at the same time lowering taxes, and, above all, to facilitate the use of techniques for making more wine from fewer grapes. This latter demand called upon the state to take the side of the producer at the expense of the consumer.

There is another side to the *vigneron* type of the Midi, which distinguished him somewhat from his counterparts in the Bordeaux and Burgundy regions and any other region where wine making remained an art. Into the Midi vintner type came a marked strain of dishonesty. The wine producers of the Midi looked upon wine—even their cheap table wine—as the nectar of the gods. They were perhaps themselves convinced and certainly tried to convince others that their wine was a tonic, a body fortifier, an intellectual inspirant, a warming companion on cold nights and a refreshing elixir on hot nights, the juice resulting from the kiss of the sun upon the good earth, etc. But while mouthing all these eulogies of wine they began the most gross adulteration of it. The drink for health, for vigor, was transformed into a chemical compound of highly toxic effect at worst, and of dubious medicinal properties at best.

Adulteration was not a deliberate trick merely to cheat consumers; it was an irresistable economic temptation to obtain more wine when prices soared because of shortages. Sick vines and young vines could only provide a limited quantity of juice for fermenting into wine. Therefore the juice had to be made to yield a greater amount of marketable wine: water was added to increase its quantity and chemicals were added to disguise the water. Another method was sugaring the grapes already pressed to make the first wine, adding water, and pressing again for a second wine. This latter was the *piquette*, formerly the wine used for family consumption by the producer, or to give to his workers as part of their wage. The Midi *vigneron* had already abandoned quality for quantity during the 1860s; he now resorted to malpractice in complete disregard of consumer interests.

The national government was mindful of the toxic effect of certain chemicals, and it did pass and seek to enforce a few laws that would prevent excesses. Undoubtedly most wine producers were not averse to these health measures; but they were more concerned with measures to facilitate the acquisition of sugar, and the lowering of transport costs, and the interest on loans. More than ever before wine became a political matter; governmental policy toward it, at first quite timid, became increasingly interventionist. The political forces which could capture the wine issue, which became its champions, had a bright future in the Midi. The Radicals took up this cause.

FOUNDING THE REPUBLIC

The invasion of France by the Germans was concurrent with the phylloxera invasion. The former came in by the northeast, the latter by the south, and while the latter proved to be far more destructive economically, the German success led to the overthrow of Napoleon's Empire.

In the history of the lower Midi, Louis Napoleon was overthrown during a period of economic expansion and general well-being. Opposition to the liberal Empire was limited, as noted above, and certainly there was no serious revolutionary movement there. Neither did the war stir up an insurrectionary wave. There was no fighting in the south. The textile industry was revived by pressing demands for woolen cloth; the destruction of the northern wine market would not be felt for some time. The revolution, when it came after military defeat in September 1870, was a Parisian phenomenon, as it had been in February 1848. And in imitation of that past event, local republicans, when apprised of the news by telegraph, seized the seats of local government. There was no resistance to them, and most of them were moderate men.

The resurrection of left-wing republicanism was a slow process, certainly not a spontaneous or phoenix-like phenomenon. On the other hand, it began early, during Gambetta's brief period as head of France. The causes were numerous: Marcou took umbrage because Gambetta would not recognize his seizure of the prefectural office and appointed his old friend Raynal as *commissaire*. Needless to say, this friendship which had endured during exile, came to an abrupt end.[13] Raynal, of Narbonne, put his own men into subprefectural posts, which further embittered the dispute.

The war also encouraged the left wing. All republicans, once Gambetta's Provisional Government of National Defence was created, insisted on winning the war in order to reaffirm a government which, they insisted, was France's new republic. What came to divide them was their views on how to fight the war. Left-wing republicans did not forget that Gambetta had been elected in 1869 as an intransigent, but they insisted that he was now, once in office, soft on Bonapartist administrators and generals. They demanded a more aggressive republicanization of all functions, and a policy of the people in arms. They revived Jacobin traditions and recalled, in their own minds, the battles of the First Republic against invaders.

In the Midi republicans also became divided over the war. The younger men reared in the republican tradition of '48 were determined to fight on if Paris fell. They were, of course, a minority of the total population. Under the Empire the peasants and small-town dwellers and the well-to-do had lacked enthusiasm for war; they displayed it even less under the new regime. Their parvenu outlook did not encourage them to join the volunteer regiments or to open their pocketbooks. Unfortunately the moderates in power did not inspire much enthusiasm. Loans were seriously undersubscribed and conscription lagged. An extreme left now emerged and vociferously called for forced conscription, capital levies, and heavy income taxes; they did not, in as clear a voice, call for mobilization of the economy. In all these respects they were at one with the Jacobin critics of Gambetta at Paris. And initially they looked to Paris for leadership. However most southerners were friendly toward Gambetta: he had been elected in Bouches-du-Rhône and Var in 1869 and would be reelected in both in 1871. Midi leftists, therefore, did not want to follow the extremists of Paris, headed by Auguste Blanqui, who sought to overthrow the provisional government; they wanted rather to complement it with regional subgovernments, autonomous and vigorous, to carry on the war to its bitter end. Two experiments were tried: the Ligue du Sudouest and the Ligue du Midi. The latter was under the leadership of Alphonse Esquiros who had successfully campaigned with Gambetta in 1869. They were supported by newly created journals, the *Fraternité* (Carcassonne), *Ligue des droits de l'homme* (Montpellier), and *L'Egalité* (Marseille). Local committees appeared in some left-wing communes and sent delegates to departmental and regional congresses. They were patriotic *à la 1793*, hailed the intransigents Louis Blanc and Victor Hugo as symbols of *défense à outrance,* and hoped to revive the revolutionary tradition.

That tradition, however, worked against them. Gambetta and his supporters accused them of being Girondins, of having federalist leanings, of threatening political unity in a time of crisis. Too, they could not bring themselves to undertake aggressive opposition to Gambetta. More important, they could not win a broad following in the South to set up regional defense centers. Most members of the leagues were journalists, lawyers, professionals; there were too few workers and peasants. Moreover, they were not as activistic as their journalism would lead one to think.[14]   The veritable activists, who were truly prepared for violence, were minimal in number and marginal in influence. The Commune of Paris won their active support and led them to detach themselves from the majority of the left who were dumbfounded by news of that bloody struggle. Autonomy as an ideal had already faded by March 1871, with the result that efforts to lead similar communal movements in the Midi failed. Emile Digeon, of an old Jacobin family, provoked an unsuccessful uprising in Narbonne, and Gaston Crémieux led a more serious but equally futile revolutionary action in Marseille.[15] These misfortunes seriously weakened the extreme left. Fearful of a monarchist resurgence it allied itself with moderate republicans and soon became hardly distinguishable from them.

This closing of ranks had begun seriously prior to the February election of 1871. Gambetta, having resigned from the government, assumed his position as a leader of all republicans rather then of the intransigents. In the lower Midi as in the rest of France the electoral campaign was waged on the issue of war or peace. Republicans insisted on winning the war because they believed that defeat would destroy their provisional republic. They were successful in the two areas where they had sunk roots in 1849–50: Roussillon and Var, and in their new conquest, Marseille. Languedoc and Bouches-du-Rhône imitated most of France and returned monarchists. But in the lower Midi, as in most of the nation, the February election was not indicative of future tendencies. On the contrary, in the by-elections of 1871 and 1872, and in the general elections of 1876 and 1877, republicans won all circumscriptions save the deeply Catholic ones of Nîmes I and Alès II in Gard, and Castelnaudary in Aude. Most of these republicans were moderates and there was not, until after 1876, a serious thrust toward the extreme left among southern politicians.

Nonetheless, there did emerge a group, in imitation of the anti-Bonapartist intransigents of the 1860s, who broke from Gambetta and followed the extreme left in its opposition to the Constitution of 1875. They were dominant in the larger cities: Toulon, Marseille, Montpellier, Bézier, and Carcassone. It is important to note that in 1876–77 this extreme left combined veterans of 1848, derisively called "old beards" and new men speaking for the second generation of southern Radicals. Indeed, the term intransigent now gave way to that of Radical to designate the extreme left. It is equally important to note that this political movement in the South was strongly dependent on Parisian leadership; consequently, its program in 1876 was almost identical to that of Parisian leaders such as Louis Blanc and Georges Clemenceau. It therefore contained little on wine which was now seriously in trouble in much of Languedoc and in most of Provence. The wine issue would emerge steadily after 1876, but during that year, it had not yet assumed a more definite political form than republicanism. On the other hand, the Radicals who won in 1876–77 were generally confined to areas more or less dependent on wine production: more dependent in an area such as Béziers, much less so in Marseille. The Radical program, of course, still contained those proposals which would directly or indirectly aid wine; it re-emphasized the economic platform of 1849, which had never been implemented.

It revived also the political platform of 1849 which was now directed against the Constitution. This political section was the most potent weapon of extreme left candidates because the elections of the 1870s were fundamentally political, fought out over governmental form and power. However, the role to be played by government was already a conscious concern of southern peasants confronted by the phylloxera and their helplessness in the face of it. By 1880 the inability of private initiative and of local agricultural societies to find a remedy the small owners could use was apparent; demands for state intervention therefore steadily increased. Henceforth elections in the lower South had a clear economic and social meaning. This does not suggest that political ideology declined. On the contrary, the governmental form prominent in left-wing ideology—power centralized in a unicameral legislature—was clearly the form most compatible with the economic demands favored now by many distressed peasants. It might here be repeated that early Radicalism was interventionist in that it favored several forms of governmental action: national ownership of railroads and lower rates for agricultural produce, especially for wine, a vastly expanded transportation system, cheaper and easier credit obtained from mutual credit societies backed by the state, the nationalization of large banks, especially the Bank of France, the lowering or removal of most indirect taxes, especially the drink taxes and *octrois,* and drastic reduction of the land tax. Since all these reforms demanded considerable expenditures, the Radicals renewed their demand for a progressive income tax so as to enlarge the forced contribution of the rich toward social reform. Their social goals were also a revival of 1848–49 ideas emphasizing cooperation and laws on hours and working conditions. These reforms were intended chiefly to benefit industrial, urban workers, and since the extreme left was, in 1876, successful mainly in towns and cities, apparently the urban workers responded more readily than rural farmers.

Of course moderate republicans also claimed to be defenders of wine interests and they were popular in the 1870s and continued to win elections in the wine districts of Aude and Pyrénées-Orientales. But they were attached to a government which, on the whole, would do little for wine producers. In the eyes of *vignerons* it spent too much money on colonial expansion into areas that did not offer new markets for southern wine. However favorable Jules Ferry's education laws, they complained that little was accomplished in agricultural and technical education, subjects in which *vignerons* were consciously aware of their own deficiencies. And the laissez faire policy of moderates seemed a willful way of ignoring distress. Most peasants and workers had never heard of Darwin; their struggle was against the phylloxera and its economic consequences and they wanted aid. Radicalism associated itself with this longing and the volatile temperament that often accompanied it.

Royalists also sought to profit from the distress. They pointed to the good times under the monarchy, without being precise; Bonapartists harked back to the golden age of the 1860s. However, save for the wine areas of Uzès and northern Arles *arrondissements,* few *vignerons* favored royalism. The attachment to tradition, to the past, was seriously undermined by the phylloxera crisis. A once stable population had been uprooted, lost much of its land, and experienced a considerable shift of population. Even the economically backward areas were affected: younger men who had, in the 1860s, gone to vineyards to work for higher wages, now returned to their highland homes because they could find no work in the lowlands. The destruction of vines had taken away their jobs. Possibly the move to the left of certain highland areas can be explained by their influence. However, there was not sufficient change in voting patterns, not even in most cantons of Lodève *arrondissement,* to warrant generalizing. What occurred in some cantons did not occur in others. Moreover, the returnees did not stay long in their home villages; when replanting began they, and more of their neighbors, took once again the difficult, rocky trails and roads leading to vineyards. They were still the awkward highlanders, only now they worked side by side with numerous local people who had lost their plots, and also with Spaniards and Italians who had entered France to help reconstitute the vineyards. Under these conditions, which produced a mixed and not always united and harmonious working class, old attachments to tradition rapidly withered. The wine grape, therefore, was the most important solvent of tradition. The vine and the *fleur de lys* were not plantable in the same soil. The trend to the left, which represented the search for new values, new solutions to the problems of livelihood, could not be stopped. The elections of the 1880s reflected these changes in outlook of two generations in crisis.

NOTES

1. The best succinct description of the phylloxera crisis is in Charles K. Warner, *The Winegrowers of France and the Government since 1875* (New York, 1960), Chap. I.
2. *B-du-R, Encyclo. depart'l.,* VII, 456–61.
3. A.D. Var 14M 19–1.
4. Chauzit, "Monographie agricole … Gard," 1548; A.D. Gard 14M 263. The figures for 1880 do not include the entire vineyard acreage which was 18,120 ha., only that of vines not killed by the phylloxera.
5. France. Ministère du commerce. Statistique générale de la France. *Annuaire statistique,* année 1886, 312–13, 340–41; année 1900, 174.
6. A.D. Gard 13M 219, reports of local administrators.
7. Warner, 2; *Le Vignoble de l'Hérault,* 33.
8. Barbut, *Etude … vignoble … Aude,* 78ff.; A.D. Aude, 3M 163, 5M 66; A.N. F[10] 1610.
9. Chauzit, 1550.
10. These generalizations are based on inadequate data and, while probably accurate, are not, like the chevalier Bayard, beyond reproach. What seems clear was that the landless working class was constantly diminished by the ease of land purchase during the 1860s. And whenever ease of credit and high wine prices occurred the proletariat rose into the ranks of petty owners. As we shall see, this phenomenon of upward mobility had a marked influence on politics.
11. See printed statistics in France. Ministere de l'Intérieur, *Dénombrement de la population,* (title varies), and Bureau de la Statistique Générale, *Résultas statistiques du recensement général de la population, 1872.*

12. For the social and economic views of Radicalism as a national movement see my studies: "Left-wing Radicals, Strikes and the Military, 1880–1907," *French Historical Studies*, 3 (1963), 93–105; "The French Left-Wing Radicals, Their Views on Trade Unionism, 1870–1898," *International Review of Social History*, 7 (1962), 203–230; "The French left-wing Radicals: Their Economic and Social Program since 1870," *The American Journal of Economics and Sociology*, 26 (1967), 189–203. For a brief study of the interventionist orientation of *Vignerons* without reference to its political implications see Warner, pp. 6–8.

13. See Jeanjean, *Proclamation*, 32–37; *Fraternité*, 14, 17 Sept. 1870.

14. See *Droits de l'homme, La Liberté* (Montpellier); *L'Egalité; Fraternité; Indépendant des Pyrénées-Orientales*, and *Gard républicain* (Nîmes) for October-December., 1870; A.N. F⁷ 12678; A.D. Hérault 39M 247.

15. Antoine Olivesi, *La Commune de 1871 à Marseille* (Paris, 1950), chaps. VI-IX; Henri Feraud, *Histoire de la commune de Narbonne, 1871* (Chateauroux, 1946). It is curious to note that Crémieux was executed, Digeon acquitted.

CHAPTER SIX

THE POLITICAL SOCIOLOGY
OF RADICALISM IN AN ERA
OF ECONOMIC CRISIS, 1881-1885

The decade of the 1880s marked the triumph of the Republic in France. Under the leadership of Jules Ferry, first as minister of education and then as premier, the moderate republicans, derisively called opportunists, consolidated their power in the Chamber of Deputies, the Senate, and the presidency. In addition, Ferry created a secular and obligatory educational system and laid the basis of France's world empire. On the right, monarchists steadily lost the influence they had once enjoyed, but they did not give up without a fight. Even in the highly republican South they showed considerable strength, especially in Gard and Hérault, but then declined steadily after 1885. Their decline was accompanied by the rise of the Radicals as a fairly distinct group on the left. Radicals emerged as a "loyal opposition" to the moderates, supporting Ferry in his determination to secularize French society but opposing him in his imperialism. The conquest of colonies, they argued, distracted attention from domestic problems, especially from the need to reorganize government and improve social conditions. What they demanded was more social and economic equality to complement political equality. In their platforms, therefore, they called for abolishing the presidency and the Senate so that full power would be concentrated in the Chamber of Deputies, the only organ of government directly elected by universal male suffrage. They also demanded the election of judges, legal protection of trade unions, shorter hours of work, improved factory conditions, and a full system of social security. There were, of course, moderate Radicals, headed by Leon Bourgeois (Marne), who were somewhat hesitant about the social role of government. But even they were firm

115

advocates of a mildy progressive income tax as a means of paying the costs of social reforms.

The fortunes of the Radical movement were not especially bright on the national level. In the provinces, however, the number of its followers varied, and the purpose of this chapter is to ascertain its strength in the lower South and to discover the reasons for its rise.

RELATIVE STRENGTH OF RADICALISM

The election of 1881 showed a marked advance for the extreme left. Out of thirty-one circumscriptions, Radicals won eighteen or 58 percent, up from 29 percent in 1876. Perhaps seventeen would be more accurate because Marcou, victorious in Carcassonne, was no longer a true-blue Radical and soon severed ties with his left-wing backers. However, he can be included because he was a symbol of the persistently left-wing majority in this circumscription. He was one of the last of the 1848 generation of *Montagnards;* and he was also a good example of one of the forces which influenced electoral outcome: personal popularity. Now as a political force, the attractiveness, or lack of it, of an individual candidate was quite important in the lower Midi. Under the system of *scrutin uninominal* or single member constituencies, the personal qualities of a candidate often counted more than his political labels. On the other hand, Radicals enjoyed greater success with the system of *scrutin de liste,* that is, a party slate for the entire department. The only experiment with the party slate was tried in 1885, a year which marked the high point of the Radical movement in the South. It is worth-while to compare the results given by both systems:

TABLE 7: ELECTIONS, SCRUTIN UNINOMINAL VERSUS SCRUTIN DE LISTE (1885)
RADICAL/TOTAL SEATS FOR DEPARTMENT

Department	1876	1881	1885	1889	1893	1898
Pyrénées-Orientales	0/3	1/4	3/3	2/4	1/4	2/4
Aude	1/4	2/4	2/5	1/6	1/6	3/6
Hérault (Includes by-election 1882)	2/6	5/6	6/7	5/6	3/6	5/6
Gard	1/6	2/6	4/6	1/6	4/6	2/6
Bouches-du-Rhône	4/7	5/7	6/8	5/8	5/8	3/8
Var	3/4	3/4	4/4	3/4	3/4	1/4
Total	11/30	18/31	25/33	17/34	11/34	16/34

The success of Radicals during the 1880s changed the lower South into a bastion of left wing politics. The multiple factors behind this success can conveniently be examined in the election of 4 October 1885, the one election since that of May 1849 when the list system was used. Comparison can serve to ascertain the progress of the extreme left since then. The 1885 election was also that in which objective factors, as distinct from personal influence, were given the freest play.[1]

To be sure it is not a perfect choice, if only because several slates of candidates were not fully composed of authentic Radicals. The group appropriated several moderates as well as a few socialists to add to their slates in Hérault, Aude, and Bouches-du-Rhône. (See Appendix VII for lists.) But since the moderates and socialists were less successful than the Radicals, the percentages in Table 8 give us an accurate account of the strength of the four political movements in the lower South in the 1880s. It is clear that opportunist republicans, whatever title they chose, were determined to run in all departments save Hérault where moderates had been crushed in 1849 and had never truly recovered.[2] It is also clear that their appeal in 1885 was not strong; it had indeed declined since 1876 and 1881. Given the resurgence of conservatives, nearly all of whom disliked the Republic, many previously moderate voters rallied to the left. This decision on their part was probably a conditioned response, and it took place at the moderate politician's expense, even where voters normally followed middle-of-the-road leaders. In 1885, therefore, Radicals gained in the lower Midi, profiting from a widespread fear of right-wing resurgence. This gain, it should be noted, was not limited to the South, it was a national phenomenon: from 14 percent of all deputies in 1881, they rose to 20 percent, whereas republicans dropped from 69 percent to 44 percent. Despite these losses, moderate republicans remained the largest political group in France; in the lower South, however, their losses put them in third place. (See Table 8).

They were strong enough, however, to cause run-offs in all the coastal departments save Hérault. And in the second or run-off elections the predominantly Radical slates emerged victorious in their entirety only in Pyrénées-Orientales, Bouches-du-Rhône, and Var. In Aude the left-wing list combined two Radicals, Pelletan and Wickersheimer, two socialists, and Théron whom the police referred to as "le timide."[3] As

TABLE 8: ELECTION OF 4 OCTOBER 1885
PERCENTAGE OF REGISTERED VOTERS, BY PARTY

Department	Radical	Republican	Conservative	Socialist	Abstention
Pyrénées-Orientales	26	14	23	4	36
Aude	21	21	27	none	29
Hérault	38	none	31	3	27
Gard	21	18	36	none	22
Bouches-du-Rhône	26	20	20	1	38
Var	30	13	21	none	35
Mean	27	17	26	none	31

front runners, Wickersheimer and Théron joined three moderates and won seats in the run-off.[4]   In Gard, a purely Radical list attracted a highly diversified vote.   Between the first and last candidates there was a spread of 9,600 votes, which was similar to 1849.[5]   And a predominantly monarchist list posed the greatest threat in the lower Midi, especially because left-wing voters were less disciplined along party lines, which explains the wide spread of their ballots.

A similar situation existed in Bouches-du-Rhône.[6]   Five Radicals allied with two moderates and one laborite and the difference between the first and last candidate was over 10,000 votes.   Despite this diversity the entire slate won in the run-off.   No such compromise was needed in Var.   Dominant since the by-elections of July 1871, the Radicals were well-organized, and, by 1885, supported by three newspapers in the three *arrondissements*.   They controlled most of the cantonal capitals, and their congress in Le Luc refused to bargain, not only with moderate republicans, but even with moderate Radicals.   Two incumbents from Brignoles and Draguignan were consequently jettisoned and "pure bred" replacements imported from Paris: Georges Clemenceau and Camille Raspail.   They joined with the two incumbents of Toulon, Honoré Daumas and Auguste Maurel, both of the extreme left in the Chamber, and won a plurality in the first election and a majority in the second.[7]

Hérault was unique in that Radicals had neither to compromise with socialists of whom there were too few, or with moderates.[8]   The political mood of vintners was such that an out-and-out moderate slate was hardly encouraged, no more so than in 1849.   The geography of Hérault militated against a moderate victory.   With the longest coastal plain of the six departments under study, it stretched along the sea with one vineyard following another. Here Radicalism grew as naturally as the vine. Add to this the economic difficulties of wool and silk textiles farther inland, there were few areas for a healthy, expansive middle group emphasizing moderation. Hérault was a crisis department where moderation was not popular. The Radical slate profited and won the first election.

GEOGRAPHY OF RADICALISM

Although a special case, Hérault formed part of the lower Midi and results there fitted quite well into the general character of regional politics. In order to understand this character we must look at the forces which conditioned it, and assess their relative weight in the precarious balance between victory and defeat. For this purpose, the results of the first election, when voters marked their ballots according to their chief preferences, is far more useful than the second, when the left and left center allied to defeat the right.

Among the variables of major importance in 1885, as in 1849, was geography. The frontiers of the Radical movement were drawn by the nonaligned forces of nature and not in the heads of politicians. Candidates in elections recognized the geographic variable and usually sought to overcome it by assembling a list of men each of whom had special appeal to a different topographical area. But the limits imposed by nature were not so cunningly overcome, and almost as a matter of course the programs and hopes of the extreme left were directed toward the more dynamic forces of society. By and large that meant the populations of the lowlands: the coast and river valleys. For this reason the left was strongest in 1881–85 where it was strongest in 1849–1851. That is, its bastions of mid-century constituted the core from which it spread out after the 1870s (see map 5).

In Pyrénées-Orientales it was solidly entrenched in most of the plain of Roussillon, particularly in the cantons of Perpignan-*Est,* Thuir, Millas, and Argelès, all fully devoted to wine. Here was the magnet area attracting population chiefly from the highlands of the department, only slightly from the ouside. The electorate in Perpignan II was remarkably faithful to its deputies: Emile Brousse literally reigned there from 1881

Opposite:

Radical Percentage of Registered Voters,
Election of Oct. 4, 1885

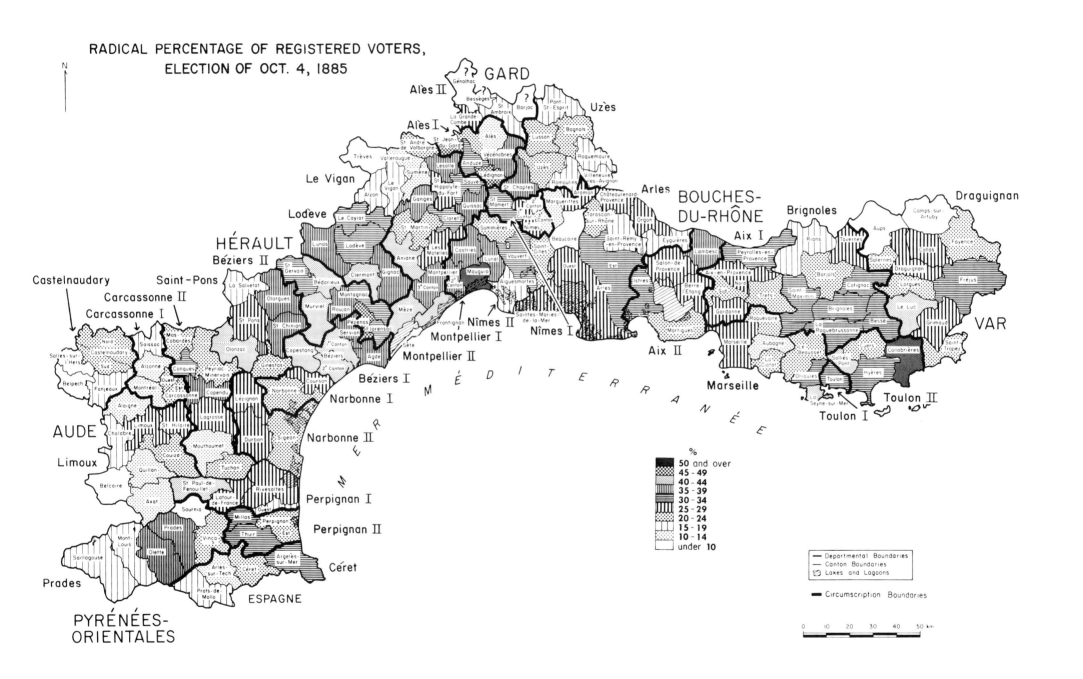

RADICAL PERCENTAGE OF REGISTERED VOTERS,
ELECTION OF OCT. 4, 1885

N

GARD

Alès II
Alès I
Le Vigan
Lodève
HÉRAULT
Béziers II
Saint-Pons
Castelnaudary
Carcassonne II
Carcassonne I
AUDE
Limoux
Prades
PYRÉNÉES-ORIENTALES
ESPAGNE

Uzès
Arles
BOUCHES-DU-RHÔNE
Brignoles
Draguignan
Aix I
Aix II
Marseille
VAR
Nîmes II
Montpellier I
Montpellier II
Béziers I
Narbonne I
Narbonne II
Perpignan I
Perpignan II
Céret
Nîmes I
Toulon I
Toulon II

MER MÉDITERRANÉE

MER

%
50 and over
45 - 49
40 - 44
35 - 39
30 - 34
25 - 29
20 - 24
15 - 19
10 - 14
under 10

Departmental Boundaries
Canton Boundaries
Lakes and Lagoons
Circumscription Boundaries

0   10   20   30   40   50 km

to 1895, followed by Jean Bourrat from 1895 to 1909, then Victor Dalbiez to 1919. All these deputies were solidly Radical; no monarchist or moderate could hope to defeat them. The chief enemies were internal division which began in 1889, and abstention which plagued an area so dominated by one party. Areas of similar domination were the coastal plain from the cantons of Courson (Aude) to Vauvert (Gard).

There were coastal areas, however, where the extreme left had to struggle for existence, and where the struggle did not always result in victory. Topography, we repeat, was a major determinant, not a perfect one. Men, whether singly or collectively, do not behave blindly but respond to situations in the light of present needs and enduring traditions. The cantons where Radicals were less popular in the 1880s were almost precisely those which the Mountain had not effectively penetrated in 1848–49. Rivesaltes, Perpignan-*Ouest*, and Sigean form a block where moderate republicanism was as powerful as Radicalism and even enjoyed a slight ascendancy in many communes. Notable is the fact that there were too few immigrants from areas invaded by phylloxera to disturb the power of tradition save briefly in the later 1880s. The plain around Narbonne and Coursan, however, was severely hit by the 1880s and the large number of immigrants, many from Radical communes of Hérault who again faced the hard times they had fled in the 1870s, were more prone to lean toward extremism. In 1881, and again in 1885, Radicals enjoyed their greatest strength there, especially when they allied with socialists for the latter election; but subsequently the allies separated and fought each other. Socialism finally won out, profiting from a sizable working class and a certain nervousness in a population affected by the alternation of rapid growth and decline of the wine market. But the wine market was itself a function of the type of viticulture characteristic of the lowlands.

The extreme left was also quite successful in lower river valleys. In Pyrénées-Orientales the lower valleys of Tech, Tet, and Agly were predominately left-wing. Conservative forces abandoned the fight, which brought about a very high rate of abstention, 35 to 42 percent. Farther north, the middle Aude was the only inland area in the Aude department that was and remained Radical. In particular the cantons of Conques, birthplace of Barbès, and Capendu were bastions of the left.

In the lower Aude Valley, Radicals often voted for socialists after 1889. In Hérault, Radical strength reached up two valleys: the Orb, from Béziers toward Bédarieux; and the Hérault, from Agde to Clermont. The central and west central region of the department retained the tradition of 1849. Here the vineyards joined hands with remaining industrial centers to form what we have called the Radical square. Another river valley, important for communication and left propaganda, was the Jaur, Radical between Olargues and Riols.

The lower Rhône River, as it spread fan-shaped into its estuaries, had once been a decisive influence in the growth and life of cities north of the Camargue, such as Beaucaire, Aramon, Arles, and Tarascon. It was still important, of course; but by the 1880s railroads had considerably lessened its influence, with the resulting decline of Beaucaire and Arles. Before the phylloxera its east and west banks had been heavily covered with vineyards. Replanting, however, was more selective and limited so as to avoid a return to monoculture. The rural economy now combined cereals, fruit and pasturage as well as extensive truck gardening on the east bank and silk production on the west bank.

Around Arles town, eastward, and especially southward, into the vast, flat plain, replanting of vineyards went on at a fairly rapid pace. Large capitalist estates emerged along the Rhône, and it was here that the Radical movement enjoyed considerable support. Its strength also depended on the urban laborers in Arles as well as on the rural workers in small towns and villages. Replanting was transforming Arles *arrondissement* into an important wine producing area, and in the small town of Fontvieille east of Arles there were by 1886 two workers for one owner. However, the northern section, lying between the Rhône and the Durance (up to Lambesc), and most of Uzès *arrondissement* on the west bank, were lukewarm to Radicals at best, and often hostile. These areas had equally been hit by the phylloxera, but replanting was limited and hesitant. Natives turned rather to fruit trees, truck gardening, and cereals.[9] These products were profitable because of adequate irrigation. There was no question of a monoculture and there never had been. Yet, wine remained an important money crop and with its high price during the eighties and nineties, there was strong incentive to replant. In fact, up and down the Rhône Valley, vineyards were migrating toward the lowlands where their production rose considerably. Arles *arrondissement* soon rivaled Aix for its vine acreage. Acreage, however, was less significant than rising production. Vines in the deeper soil of the valley floor, well fertilized, produced twice the juice of the older vineyards on sparse hillsides.

Nonetheless, farmers north of the town of Arles and in Uzès were less dependent on wine than those in Arles canton and were less radicalized. Fewer of them were workers because the limited scale of replanting did not require many; instead there were numerous independent owners living in a more dispersed, and therefore more individualistic fashion. Truck gardening was highly compatible with their temperament. The area did not experience the leveling process which accompanied capitalistic agriculture along lower river valleys and in coastal plains.

But quite similar conditions prevailed in the middle Durance Valley (Lambesc and Peyrolles cantons) and a majority of the population there was decidedly Radical — as they had been in 1849. It appears then that the only valid explanation of a left-wing victory is tradition. Since mid-century left ideas came down the Durance Valley from Vaucluse and Basses-Alpes, especially from the towns of Manosque, Valensole, and Pertius just to the north, and spread into both Bouches-du-Rhône and Var. This mid-century block of the left held good into the twentieth century, long after the falling off of Manosque's population and its leftward impulse.

Other river valleys, the Touloubre and Arc, descending from Sainte Victoire to the west do not seem to have played an important role, possibly because they did not flow into dynamic areas of Radical influence; they emptied, rather, into the Etang de Berre, politically a dead sea for the Radicals. Population was abandoning these valleys and moving southward toward the more dynamic sectors. The same conclusions apply to the Argens River in Var; it was small, nearly dry most of the year, and of almost no economic consequence. Other rivers were shorter and of even less importance. Rivers in lower Provence could not serve the same political function that they did in Languedoc and Roussillon of forming a connecting link between the lowlands and the highlands. In Provence mountains came right down to the shore.

Consequently there was not a continuous prosperous plain between mountains and sea. In the southwestern corner, the Camargues, where there were some islands of dry land, capitalist vineyards had been created to escape the phylloxera. In the sparsely populated canton of Saintes-Maries-de-la-Mer, Radicals enjoyed a firm majority among the vineyard workers. To the east, however, stretched a rugged, rocky coast between the Rhône mouth and Marseille. There the extreme left found only a sprinkling of followers. This area was almost as barren of workers as the upper Arles *arrondissement* and as moderate or conservative. Only the ports offered an opening to the left because the social structure favored it, as was generally true in ports. In the eastern cantons of Marseille *arrondissement* most voters remained, as in 1849, indifferent to the left. This was an area of steep hills and valleys from Roquevaire southward to La Ciotat. There was a good deal of petty industry and small scale agriculture; vineyard acreage had been considerably reduced before and after the phylloxera; independent farmers, favored by adequate irrigation, prospered from truck gardening and meat and milk production. At best, only a moderate Radical, Joseph Chevillon, could win wide support. This area was, indeed, the Chevillon bailiwick, characterized by a long tradition of moderation, even where vineyards dominated agriculture, as was the case in western Var.

The Toulon *arrondissement* was the most economically active of Var, in part because large-scale industry was located there, in part because of extensive vineyard replanting on such a scale as to approach a monoculture west of Toulon and to achieve that goal east of it as far as Collobrières. The wine classified as Côtes de Provence was produced here, as well as in the plain of Cuers, around La Roquebrussanne. Here was the stronghold of the extreme left, save for communes such as Le Beausset and Brignoles, and Cuers, where moderates or conservatives had a larger following. Since the extreme left controlled the areas attracting population, its position became more assured. But the extreme left in Var, earlier than in other departments, split irreparably into Radical and socialist groups. The list system of 1885 had avoided that, but the return to *scrutin uninominal* in 1889 led to divisions that became permanent and often bitter. This produced a wide dispersal of the left wing vote over numerous candidates and a return to massive abstention. Political activists, however, came chiefly from the left and the Radicals profited from their activity in 1885 and until about 1900.

The same factors prevailed in the hilly terrain of Aix *arrondissement*. There was replanting of vines on a limited scale, which had generally aided left-wing political movements, and the Radical slate won most of the communes which were more or less dependent on wine.[10]

The Radicals were also strong where there was some fairly active industry: Arles, Istres, La Ciotat, Berre l'Etang, and Gardanne. Save in Berre l'Etang, they received 30 percent or more of the registered votes in these districts. An even greater success was carried out in the mining area in the northern part of Roquevaire and the western part of Trets cantons. Unlike their counterparts in Languedoc, miners of Bouches-du-Rhône early turned to the extreme left. They were less isolated and more easily influenced by labor ideologies and left-wing politics than the mountain people of Languedoc.

What does not appear in lower Provence during 1885 is a clear geographic pattern of Radical strength. With both terrain and economy more diversified, it is difficult to discern the factors bringing about the extreme left's rise. The most cogent generalization is that its chief bastions lay in important wine producing districts: lower Arles, northern Aix, Toulon, and Draguignan *arrondissements*. Therefore, where the land was too high, or too rugged, as in Ste. Victoire, Ste. Baume, and Plan de Canjuers, neither the vine nor the Radical could make much headway, unless, to aid the latter, there was industry and an industrial work force.

This generalization is even more applicable to Languedoc. The Cévennes and Garrigues of Gard and Hérault, the upper Minervois, the Montagne Noire, and all the highlands from the upper Aude Valley to the Spanish border, including the Fenouillèdes, Cerdagne, and Vallespir, were least receptive to the extreme left. As explained earlier, individuals who were especially popular could win in these unfavorable areas, but these were personal rather than ideological victories.

Without a locally popular candidate, the extreme left was unable to win wide appeal with its political program. Weakening of the Presidency, abolition of the Senate, election of judges, and secular schools did not attract populations that were authoritarian, patriarchal, and proclerical. Indeed, as young persons emigrated, the older population often became more set in its traditions. The demand for lay education undoubtedly had wider appeal in 1885 than in 1849; republican followers of Jules Ferry made notable gains in the highland cantons and numerous administrative reports underscored the decline of religion as a vital factor in highland culture. But it was precisely the moderates who profited from this new situation, not the Radicals who seemed extreme, who appeared not only anticlerical but antireligious.

One might also state that not until Midi Radicals became protectionist could they win large numbers of followers outside of wine areas. The highland people had many economic ills and the Radical's program of cheaper transport and easier farm credit might have won them over but moderates promised as much. More decisively working against the extreme left was its image as a group advocating free trade in cereals to provide cheaper bread for wine laborers and urban industrial workers who had to purchase their food. Cereal producers, like raw silk producers, viewed the left as representatives of urban interests, as city slickers. At least the conservative press depicted them as such. These conditions made it particularly difficult for Radicals to politicize the economic distress of the highlanders. Not until the appearance of another generation of peasants—and of Radicals—would there be mutual understanding and electoral victories.

A frequency table for Hérault, where the Radical slate achieved the highest percentage of registered voters of the six departments, makes clear the highland-lowland dichotomy. Out of 336 communes, 294 showed a political inclination by giving a majority (55 percent plus) either to the Radical or the conservative slates.

TABLE 9: HERAULT, TOPOGRAPHY AND THE 1885 ELECTIONS

| | Radical majority | | Conservative majority | |
	Lowland	Highland	Lowland	Highland
Total of Communes N—294	84 (29%)	44 (15%)	60 (20%)	106 (36%)

The Radicals won in the lowlands almost double the number of communes they won in the highlands. Radicalism undoubtedly had a strong appeal for both landowning and non-landowning peasants in the lowlands, and in particular for laborers in industry.[11] Proposals to regulate hours, enforce industrial hygiene, limit child and female labor, raise wages, encourage professional trade unions and provide cheap credit for farmers did have much meaning for full time laborers. But all efforts in the Chamber of Deputies to enact this type of legislation had the industrial worker as their goal; not until the late 1890s was there a serious debate over the protection of the agricultural worker. Undoubtedly the Parisian leadership of the extreme left and also most of the moderate Radicals tended to ignore rural working conditions. Rather the fiscal and economic planks of Radical programs were designed for small producers, whether artisans or landowning peasants. And in the lower Midi the small and medium producer of wine formed the most impoitant single element in the electoral corps of Radicalism. But it is undeniable that many workers, without land or with minimal holdings, aspired to ownership and identified with small owners and therefore with the Radical programs favorable to small producers of wine. On the other hand, there are numerous indications that the real rural proletariat, found chiefly in the plain of Roussillon, the Narbonnais, Bitterois, and Vaunage were drawn to the Radical movement because it constituted the extreme left. When socialism emerged they would become socialists.

LABOR VOTE

To complement these generalizations it is desirable to look more closely at the labor vote in 1881 and particularly in 1885. Such a study requires an examination of the social structure of each circumscription and the sampling of as many communes as the documents allow.[12]

In 1886 the department of Pyrénées-Orientales had about 16,800 farmers with patronal rights, that is, who could hire workers as needed. Excluding tenants and sharecroppers, about three-fourths of the above total were land owners. Distinct from this group were 16,586 workers (ouvriers). The census did not distinguish between owner-workers and full-time workers, but certainly a large number of the full-time workers owned some land. In 1881 there were 6,300 self-employed, 5,600 owner-

TABLE 10: MALE POPULATION CLASSIFIED BY PROFESSION (1886)

| | Agriculture | | Industry, Transport, Commerce | |
Department	Employer	Worker	Employer	Worker
Pyrénées-Orientales	16,844	16,586	5,358	2,818
Aude	32,900	22,962	6,578	4,855*
Hérault	24,485	14,595	13,261	12,140*
Gard	38,878	14,411	10,103	18,535
Bouches-du-Rhône	22,043	9,566	21,367	37,051
Var	25,793	12,268	6,843	4,238

*Textiles lacking

Source: *Résultats statistiques du recensement général ... 1886*, 180.

workers, and 5,400 workers in Perpignan *arrondissement*. In 1886 about one-third of the department's self-employed and two-thirds of the workers resided there, and labor concentration was notable in the plain. When the phylloxera arrived in the early 1880s the major part of the population was severely affected. Wine production fell sharply there and throughout the department.

TABLE 11: WINE PRODUCTION PYRENEES-ORIENTALES.

Year	Hectares of Vines	Hectolitres of Wine
1882	76,030	1,340,465
1884	54,991	1,407,477
1885	52,602	806,307

Economic distress combined with the personal popularity of the Radical candidates undoubtedly explains why there was a marked shift to the left between the elections of 1881 and 1885. Emile Brousse was particularly favored. Not only was he a first-rate campaigner, he was equally skilled in wine issues, which, as his voting records show, took precedence over social and labor reforms. The defense of vintners rather than of workers gave him his reputation, and he was the frontrunner of the Radical slate. Even though the Radicals' personal popularity brought them remarkable success during 1885 in nonviticultural highland cantons such as Saint-Paul and Olette, their abiding strength was limited to wine areas where there were full-time and part-time workers; this meant the low hills and coast. The radicals mean vote was 26 percent for the department. Most of the communes which provided them a vote above this percentage were in the coast, low hills, or valleys, and where there were at least some elements of a working class.[13]

A quite similar situation existed in the department of Aude. It and Pyrénées-Orientales not only had large areas and population devoted to crops other than wine, they were fortunate in that the phylloxera came late and damaged them less. This was certainly a factor contributing to the hesitancy which marked their move leftward. Aude was similar to Roussillon and the rest of Languedoc in that its labor force was concentrated in the coastal plain and in river valleys, especially the middle and lower Aude Valley. This laboring force as well as the departmental population were chiefly agricultural, with a small number of artisans and commercial workers in towns and larger villages, a situation similar to that of Pyrénées-Orientales. Of the six departments, these two had the largest percentage of their populations engaged in agriculture:

TABLE 12: PERCENTAGE OF POPULATION BY PROFESSION, 1886

Department	Agriculture	Industry	Transport	Commerce
Pyrénées-Orientales	61.0	9.7	3.6	11.2
Aude	62.3	13.3	2.6	10.8
Hérault	39.3	16.0	5.3	16.7
Gard	46.9	19.8	4.5	17.4
Bouches-du-Rhône	22.6	31.6	6.7	25.0
Var	47.1	12.2	2.6	9.7

Source: Résultats Statistiques du recensement général...1886,135.

Politics of any kind, including Radicalism, would have to find its mass base in the countryside, and, to be victorious, would have to win over the vineyard workers of the coastal plain and Aude Valley. But, as in mid-nineteenth century, the working class was complex, with numerous owner-workers, and they could go down several political paths. In Aude, much of the laboring class in the 1880s was too unsettled to have acquired a strong class consciousness. As in Roussillon, many had come from phylloxera-stricken areas, as well as from the highlands. In 1886 nearly 16 percent of Aude's population was born in a different department, the highest rate west of the Rhône. And just over 25 percent of the population was born in a different commune, the highest rate of the six departments. There was a remarkable fluidity in population; indeed,

TABLE 13: POPULATION BY BIRTHPLACE, 1886

Department	% Born in Commune where living	% Born in Other Commune	% Born in Other Department
Pyrénées-Orientales	84.6	12.1	3.3
Aude	58.9	25.5	15.6
Herault	89.3	7.2	3.5
Gard	87.5	7.2	5.3
Bouches-du-Rhône	58.9	12.7	28.4
Var	61.1	19.6	19.3

Source: *Résultats statistiques du recensement général...1886, 69.*

Aude was in the same category as lower Provence. Much, but not all, of this migration consisted of workers and it seems likely that most of them were landless. Unfortunately the manuscript census, as well as the documents of the agricultural investigations, are missing for the wine cantons where most workers resided.[14]

This study of the labor vote has, up to now, relied on general analysis, more qualitative than quantitative, because hard data has been too limited to encourage the use of it for close statistical analysis. With Hérault and Gard, however, there is sufficient information about social structure to allow a more quantitative approach. As in other wine departments, the victory of the Radical list was heavily dependent on the vote of small and medium landowners, even though it could not have been gained without the support of a segment of the labor vote.

The political role of agricultural workers is evident. As in other departments they were rarely active as political leaders, even at the communal level; they did not have the time and money to devote to politics. One searches in vain for them among cantonal committee members or among the members of delegates of the central committees which chose electoral candidates. Artisans, on the other hand, were active, but it is impossible to discover whether they were self-employed, employers, or wage laborers. What is certain is that most men active in politics at the *arrondissement* and departmental levels were independent landowners, or in the professions, or both owners and professionals. The agricultural wage workers, then, were more important as voters than as leaders, a situation which had not changed since 1849. In Hérault, the electoral campaign of 1885 was rather similar to that of mid-century when the moderate slate had been too weak to count for much. Once again a predominantly Radical list was running against a predominantly monarchist list, and republican conservatives, fairly sizable in number, split between the two extremes.

This dichotomy probably explains why the labor vote—that is, the agricultural labor vote—was rather badly divided; the pressure of socially conservative landowners must have strongly influenced their hired help.

Given this situation the victory of the Radical list would have been unattainable without considerable support among left-wing landowners in the lowlands. If one studies the election, commune by commune, this situation emerges clearly. For this analysis communes with three employers *(patrons)* to one worker are classed as patronal, those with two employers to one worker are classed as mixed–patronal, those with a nearly equal ratio as mixed, those with two workers to one employer as mixed worker, and those with three workers to one employer as worker.[15]

The following table correlates topography and social structure, using 294 communes out of 336. This sampling includes only the communes in which one slate received a majority (about 55 percent) of registered voters, that is, communes with a fairly well-defined political preference.

TABLE 14: HERAULT, SOCIAL STRUCTURE, TOPOGRAPHY, AND ELECTORAL RESULTS

Type of commune	Radical Majority		Conservative Majority	
	Lowland	*Highland*	*Lowland*	*Highland*
	Number	*Number*	*Number*	*Number*
Patronal	25	24	15	51
Mixed-Patronal	12	7	10	23
Mixed	26	8	18	16
Mixed-Worker	14	2	10	9
Worker	7	3	7	7
Total	84 (29%)	44 (15%)	60 (21%)	106 (36%)
N—294				

It is obvious that Radical strength—the Radical frame of mind—had its topographical locus in the lowlands and its true social roots in the mixed communes there.

It is worthwhile to correlate the 1885 electoral results with the census of 1891, which was somewhat more realistic about the ratio of landowner to worker. There was not much change in the social structure of Hérault between 1886 and 1891 and the correlation is a reasonably accurate one. Unfortunately, the data by communes is available only for the *arrondissement* of Montpellier and therefore, the comparability of Table 14 and Table 15 is limited. (For the totals by *arrondissement*, see Appendix II).

TABLE 15: MONTPELLIER, SOCIAL STRUCTURE, AND ELECTORAL RESULTS

Type of Commune	Total	Radical Majority	Conservative Majority
Patronal	33	13	20
Mixed Patronal	12	6	6
Mixed	28	10	18
Mixed Worker	17	8	7
Worker	27	16	10
Total	117	53	61

The conservatives have still won a majority of communes, but there is a more positive correlation between the vote for Radicals and the number of workers in the population in the eastern part of the department. For Radicals, it was not disquieting that the conservative list won an absolutely larger number of communes in each classification. If they did not have a numerical superiority in the total number of communes, they did in the total number of people and of voters. Conservative strength lay chiefly in the small communes in the highlands, that of the Radicals in the mixed, larger communes of the wine areas where population was growing. In the seven worker-and-Radical communes of the lowlands (Table 14) there was a population of nearly 12,000; in the seven worker-and-conservative communes, there was a population of only 3,500. In the larger coastal towns were the masses of workers and peasants; here was the true *vigneron* type of Languedoc, fully devoted to vines, to monoculture and speculative production, and almost naturally left-wing in mentality. When later Radicals no longer appeared sufficiently advanced, he would turn to socialists, as would the town-based industrial workers.

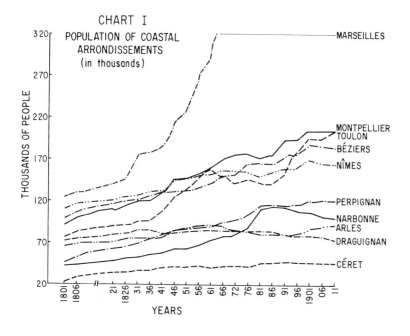

CHART I

POPULATION OF COASTAL
ARRONDISSEMENTS
(in thousands)

THOUSANDS OF PEOPLE

320
270
220
170
120
70
20

MARSEILLES
MONTPELLIER
TOULON
BÉZIERS
NÎMES
PERPIGNAN
NARBONNE
ARLES
DRAGUIGNAN
CÉRET

1801 1806 21 1826 31 36 41 46 51 56 61 66 72 76 81 86 91 96 1901 06 11

YEARS

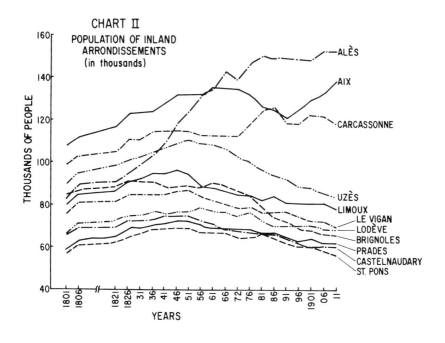

CHART II

POPULATION OF INLAND
ARRONDISSEMENTS
(in thousands)

THOUSANDS OF PEOPLE

160
140
120
100
80
60
40

ALÈS
AIX
CARCASSONNE
UZÈS
LIMOUX
LE VIGAN
LODÈVE
BRIGNOLES
PRADES
CASTELNAUDARY
ST. PONS

1801 1806 1821 1826 31 36 41 46 51 56 61 66 72 76 81 86 91 96 1901 06 11

YEARS

When considering the labor vote, it is necessary to study the votes of industrial workers. In 1886, about 16 percent of the departmental population was engaged in industry. Much of this activity was artisanal, and the artisans were more concentrated in the lowlands now than at mid-century because of the intervening change in the density of population. The only activity which attracted sizable numbers of workers to the highlands was mining, located in the cantons of Bédarieux and Lunas. Here the miners strongly supported the Radical slate. So did the textile workers of Bédarieux, Clairmont, and Lodève; however, the labor force in the highlands had undergone some important changes. Most weavers preserved their left-wing traditions of 1848. They consistently turned more to politics than to trade unions to resolve their grievances, because their chief grievance was the decline of jobs, a problem that was beyond the powers of unions. The weavers' preference for politics over unionization resembled that of the vineyard laborers who were generally indifferent toward professional organization until the twentieth century. Many textile workers also resembled owner-workers in the vineyards in that they owned homes and some land which they cultivated during the slack season and which enabled them to survive the regime of the short week. Weavers without land often could not survive and moved away, causing thereby a steady decline of population at first from emigration and finally as a result of lower natality. The remaining workers were solid citizens, older, and good family men, hardly given to concubinage or excess drinking. The cafe, much frequented in textile as well as in wine towns, was more of a place for social intercourse and politicking than debauchery. Industrial relations were calm and strikes infrequent.[16] The moderate Radicalism represented by Eugene Arrazat, Paul Ménard-Dorian, and Michel Vernière fitted in with the scheme of things in these industrial centers.[17]

Radicals in Gard did not have a large coastal population to back them; Gard had no more than a finger of its great hand-shaped mass touching the sea. Moreover, most of its communes with an agricultural population had a preponderance of landowners with patronal rights. To have a clearer understanding of the Radical's strength, we can look at Table 16 which is based on a sampling of about 43 percent of the communes of Gard.

TABLE 16: GARD, SOCIAL STRUCTURE AND ELECTORAL RESULTS

Type of Commune	N	Radicals Won under 27–30%	Radicals Won 30% or more
Patronal	46	26	20
Mixed	83	50	33
Worker	22	16	6
Total	151	92	59

Of the twenty-six patronal and unfavorable communes, twenty (77 percent) gave less than 20 percent to the Radicals, that is, less than the Radicals' departmental average (21 percent). Clearly the left was at a disadvantage in these communes, not only as regards social structure, but also religion. At least seventeen of the twenty-six unfavorable communes were Catholic, and four were both Catholic and Protestant.

Particularly significant were the results of eighty-three mixed communes with a more or less equal ratio between employers and workers. The position of the Radical list had already worsened; 38 percent of this sample were favorable, 56 percent were unfavorable. Now we come to the *pièce de résistance*. There were twenty-two communes with three or more agricultural workers to one employer. This sample includes nearly all such communes; it is evident from Table 16 that the Radicals did not win a significant percentage of the farm-labor vote. Ten of the sixteen unfavorable worker communes gave them under 20 percent, and at least seven and undoubtedly more were Catholic. Sixteen of the total of twenty-two were in the wine area and the performance of Radicals varied there.

This variation resulted, as in 1849, more from religious than social or economic differences. For example, the coastal communes of Le Cailar, Vauvert, and Vestric, with four workers to one employer, were strongly Radical. They were predominantly Protestant, with some Catholics in Le Cailar. On the other hand, the Catholic communes of Aiguesmortes (three workers to one employer) and Fournès (five plus to one) were strongly hostile to the left; Radicals won less than 10 percent of the registered voters. Saint-Gilles, Saint-Hilaire d'Ozilhan (both five to one) gave only 10 to 14 percent. Saint Laurent (six to one) gave only 20 to 24 percent; it was both Catholic and Protestant. Of course, not all Protestants were Radical. Sommières (three to one), in the Pro-

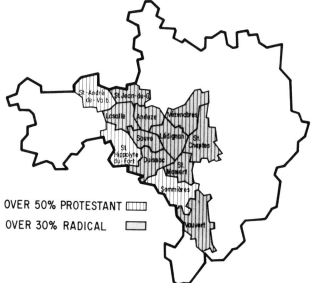

GARD
POLITICS AND RELIGION, 4 OCT. 1885

St André
de Valb.   St Jean-de-G

Lasalle   Anduze   Vézenobres

Sauve   Lédignan   St.
Chaptes

St
Hippolyte
du-Fort   Durfort

St.
Mamert

Sommières

Vauvert

OVER 50% PROTESTANT

OVER 30% RADICAL

testant belt, provided the left with only 10 to 14 percent of the registered vote (see map 6).

Voting among industrial workers followed a similar pattern; that is, artisans in the western or more Protestant half of Gard were divided between Radicals and moderates; many in the eastern half were conservative, save in several cantonal capitals along the Rhône. The Radicals' chief weakness was their failure to win over the major concentrations of industrial workers: those in Le Vigan tended to favor moderates; those in Nîmes and Alès II (chiefly the mining basin) voted strongly for conservative royalists. Silk textile workers in the second and third cantons of Nîmes and miners in Alès II were devoutly Catholic rather than class conscious. Their religious fervor was reinforced by the anticlerical legislation of Jules Ferry. They were not as fanatical as their progenitors in 1848 and earlier—although fights continued to break out among Protestant and Catholic circles—but they had been aroused since 1881 by Ferry's policies which closed their schools and expelled certain religious associations. Many Catholics saw Jules Ferry as the diabolical incarnation of Freemasonry and Protestantism. Now this does not mean that all Catholics were antirepublican, or even anti-Radical. In the sampling of forty-six employer-dominated communes, at least six Catholic ones and perhaps more (there was not information on religion for all comunes) favored the Radicals. Among the eighty-three evenly balanced communes, at least eight and perhaps more were in the favorable group. And among the twenty-two worker-dominated communes, at least three were in the same group. Most of the pro-Radical Catholic communes were in the plain and Rhône Valley, indicating a growing class consciousness among some Catholics. On the other hand, most of these communes were located in areas of increasing de-christianization which official data on religious affiliation did not take into account. Possibly—and it is likely in some cases—freethinkers or religiously indifferent persons were classified as Catholics simply because they had been baptized or because they went to church once or twice a year, "just in case," as they put it, "God really does exist." Recognizing these possibilities it is nonetheless clear that the Catholic vote had evolved since 1848–49; much of it went to moderate republicans whose list contained at least one practicing Catholic, Emile Jamais. The Radical slate, however, had all Protestants save Fernand Crémieux who was a Jew.

This tactically unwise choice of candidates undoubtedly helps explain why the slate did so poorly in the mining communes. With the exception of Bessèges, where metallurgical workers taught left-wing politics to coal miners, there was a strong tendency to favor royalists. That class consciousness was not lacking in nearly all the pits was evidenced by the extensive strike movement there in 1881–82. Although Georges Clemenceau and a few other Radicals had defended the demands of the strikers, the mining population remained deeply conservative.[18] The Radicals and moderates were fortunate in that the *scrutin de liste* balanced out the highland conservative voters with the moderate and Radical majority; the return to single-member constituencies in 1889 destroyed this balance, and ended the possibility of Radical penetration of Alès II.

Quite clearly, then, there is not so positive a correlation between the labor vote and the extreme left in Gard as in other departments. The situation in 1885 was remarkably similar to that of 1848–49 in that cultural variables were still at least as important as economic and social ones, and one may cogently argue that the religious issue, which has been impossible to isolate adequately because of insufficient data about de-christianized communes, was paramount. It is the only variable which produces a nearly consistent response: the larger the Protestant population the more favorable was the vote for Radicals.

In Bouches-du-Rhône, it was not Protestants, of which there were very few, but the population of Marseille and the working class there, that played a preponderant role. Thanks to the census of 1881, nearly complete, it is possible to make a more detailed analysis of the relation between socio-economic conditions and electoral results. The census data of 1881 can be used for 1885, for in the elections from 1881 to 1893, the Radicals and their allies dominated the department. In fact, there was hardly any change in the personnel, which indicates a relative stability, both in politics and in social structure. Therefore the correlations valid for 1881 hold good both for 1885 and 1889, to a lesser extent for 1893.

As in other departments, the Radical slate derived support from a cross section of the communes, as is shown in a representative sample of 55 communes out of 119 for the department.

Table 17: Bouches-du-Rhône, Social Structure and Electoral Results

Type of Commune	N	Radicals won under 26%	Radicals won 26–30%	Radicals won over 30%
Patronal	30	19	3	8
Mixed-Patronal	7	5	1	1
Mixed	10	4	1	5
Mixed-Worker	3	1 } 2	1	1 } 6
Worker	5	1 }	3	1 }
Total	55	30	9	16

25

Note: The cantons of Marseille are each listed as communes in order to avoid under weighing the influence of Marseille , which would happen if its cantons were counted together as simply one commune. Likewise Arles-*Est* and *Ouest* and Aix *Nord* and *Sud* have been counted separately.

As in Hérault, the Radical slate seems weakest in patronal and strongest in worker communes, if one considers only the number of communes. But Bouches-du-Rhône had a larger segment of its active male population in industry and commerce than in agriculture; therefore it is necessary to look both at the number of communes and at their type of economy. Later in this chapter their size will be studied. For the present, they can be grouped into three types: agricultural (about 70 percent of the active male population engaged in farming), industrial-commercial (about the same percentage in industry, commerce, and transport), and economically mixed or herterogeneous.

Table 18: Bouches-du-Rhône, Type of Economy and Electoral Results

Type of Commune	N	Registered Voters	Mean Radical Vote	Radicals' percent of: voters of type	their mean vote of sample	all registered voters of sample
Agricultural	74	28,161(x)	6,986(x_1)	$\dfrac{x_1}{x} = 25$	$\dfrac{x_1}{y_1} = 19$	$\dfrac{x_1}{y} = 5$
Mixed	33	56,168(x)	15,027(x_1)	27	41	11
Industrial-Commercial	12	53,992(x)	13,456(x_1)	22	37	10
Total of Sample	119	138,321(y)	35,469(y_1)			

Since this table is based on 138,321 registered voters out of 139,346, it is nearly a complete sampling of the department. It is quite evident that the Radicals' strength lay in the mixed and industrial-commercial communes rather than in the agricultural ones. This was to be expected. What was, perhaps, less expected was their stronger position in centers with a mixed economy where they could win over town-dwelling peasants, numerous artisan wage earners and some elements of the middle class. In highly industrialized centers, however, class lines were more strongly drawn. While workers might lean toward the left, the middle-class population tended to favor moderate republicans or conservatives, and in the small industrial communes east of Marseille, peasants, employers, and undoubtedly some workers, strongly backed the moderates at the expense of the Radicals. Only in the mining commune of Gréasque did the left win a majority; in the shipbuilding commune of La Ciotat it won a plurality.

In numerous small industrial and middle-sized mixed communes, there were still workers with peasant outlooks on life and who voted accordingly, even if they were employed full time. In some agricultural and mixed communes there were also sizable numbers of owner-workers. This latter situation probably strengthened the left. In nine of the patronal communes at least half of the landowning group consisted of owner-workers and four of them gave the Radicals either a majority or sizable plurality. Twelve communes in which 20 to 50 percent of the owners were part-time workers divided evenly among the three slates, and finally, of sixteen communes in which only about 20 percent of the owners were also workers seven gave majorities or large pluralities to the left. But the fact remained: to win in 1885 and after, a left wing political party would have to win over a larger working class following. And the Radicals clearly had not won over all the workers.[19]

The city of Toulon was typical of Var and more decisively left wing. Although there was a higher rate of abstention than in Marseille, 44 to 35 percent, the slate won an absolute majority there. The workers of the naval yards, the numerous artisans and laborers in commerce and transport, certainly rallied to the extreme left or abstained. And in the entire Toulon *arrondissement*, highly urbanized with a sizable lower class in town and countryside, the extreme left won an absolute majority thanks to important industrial centers such as La Seyne with over 2,000 industrial laborers, Hyères with over 900 vineyard workers, and Six-Fours and Solliès-Pont, each with lesser but important rural labor contingents.

However, even within the Toulon *arrondissement*, and certainly in those of Draguignan and Brignoles, the Radical-Socialist slate obtained its winning votes in patronal or owner-dominated communes. In a sample of thirty-six communes, nearly a fourth of the total, the extreme left was strongest—30 percent or more—in owner-dominated areas.

TABLE 19 : VAR, SOCIAL STRUCTURE AND ELECTORAL RESULTS

Type of Commune	N	Radicals won under 30%	Radicals won 30% or more
Patronal	11	3	8
Mixed	23	13	10
Worker	2	0	2
Total	36	16	20

The above sample includes a random choice of patronal communes, as well as all communes with a sizable labor force, agricultural and non-agricultural, that is, in which laborers were more or less equal to owners, and the two in which there were three or more workers to one owner: La Seyne in Toulon II and Puget-sur-Argens in Fréjus canton. In both, the Radical-Socialists won absolute majorities. But their departmental victory resulted from their popularity in patronal and in mixed communes; as in most other departments, there simply was not a labor force numerous or concentrated enough to assure success outside of Toulon and La Seyne. In the ten mixed communes where Radicals won over 30 percent of the registered voters, only three had a somewhat higher total of workers than owners, and five communes were evenly balanced. But these ratios were identical to the thirteen unfriendly communes. The workers' vote was split and large numbers of landowners brought victory to the Radicals, as in 1898 and after, they would to the socialists.

When considering the social and economic background of the Radical vote in the Midi during the 1880s, the percentage of labor in the total male population is a fairly good indicator of left-wing strength, however it is not a perfect one and not always conclusive. Whether we consider agricultural or nonagricultural labor, there was not a consistent positive correlation between the percentage of labor and electoral outcome. There was, rather, a tendency for Radicals to win or to run well in areas with a sizable working class. The one serious exception to this tendency was Gard, and, after 1885, the coastal areas of Aude. In order to prode more deeply into the sociology of the Radical vote it is necessary to consider another variable and its connection with the labor vote, that is, the urban vote.

URBAN VOTE

Defining the term urban in a wine producing area is most difficult. The definition of the French census bureau, a commune with 2,000 *habitants agglomérés* (inhabitants concentrated in the town), only partially serves the purpose; by the 1880s such a commune might, and in the highlands often did, have a distinctly rural character, because even its concentrated population was predominantly peasant. In the plains, on the other hand, a far smaller commune often had a distinctly urban character derived from its location in a zone of dynamic economic and population growth which set it apart from larger communes in zones of both economic and demographic stagnation. In general, communes in the larger wine zones proved to be the most urbanized in terms of complex social structure, commercial activity, population growth, municipal forms of government, capital accumulation, and frame of mind. This situation was inevitable. After all, the large-scale production of wine was for a vast, unknown market, therefore local producers and their agents had to have ease of transportation, contact with the outside world, willingness to speculate and to favor change, access to credit facilities, sophisticated means of influencing the government in Paris, and open-mindedness toward cultural activities which the accumulation of wealth and leisure encouraged. Only the major port and industrial towns encouraged the concentration of population superior to that of the wine districts. (See Table 20.)

TABLE 20: POPULATION DENSITY BY ARRONDISSEMENT: 1801–1886
(Persons per square kilometer)

Highland

(Polyculture without wine)	1801	1846	1886
Prades	21	29	26
Castelnaudary	51	61	52
Alès (mining)	47	75	98
Le Vigan	40	48	41
Lodève	38	48	42
(Polyculture with wine)			
Céret	21	29	26
Carcassonne	38	47	53
Limoux	33	42	35
Saint-Pons	30	41	37
Brignoles	33	35	28
Aix	42	52	49

Lowland

Rhône Valley (Polyculture with wine)	1801	1846	1886
Uzès	47	60	50
Arles	30	37	36
Coast (Wine monoculture)			
Narbonne	26	40	71
Nîmes	69	89	96
Toulon (includes town)	60	99	111
Marseille (nonwine)	193	329	633
Coast and Highland (Wine monoculture in coastal sections)			
Perpignan	36	63	86
Béziers	56	75	89
Montpellier	47	74	89
Draguignan	27	31	31

If one accepts the definition of the French census bureau, lower Provence was decidedly more urbanized than lower Languedoc and Roussillon.

TABLE 21: PERCENTAGE OF TOTAL POPULATION CLASSED AS URBAN

Department	1856	1872	1886
Pyrénées-Orientales	29.8	37.6	40.7
Aude	24.6	24.9	33.0
Hérault	50.4	53.9	56.7
Gard	44.4	47.2	49.0
Bouches-du-Rhône	76.1	80.3	83.5
Var	53.2	56.4	56.2

Source: Résultats statistiques ... 1886, 38.

For electoral sociology these departmental statistics are, at best, useful indicators, at worst, deceptive. They are particularly deceptive as regards lower Provence where each department was dominated by a single city: Bouches-du-Rhône by Marseille and Var by Toulon, which unduly raised the percentage of the urban population. Since there are other weaknesses in the arrangement of the census figures we have decided to use a different set of figures, the number of registered voters, in order to determine urban character. Since women and males under twenty-one were not allowed to vote, electoral results reflected the number and the condition of adult males. For purpose of analysis, communes with 650 to 950 registered voters are classed as semiurban and those with 950 or more as urban. This system is not perfect either; it is simply more meaningful for analysis. Its major usefulness lies in its inclusion of coastal communes west of the Rhône without 2,000 *habitants agglomérés,* but with a large dispersed population who, although dispersed, yet had easy and frequent contacts with urban centers. A dispersed commune of the coastal plain was quite different from a dispersed commune of the highlands where communication with the communal center was difficult in good weather and impossible during winter months.

Since left-wing propaganda more successfully found converts in areas of easy communication, radical candidates won more voters where urbanization had advanced. In Table 22 columns 1 and 2 offer a good part of the explanation as to why radical slates were weakest in Aude and Gard. Columns 3 and 4 reinforce the explanation: Aude was too rural; Gard, while evenly mixed, had too large a conservative peasant and catholic population living in her small towns.

TABLE 22: URBAN POPULATION AND ELECTORAL RESULTS

	(1) Radical Departmental Percent of Registered Voters	(2) Mean Radical Urban Vote as Percent of Registered Voters of Department	(3) Urban Percent of Radical Vote: 650+ of Registered	(4) Percent of Urban Population in 1886. *Résultats Statistiques*
Pyrénées-Oientales	26	11.4	44	40.7
Aude	21	8	25	33
Hérault	37	22	59	56.7
Gard	21	9	43	49
Bouches-du-Rhône	27	23	86	83.5
Var	30	19	60	56.2

Save for Aude, the correlations between columns 3 and 4 are obvious.

Marseille and Toulon present special problems; they account for the high percentages in the above table. The great port city of Bouches-du-

Rhône was to the lower Midi what Paris was to France; a demographic magnet and a melting pot where provincials from east Languedoc, upper and lower Provence, Dauphiné, and the lower Alpes were mixed together and became *Marseillais*. Its political impact on Bouches-du-Rhône was more important now than in 1848–51. In the 1880s the city returned five out of eight deputies and in 1885 the predominantly Radical list won over 40 percent of its votes there. The Radicals were strongest in the first and second circumscriptions (which contained a large industrial working class and a host of petty producers and shopkeepers) and, thanks to Chevillon and Antide Boyer, in the fourth and fifth (a semi-rural area with large numbers of artisans in suburban crafts, the industrial workers in La Ciotat, the miners in Roquevaire canton, and a host of small farmers engaged in truck gardening in the L'Huveaune Valley).

As in other departments the Radicals held their own in the countryside, but most of their strength came from the cities. Including Marseille, 63 percent of their total vote came from towns with more than 950 registered voters, and the big city accounted for 42 percent of this Radicalized urban vote. To be sure, Radicals were still fairly strong in other urban and semiurban communes; but with *scrutin de liste,* Marseille carried the left to a plurality and therefore to victory in the runoff.

TABLE 23: PERCENT OF TOTAL RADICAL VOTE FROM URBANIZED COMMUNES

	Communes with 950 + registered voters	Communes with 650+ registered voters	Mean Radical urban vote (650+) as % of all registered voters in department
With Marseille commune	63	81	21
Less Marseille commune	20	39	10

This table makes clear that Marseille held a preponderant place in the plurality won by the Radicals. The urban vote was more decisive in Bouches-du-Rhône than in Hérault where the economic factor was different. East of the Rhône the urban populace was more decisively connected to industry, commerce, and transport, that is, the secondary sector of the total economy. There were twelve communities in which

70 percent or more of the population was in the secondary sector, with a preponderance of wage workers. That only the industrial cantons of Marseille and La Ciotat were populous enough to be classed as urban, however, reinforced the dependency of the left on Marseille.

The rural *arrondissements* in Var were somewhat more independent of Toulon in 1885 than their counterparts in Bouches-du-Rhône were of Marseilles. Toulon *arrondissement* did not elect more deputies than Brignoles and Draguignan, but only two, and the city itself comprised only one circumscription, the first. The second was partly rural, but, in reality, quite urbanized because of the large, active communes of La Seyne, Hyères and Cuers. Political views were not seriously different between the first and second circumscriptions. Nor were they seriously different between Toulon and the central and eastern sector of the department, where the remaining urban centers were located. The leadership of Toulon can be recognized in the fact that the large port and naval base provided the Radical slate with one-half of the votes it won in the nine strongly urban communes of Var and one-third of its votes in all communes with over 650 registered voters. The electoral weight of Toulon was a major factor in the leftward tendencies of Var both in 1848–49 and after 1870. With Toulon included in the total, the Radical slate derived 36 percent of its average vote from urban centers with 950 registered voters and 60 percent from all communes with over 650 voters. It is significant that Radicals were weakest in Brignoles *arrondissement,* not in their percentage (30) but in relation to conservatives (35. 4). In Brignoles, the most rural sector of the department, the Radical slate was more successful in the lower wine-producing communes, and in the city of Brignoles. The future of the left in Provence was guaranteed by the constant rise in the urban population, a result of the drift of people toward the more habitable lowlands.

West of the Rhône, the impersonal factors of demography certainly had a more lasting effect on politics than the personal one, which does not eliminate the personal factor but rather recognizes its limitations. It has already been noted—and underlined—that the personal factor during 1885 was extremely important in Pyrénées-Orientales. But personal appeal and the urban vote must be seen as complementary. Vilar and Floquet, while popular in the uplands where there were few urban centers, ran less well in the lowlands which were more urbanized. Yet, the entire slate was highly successful, in large measure because of its ability to win the urban population. Forty-four percent of its departmental vote came from communes with over 650 registered voters, and most of these communes were in the coastal plain. In all, there were seventeen urbanized communes in the department. Eleven of them were in the plain and of these latter, the Radical list won an absolute majority in nine during the first election. Undoubtedly the Radical strength in Perpignan was an important weight on the electoral scale, but, in general, they attained higher percentages in small urban centers. In fact, the monarchist list won a plurality in the commune of Perpignan thanks to their strength in the northern and western sections, whereas the Radicals won decisive majorities in the port towns of Banyuls, Collioure, Port Vendres, and in most lowland, urbanized wine towns such as Rivesaltes, Thuir, Elne, and Argelès. The list did well in some upland communes, such as Prades, which was already pro-Radical; but it lost in Céret and Prats-de-Mollo which were traditionally conservative or moderate, and also where the population consisted largely of peasants or rural-minded people many of whom were transient farm laborers. Upland towns, because of emigration and declining wealth, lost enough of their service and professional population to become transformed. Urban by numbers of inhabitants, they were rural by mentality. Where this phenomenon occurred, true Radicalism could make no headway.

The same was true in Aude, and Radicalism was weakest there largely because its urban base was neither sufficiently concentrated as in Provence nor widespread along the coast as in Pyrénées-Orientales and Hérault. According to the census, only 33 percent of Aude's population was urban in 1886. Had the Radicals captured this population, they could have sailed easily to victory, but they did not. In the urban centers with over 950 registered voters, they won 29 percent which was eight points above their departmental average. In the semi-urban centers, they won only 21 percent, which was equal to their departmental average. Their entire urban mean vote represented only 8 percent of registered voters in the department. Their weakness lay in their failure to carry greater weight in the two largest cities, Carcassonne (24 percent) and Narbonne (25 percent). The moderates, backed by strong traditions and the personal weight of ex-Radicals such as Marcou, were almost as strong in these towns, and particularly influential in the semiurban centers along the coast as well as inland. Radical strength, whether in urban or rural areas, was largely confined to the lower and middle Aude Valley, that crucial stretch of sacred soil between the coast and Carcassonne. Elsewhere it chiefly held outposts among urban centers: Castelnaudary to the west, Limoux to the south.

Both Hérault and Gard were considerably more urbanized than their western neighbors. Hérault had 56.7 percent of its population in urban communes according to the census of 1886 and Gard 49 percent. Therefore electoral strength would be far more determined by townspeople. In Hérault, the Radical list, without a moderate list to oppose it and with a weak socialist contingent, was in a particularly strong position. The Radical list won 38 percent of the registered voters of the department. Just over half of this percentage came from communes with 950 or more registered voters, and just under two-thirds of it came from all communes with over 650 voters. In the twenty-four communes with over 950 voters, Radicals ran well in eighteen, and of the six where they performed poorly, three were in the highlands, two in the low hills and one in the plain. Of the eighteen where they won over 30 percent of the registered voters, three were in the highlands, four in the low hills and thirteen in the plain. To be sure, 30 to 37 percent of the registered voters did not guarantee and absolute majority, because there were only two serious slates. But 30 percent or more in a large commune counterbalanced the strong conservative vote in numerous small communes. In Hérault, therefore, the urban vote, which included much of the labor vote, made the Radicals' position almost unassailable until the twentieth century when they began to lose the towns. When that moment arrived they were doomed. (See Appendix I.)

Radicals eventually lost out in Gard too, but for different reasons. Their eventual demise there was due neither to the loss of the labor vote, for they did not control enough of it, nor the loss of the urban population which they never commanded. Even had the Radical slate included men as moderate as Elisée Déandreis and G. Galtier in Hérault, it is doubtful that it would have won a significant portion of the urban vote. This weakness does not mean that Radicals had no urban following.

In the department they won about 21 percent of the registered voters,[20] of which 13 percent came from semiurban communes with 650 to 950 voters and 30 percent from urban communes with more than 950 voters. Its urban vote therefore came to 43 percent of its total, a quite significant figure. However, its urban vote came to only 9 percent of the total registered voters in a department that was nearly half urban according to the census of 1886. This weakness can be underlined: the Radical list won more than 20 percent of the registered voters in only eight of the twenty-five communes with over 950 voters; it therefore made a respectable showing in only about one-third of the truly urban centers, and most of the eight were either Protestant, or part Protestant, part dechristianized.

The failure of the Radicals to penetrate sufficiently the urban milieu resulted in part from the most constant of all variables in Gard: religion. They did well in the Protestant first canton of Nîmes, with 27 percent of the voters, well above their departmental average, but they hardly touched the Catholic second and third cantons. They also were unable to win over a sizeable following in the Catholic wine and Commercial towns in the Rhône Valley: Beaucaire, Bagnols, and Armon. And a crucial weakness was their failure to win over the republican Protestant-Catholic towns of Sommières and Le Vigan which supported the moderate slate.

CONCLUSION

By the 1880s the economy of the entire Mediterranean coast, so heavily dependent on wine, had been seriously upset by the phylloxera. The result was widespread unemployment, population shifts and decline, bankruptcies, forced sales of land, downward mobility for many, frustration for everyone, and widespread, even intense, antipathy toward the opportunist politicians who were too slow to mobilize resources to meet this crisis. Consequently political opinion took a marked shift toward the left; not a sudden shift, but rather a sharper turn in the direction that southerners had been heading since the late 1870s. The Radicals profited from this general conjuncture of events and emerged after the 1885 elections as the single most powerful force in public affairs. Vintners turned to them en mass, hoping to find a solution to their problems, and indeed, the Radical program offered them specific measures which would assist wine production in its slow recovery (See Appendix IX).

The situation was not so greatly different from that of 1849: there was an afflicted economy, and there was a government bent on foreign intervention, not in Rome to save the pope, but in Indochina. Foreign adventures were highly unpopular in the lower Midi. Viewing the entire electoral results, there was a remarkable similarity between the elections of 1849 and 1885. The major differences lay in the left's conquest of Bouches-du-Rhône and in the open conflict between moderate republicans and Radicals, at least for the *premier tour*. For the run-off they united forces to defeat the right, with the result that not one conservative was sent to the Chamber.

The key to understanding political continuity since mid-century is geography, in particular topography. The turn to the Radical left was most notable in the lowlands. In the plain of Roussillon and the plain of Languedoc existed those objective conditions which made Radical politics attractive: vineyards in distress and an urbanized population ready and willing to follow Radical leaders in the direction of reformist innovation. The state, with its resources of credit, its power to aid citizens in distress, its ability to mobilize human knowledge in the struggle against natural disaster, loomed now, not as an oppressor but as a friend, provided, of course, it was responsive to the popular will, provided it was a Radical state, elected by and responsible to the people, that is, the vintners. From here on, politics in the lower South, especially west of the Rhône, was to be the politics of wine.

Where topography and climate encouraged extensive viticulture there were also many towns and cities. Topography determined not only crops but the locus and growth of towns most of which were important wine markets. They were natural centers of political education and action. In the coastal plains and the river valleys townsmen brought victory to the Radicals. The urban vote was the primary human factor in their successful election. Whether west or east of the Rhône, urbanism and Radicalism went hand in hand. Of course, it is important not to oversimplify. Southern towns were usually commercial rather than industrial centers, and their support of left wing politicians, while decisive if they are taken as a group, varied if they are studied individually. In the core or center of most coastal towns there was a conservative or moderate republican population that either voted according to their ideals or abstained. Radical strength tended to find its true locus less in the central districts and more in the suburbs or in the urbanized villages and towns surrounding the larger city where workers in commerce, transport, small industry, and agriculture usually resided. The urban vote, then, blended in with the labor vote.

On the whole workers tended to support the Radical left, especially those who lived in or near the urban centers. The latter were, of course, complex; urban centers were populated by different classes and neighborhoods voted differently. The bourgeois, who lived usually in the vicinity of the court house or town hall, were republican or conservative. The working class quarters generally favored the left. But workers of small communes in the hills or mountains often shared the political moderation characteristic of their area. To become consistently Radical meant not merely to cast a ballot, it meant to break with conservative traditions, often with parents and friends, and the generation of the 1880s was not yet prepared for that. In fact many young men found it easier to emigrate than to oppose the conservative opinion there. Even in the lowland the purely labor vote is difficult to single out. Most workers were in agriculture, chiefly in vineyards. This meant that many of them, perhaps half, were part owners with small plots. Their mentality, in consequence, was complex, as was their income and social status, with the result that they ranged over the entire spectrum of parties. Certainly their votes were indispensable to the left, but they alone could not usually decide the political color of an entire region. As a decisive factor their influence was limited to the plains around Perpignan, Narbonne, Béziers, Montpellier, and Toulon. With rare exceptions, workers here became firmly Radical and fixed in their left-wing orientation.

Political leadership, however, lay not in the hands of workers, but in those of professional men, and its coloration, on the regional level, was determined by middle-class ideals of the Rights of Man, and by large numbers of small and medium landowners who were omnipresent and whose motivation combined self-interest and a kind of agrarian idealism which glorified wine.

The radical movement which had grown up chiefly in urbanized areas had spread into the countryside as a populist agrarian movement. Its emphasis on liberty and equality brought a more democratic idealism to peasants who were themselves passing through far-reaching economic and social changes, who were, indeed, well on the way to becoming a rural petty middle class, with property and producing goods for both the local and national markets. In fact, it was precisely where agricultural production had ceased to be devoted to self-subsistence that left wing forces made their deepest penetration, where they endured.

Radical slates found voters in areas of traditionalist agriculture, the Pyrenees, Cevennes, and Alpes. However, their hold here was precarious, more the result of personal popularity than of doctrinal affinity and economic need. Or else it was the result of cultural factors, chiefly the Protestant religion or a decline in the persuasive powers of Christianity. The election of 1885 marked the last significant crusade on the part of Catholic forces to influence voters. With conservative, pro-Catholic lists in every department, the right proved that religion was by no means a dead issue. On the other hand, their failure to win a single seat, even in Gard where they were strongest, greatly discouraged their followers. Henceforth, clergymen became, if prefectual reports were accurate, neutral in politics, and the way was prepared for the *Ralliement*. Save in the extremely conservative highland cantons Catholic voters often abstained or rallied to moderate republicans. In consequence, the Boulangist movement came at a most opportune time and offered them a means of disrupting republican unity.

NOTES

1. For a description of Radical electoral activity in France, see J. Kayser, *Grandes batailles*, 138-43.
2. They enjoyed a brief revival between 1869 and 1876, but then lost out everywhere save in Montpellier.
3. A.D. Aude 5M 93, report of August 1885

4. Electoral returns can be found in A.D. P-O 2M 1–80; Aude 2M 66, incomplete, Hérault 15M 38, incomplete, and A.N. C5304; Gard 2M 79–81.
5. For the electoral maneuvering see A.D. Gard 2M 81, prefectural reports of Sept. 1885, and *Suffrage universel* and the moderate *Progrès du Midi,* June-September 1885.
6. See A.D. B-du-R 2M 3–46, various reports of June-July 1885; *Petit Marseillais,* 7 October 1885.
7. A.D. Var 2M 3–341.
8. A.D. Hérault 39M 277, 283–84; 15M 34, police reports.
9. See Pierre Georges, *La Région du bas Rhône* (Paris, 1935).
10. For a list of communes and the value of their cash crops see A.D. B-du-R 13M 248. These data, although drawn up in the 1890s, can be used as indicative for 1885. The replanting of the 1880s determined the values of the 1890s and the dependency of a commune on wine or other crops was conditioned by decisions about capital investment in the 1880s.
11. For programs see *Républicain de Pyrénées-Orientales,* 4 July 1885; *Radical de l'Aude,* Aug.-Sept. 1885; *Petit radical du Midi* (Montpellier), 28 June 1885– *Petit méridional,* Aug.-Sept. 1885; *Suffrage universel* (Nîmes) 28 September *Indépendant du Midi* (Nîmes), 2, 4 Aug. 1885; *Radical de Marseille,* and *Petit provençale,* Sept.-Oct., 1885; *Justice du Var* (Draguignan), *Région radicale* (Brignoles,) *Petit Var* (Toulon), Aug.-Oct., 1885.
12. This survey is based on four major documents: the censuses of 1881 and 1886 in manuscript, and the 'Statistique décennale agricole," 1882 and 1892, also in manuscript. See A.D. Pyrénées-Orientales M2570, incomplete; A.D. Aude 11 M 35–38, incomplete, 13M 308–11, incomplete. A.D. Hérault 114M 18–19 "Dénombrement de 1886", A.N. C3021 "Enquête parlementaire ... sur la situation de l'industrie et de l'agriculture en France," 1884. A.D. Gard, 10279 "Dénombrement de 1886" A.D. Bouches-du-Rhône 10M 1–170 "Dénombrement de 1881"; A.D. Var 14M 19–4, 4 "Statistique agricole," 1871–88, 1892; 16M 1–11, "Industrie, situation mensuelle par commune, 1887–94"; in the "Dénombrement de la polulation," 1886, see especially Modèle 10.
13. The Radical slate won most of the workers and small owners in the cantons of Millas, Thuir, and Argelès. The response in Rivesaltes and Perpignan cantons, however, was mixed. There was, on the one hand, serious abstention; over a period of several elections it oscillated between 40 percent and 50 percent! After the phylloxera, many workers were leaving and undoubtedly their names were left on the rolls. It is also likely that many workers, fearful of their employer's vengence, chose not to vote. Those who did cast a ballot, however, chose moderate Radicals such as Floquet, or simple republicans, that is, men such as Edouard Rolland, who were close to the Ferryites, but willing, at times, to join the Radicals. On the other hand, there were several communes, with a sizable agricultural labor population, which were staunchly conservative: Saint-Hippolyte and Claira in Rivesaltes canton. An old legitimist tradition survived even the influx of worker immigrants in the 1870s and their departure in the late 1880s. And their instability may also explain the high abstention rate. This conservative phenomenon was most notable in the canton of Perpignan-Ouest which had furnished a large contingent to the resistance against the coup d'état of 1851. The fervor of those days had died, regardless of cummunal social structure. The Radical slate was weakest precisely in those communes, save Bompas, which had the largest number of workers. In subsequent elections, even the combined vote of several Radical candidates indicated retreat rather than progress, perhaps because the number of workers declined considerably between 1886 and 1892 as a result of the phylloxera. The cantons of Perpignan-*Est* and Thuir were more successful in conserving their populations and social structure and their Radical tradition based on a remarkable balance between owners, owner-workers and workers. Perpignan

I was missionary land, but Perpignan II was friendly territory. In the latter was the change and limited instability which often encouraged left wing politics: persons born in another commune came to 36 percent in the east canton, only 16 percent in the west canton. Nearly a quarter of the population of the commune of Perpignan, most of which was in the east canton, were born in another department. Of course, many of the newcomers abstained—41 percent in Perpignan—they nonetheless brought a dynamic force which encouraged the politics of change—as it had at mid-century. In contrast, the communes of the west canton consisted chiefly of small owners and owner-workers who were native, republican by temperament but of limited vision, and moderate or conservative as are closed groups. They hired fewer workers than their counterparts in the east canton. Hard hit by the phylloxera, they perhaps feared immigrants who competed with them, and contentedly watched the outsiders leave after the boom of the 1870s and early 1880s.

14. Given this deficiency of data, I can do no more than offer some general observations based on administrative reports and electoral returns. First, royalist conservatism was dead in major vineyard areas, with the exception of the Minervois. Workers and landowners voted overwhelmingly for proponents of the Republic, and in areas of major labor concentration, Coursan and Narbonne cantons, the Radical-Socialist list ran slightly ahead of the moderate list. Where laborers were about equal with or somewhat less in number than owners, Lézignan, Durban, and Sigean, the two lists ran neck and neck. Ginestas, however, with a large labor force, was predominantly moderate. In these latter four cantons, workers were already departing as a result of the phylloxera and moderate republicans won in subsequent elections in Narbonne II. Narbonne I (Narbonne and Coursan cantons), which retained much of its labor force for the replanting, became increasingly but not predominantly socialist under the able and fiery leadership of Dr. Ernest Ferroul. Radicalism, then, retreated up the Aude Valley and away from the coast. It became less dependent on rural workers; its two strongholds were located in the cantons of Capendu, with a population composed largely of land owners and owner-workers, and Conques, with almost no workers but where the voters still venerated the memory of Barbès who was born there. In the Carcassonnais the Radical list ran only slightly ahead of the moderate list, save in the wine commune of Saint-Hilaire where most owners looked to the extreme left. In Carcassonne canton, more than half of the arable consisted of medium and large holdings, requiring a sizable labor force which resided in the town. In Carcassonne *arrondissement*, especially in the cantons east of the town of Carcassonne, it would be more accurate to state that about one-third of the winemen rather than owners or laborers voted for Radicals. This was an area dominated by owners, especially small and medium vintners, with some workers, whose Radicalism leaned toward socialism because they were strongly interventionist. Where there was little wine production, in Mouthoumet canton, the extreme left received few votes. Workers west of Carcassonne were few in number. In Castelnaudary, especially in Belpech and Salle-sur-l'Hers cantons, they were a special breed, clerical and conservative, voting the same royalist slate as their employers and easily controlled by them. Workers in the Minervois must also have rallied to the right whose list won over 50 percent of the registered voters. In Limoux *arrondissement* workers usually voted for moderate candidates, but there were very few workers there anyway. The upper Aude Valley, into whose narrow confines the population was concentrated, was an area dominated by small and medium property, with a fairly prosperous mixed agriculture of which vines were only a limited part. The wine producer here, as owner or as owner-worker, was a different social type from the vintner of the coast. He produced cereals as well and reserved his best bottom land for them, using the less fertile hillsides for vines. He was an intermediate type, between the cereal producer, usually conservative, and the vintner, usually left-wing. In politics he was moderately republican, moderately anticlerical, and moderately interventionist.

15. In the "Dénombrement de 1886," many persons classed as patron did not hire workers, at least not on a full-time basis. They were simply landowners who hired workers for special tasks and who were self-employed most of the time. Undoubtedly some of these *Patrons* were really owner-workers and would tend to identify with small landowners.

16. See testimony on conditions in A.N. C3021, "Enquête parlementaire sur la situation de l'industrie et de l'agriculture en France, 1884."

17. Clermont canton, demographically the most dynamic, was also the most advanced politically, and gave the Radicals over 500 more votes than the conservatives. In the town of Lodève, however, the Radical slate won by only 55 votes; in the small textile center of Riols it won by 28 votes; in Bédarieux it lost by 40 votes; in Saint-Pons by 201 votes. Without the labor vote, then, Radicalism would have undoubtedly suffered defeat at the hands of the merchants and local landowners who lived in these urban communes.

    The political character of textile centers had been drastically changed by the emigration of younger workers. A new generation of youthful spinners and weavers appeared every ten years before the child labor law of 1874, every thirteen or fourteen years after it, because lower-class families sent their children to work at the minimum legal age. When natality was high there was a rejuvenation of the labor force frequently; but with the decline of government orders, this situation had changed. Another innovation, resulting from mechanization and concentration, was the greater use of female labor in weaving, formerly a male job. More males, in consequence had to rely on agriculture; in fact, they became more agrarian in outlook than industrial, more rural than urban even though they continued to live in towns. The Radicals, therefore, could no longer count as heavily on the textile labor force. Vineyards rather than textiles determined the outcome of elections in Béziers II and Montpellier II, two circumscriptions stretching from the plain to the mountains. And, of course, so did the more populous lowland towns. For example, the port of Sète had nearly 2,000 more registered voters than all of the textile towns mentioned above, and the Radicals were predominant there in 1885 and well into the 1890s.

18. See my article, "Coal Miners, Strikes and Politics in the Lower Languedoc, 1880–1914," *Journal of Social History,* 2 (Fall, 1968), 25–50.

19. In Tarascon, full time workers of all trades made up 40 percent of the active male population, but Radicals attracted only 25 percent of the registered voters. Practically the same imbalance held for Martiques (50 percent and 13 percent) and several other small communes, such as Les Baux (80 percent and 27 percent), in the canton of Saint-Rémy. Nonetheless, Radicals were dependent upon workers of all sorts as well as upon numerous small independent owners. Where their slate received less than 20 percent of registered voters there were usually few workers, and the owners had succeeded in passing on their conservatism over many generations. Even where workers did not make up a large majority, their vote was decisive. Traditionally conservative Arles *arrondissement,* with only 400 or so more workers than owners, was fairly receptive to the left in 1885 (26 percent). The canton of Arles-*Est,* with a large contingent of workers residing along the road to Salon, gave the extreme left 38 percent, an important conquest given the high rate of abstention, nearly 50 percent. In the commune of Aix workers, both agricultural and industrial, made up 25 percent of the active male population and Radicals won 27 percent. In the city of Marseille , where there was relatively light abstention for the city (35 percent), the cantons with fairly large laboring populations, first, third, fourth, and fifth, brought the Radicals' votes up to 28 percent, a plurality. The laborers' contribution to the left, therefore, was important but as uneven as it was unpredictable.

20. This percentage should be slightly higher because it does not include the mining commune of Bessèges whose results I could not locate.

CHAPTER SEVEN

THE ERA OF POLITICAL CRISES, 1889-1900

The period from 1889 to about 1900 witnessed a marked change in the line-up of political forces in France. On the extreme left several socialist parties sought to replace the Radicals as defenders of lower-class interests. On the right some monarchists, abandoning all hope of a restoration, allied with moderates who were also fearful of socialism, and their union produced a parliamentary group known as *progressistes*. On the extreme right emerged a truly novel group, authoritarians who became vehemently nationalistic and who rallied first to the cause of General Georges Boulanger in 1889 and then to that of the army in the Dreyfus affair of 1898–99.

BOULANGISM IN THE SOUTH

The decade which began with the Boulanger crisis witnessed a severe moral strain within the Radical movement. General Georges Boulanger, a rare type at the time in that he was both a general and a democrat, was placed in charge of the war ministry as a result of pressure from Clemenceau and his colleagues shortly after the 1885 elections. Now that education had been secularized, they sought to bring democracy into the army. Moreover, they had behind them a long tradition of fervent patriotism and, since the Franco-Prussian War of 1870–71, they were vehemently hostile to Germany's hegemony in Europe. They had in mind, in addition to the general's political role, revived hopes for both the recovery of the provinces lost to Germany and of France's primacy in Europe. They had acrimoniously denounced Ferry before and during 1885, accusing him of sacrificing the nation's European mission in favor of colonial conquests.

Since they placed so much hope in Boulanger, most of them found it difficult to believe that he was becoming a menace to the Republic. His personal ambitions, his negotiations with the monarchist right, were quite apparent by 1887, and some Radicals began to express open distrust. But the most influential of them, Clemenceau, Pelletan, Desmons, either persisted in their support of him until quite late, or else they refused to take a stand against him.

The extreme left in the lower Midi, as in the rest of France, was first shaken by the indecisiveness of many of its members toward the general; only seven out of twenty-four southern Radicals signed the March 1888 manifesto of the extreme left condemning him as a menace to the Republic. However, not more than four members, Emile Brousse, Edward Théron, Edward Gaussorgues, and Joseph Chevillon resigned from the group in protest against the manifesto; most of the others came out against Boulangism shortly before the 1889 elections. Brousse of Perpignan eventually turned against the Boulangists and rejoined the group, yet, like other Radicals, persisted in his demand for revision of the constitution. So did Vilar, his fellow Roussillonnais.[1] Boulangism in consequence, did not have a noticeable influence in Pyrénées-Orientales.

It had a far more serious effect in Aude where the official forces of Radicalism were sympathetic almost up to the eve of the election. The situation in the Carcassonnais and the Narbonnais encouraged a form of extremism. Among Radicals as well as among socialists there was a keen desire to form a united front against the popular moderate republicans. In other departments the Radical lists, especially those with one or two moderates on them, had been highly victorious in 1885. This was less true in Aude, where moderates and the extreme left were mutually hostile and the extreme left, to defeat their moderate enemies, found it necessary to attack parliamentary democracy. A form of left wing Boulangism therefore appeared quite suitable. Pierre Massé, editor of *Le Radical du Midi*, Théron in Carcassonne, and Ernest Ferroul in Narbonne continued the 1885 ideal of uniting Radicals and socialists in an alliance to attack and destroy the middle-class parliamentary regime dominated by the moderates. In Aude, then, the term Radical-Socialist had a more revolutionary connotation than elsewhere and became the rallying cry for all dissident left-wing elements. As it turned out, the bond of this left alliance was nationalism, as well as an incipient anti-Semitism. Radical opponents of this tendency were led by Wickersheimer but he was defeated in Carcassonne II by Théron who now repudiated his Radical connections and, in the Chamber, joined the small parliamentary faction of Gustave Cluseret who represented Toulon II. Since all the moderate Radicals of Aude were defeated in 1889, the wine issue, as a weapon to attack the opportunist regime, was to be wielded by extremists such as Théron and Ferroul who won in the Narbonnais. In this developing mentality can perhaps be found a partial cause of the violent wine demonstrations of 1906–7 in Aude.

In Hérault, Boulangism was less attractive to recognized Radicals, but there did appear left-wing nationalists who ran under the title of radical and who attracted a sizable number of followers among native vineyard workers. In Béziers I and Montpellier II, where there were large estates and highly capitalized wine production, the number of immigrant laborers from Spain and Italy was high. Boulangists appealed to the xenophobia of the rural population who complained of unfair competition for jobs and of wages dragged down by cheap foreign labor. Boulangism became a form of economic protest. But even voters less directly threatened by foreign competition, textile workers in the uplands and railroad workers in Béziers, rallied to Boulangists to protest against their working conditions. And at election time, only a fourth to a half had returned to the Radicals.[2] Despite these gains, no Boulangist won in Hérault, and no true Radical went over to the Boulangist camp.

In Gard two Radicals, Numa Gilly in Nîmes I and Edouard Gaussorgues in Le Vigan, defected. And they were both thoroughly defeated. In Gard Boulangism really could not aid the left because it became the instrument of the conservatives to attack the Republic. After all, the Duchess of Uzès was Boulanger's biggest financial backer, and conservative Catholics, in the guise of Boulangists, made the general distasteful to many republicans whatever their color. Nonetheless, Boulangism was as disruptive a force in Gard as it was in Aude, and it had the effect of dividing republicans, both moderate and left wing.[3] Radical voters were confused upon seeing several of their deputies running under a title which the right wing claimed as its own. Consequently most of them voted for opportunists firmly opposed to the general, and the number of Radical deputies fell from four to one, Desmons. On the surface Radicals came back strong in the 1893 elections, but this was a temporary recovery in a brief period of calm.

Boulangism was less significant in Provence than in Languedoc. Only one recognized Radical remained a true Boulangist in 1889; he was the moderate Radical Joseph Chevillon, but unlike Théron, Numa Gilly and E. Gaussorgues, he went off to the Seine to run in the elections and was defeated. Clearly most left-wing voters, and they were the majority, continued to regard the Radical movement as the embodiment of their ideals. More important, the economic crisis of the 1870s was sufficiently diminished so that voters did not turn to Boulangists or to socialists to express their discontent. In fact, a majority in Arles, when Granet replaced Chevillon in Marseille IV, voted for a vigorously left-wing Radical, Antoine Lagnel, a farmer of Noves. This choice further divided the *arrondissement* between right and left.[4] However, the Radicals, running as individual candidates rather than on a slate, considerably improved their percentages, especially in Aix and Arles.

The department of Var was as deeply left wing as Bouches-du-Rhône. Boulangism was of no aid to conservatives who hardly dared enter an election openly calling themselves such—save in Brignoles which resembled Arles in its politics. But even there conservatives could win only local office.

In Provence, Boulangist candidates threatened Radicals in only two circumscriptions: Aix II where Pelletan obtained twice the votes of his Boulangist rival, and Draguignan where Clemenceau did even better. Ironically, both men were among the general's earliest and most fervent supporters. The only circumscription where Radicalism fell to nationalism was Toulon II, the rural and semiurban area around the city of Toulon. The situation here was somewhat similar to that of Narbonne; Cluseret was as fiery a character as Ferroul, full of fury against republicans and most Radicals, and a pro-Boulangist. In addition, both he and Ferroul, although running as socialists, had conservative backing for the second election. The situation was different, however, in that the city of Toulon, unlike Narbonne, remained solidly Radical. Had it been part of the second circumscription Cluseret might have lost. In fact he won his majority outside of the city because the Radical vote was divided, even in the run-off election.[5]

In the lower Midi, Boulangists as such were not candidates to be feared; men running openly under the general's banner did not win any seats. By 1889 there was little reason for voters to swing behind an unknown political movement which offered no solution to economic grievances. Save in a few areas where distrust of foreign workers aided the cause, most voters had no impelling economic complaints. Replanting was well advanced, wine prices were high, and workers were again buying their precious parcels of land. Although without positive success for itself, the Boulangist movement did have a negative effect in the South. It became the means by which extreme right factions disrupted the *entente cordiale* established between Radicals and moderates during 1885. It did this by bringing right-wing support behind the dissidents of the left in the run-off elections, and in several instances carrying them to victory over "official" Radicals or moderates. This tactic provoked disunity within republican ranks, the desired aim of conservatives. Boulangists prevented true Radicals from possibly winning three seats: Carcassonne II, Narbonne I, and Toulon II. Such losses were serious because these districts were natural Radical strongholds having social structures and economies compatible with the Radical movement. They were, in fact, traditionally left wing and only Narbonne was permanently lost to the Radicals. Three other lost seats, Perpignan I, Narbonne II, and Uzès were marginal, sometimes Radical, sometimes not; their fluctuations did not have a direct relation to Boulangism. The return to normalcy in 1893 brought reassurance and Radicals won back Uzès and gained Nîmes I.

The election of 1893 was a mixed one. It brought marked success in Gard but the loss of Clemenceau in Draguignan and temporary losses in Hérault. However, the calm of the early 1890s, the result of economic recovery, was abbreviated by a new crisis.

DREYFUS CASE

In lower Midi the Dreyfus affair was a purely political and, one may say, a moral crisis. The economy was healthy, after a brief recession in 1893; wine production had become plentiful; and prices rose to a profitable level by the later 1890s. On the whole, however, Radical politicians were not at their best in political and moral crises. December 1851 had been their finest hour, and their part in the hard struggle to consolidate the Republic had reflected their highest ideals of freedom and equality. It was those ideals which led them, in alliance with other republicans, to strip the clergy of its political and educational role and to support Boulanger as Minister of War in the hope of bringing democracy to the army. That he could betray their trust was a reality they were slow to recognize, and some never did.

By the 1890s however, most of them were still as patriotic as their forerunners during the Franco-Prussian war; some of them had lived through that experience and had high regard for the army, even though many general officers were not heart-felt republicans. These Radicals also represented petty middle classes and peasants among whom anti-Semitism was an economic reaction. Their attacks upon high finance, the "mur d'argent" to use an expression made popular by Pelletan, led many of them to see in the Jew the bitter enemy of easier credit for the "little people." In fact, Pelletan is a good example of this mentality. Like him, they were vindictive against Dreyfus, blatantly patriotic, slow to recognize his innocence when proven, and then, as though to hide their past errors, vociferous in proclaiming that he had been the victim of a clerical conspiracy. Jean Bourrat, who had won Perpignan II in the 1895 by-election, was also not untypical. In 1898 he ran on an antirevisionist platform and was convinced of Dreyfus's guilt.[6] But the most intransigent anti-Dreyfusard was Dujardin-Beaumetz of Limoux; he continued to insist on the guilt of Dreyfus long after most Radicals came out for revision. More typical was the *Petit méridional* of Montpellier. When in 1895 it editorialized about Captain Dreyfus, it demanded that all soldiers be allowed to spit in his face. Up to October 1898 it condemned Dreyfusards and their revisionist campaign; Emile Zola was its *bête noire*.[7] After October and the revelations of Colonel Henry, it came out for revision, as did most of the Radical left. On the other hand, it was never anti-Semitic during the affair. Rather it condemned Edouard Drumont and his gang whose bitterness launched itself not only against Jews but also against Protestants and Freemasons. This seemed a personal attack upon Protestant Radicals and upon the journal's editor who was a high dignitary in the Masonic Order. The most extreme anti-Semite among southern Radical-Socialists was Paul Vigné d'Octon, exceptionally popular in Lodève *arrondissement* from 1893 to 1902. He referred to himself as an "aryan" and expressed sympathy for Drumont's *Libre parole*. However, he denied that he was an "antisémite à tous crins," and admitted that Jews had made some valuable contributions to civilization.[8]   He was, it is evident, not particularly extreme. At about the same level was the distrust of Jews expressed by Poisson in Uzès. These manifestations were isolated incidents. There was no pattern of anti-Semitism or of extreme nationalism either among the Radicals or among their voters in the Midi. In fact, Vigné was later repudiated by the extreme left and most of his backers after 1902 because of his collusion with the nationalist right to prevent an investigation of his election. And in 1902 Poisson used all the devices at his command to defeat the arch conservative nationalists, among whom was the Duke of Uzès, in an *arrondissement* that had largely repudiated Crémieux, a Jew, in 1898.

The Dreyfus case does not seem to have had a serious influence on the electoral position of the Radical movement, save in Uzès, where,   as mentioned above, Crémieux was defeated by the nationalist mayor of Uzès town. Few of the candidates brought up the issue save in Toulon; it did not figure conspicuously in most platforms and their enemies found it difficult to use the Dreyfus affair against them since not one assumed a heroic position. Clemenceau, of course, charged into the affair, but he had been defeated in 1893 and was no longer a party man. Moreover, it is really doubtful that Draguignan voters in 1893 were so naively patriotic as to believe that the *Tigre* was an English spy. They repudiated a patriotic Radical, Jourdan, in 1898, to elect an antinationalist socialist, Maurice Allard.

In fact, where Radicals lost, and here we exclude Crémieux, they were defeated by socialists. Now these socialists were neither nationalists or anti-Semites—except G. Baron in Aix I, an ex-Radical expelled from the federation in 1897 because he attacked Freemasonry and appealed for clerical support while running as a socialist—and Cluseret, if one can call him a socialist although he was elected as such. The 1898 election revealed two tendencies, neither of which had anything to do with the Dreyfus affair. First, it showed the concentration of the Radical movement in the major wine producing areas of Roussillon, Languedoc, and Provence. Here it was reinforced numerically by men who were formerly moderate republicans but who now began to refer to themselves as Radical-Socialists. Jules Pams in Céret, Edouard Rolland in Perpignan I, and Dujardin-Beaumetz in Limoux fell into this category. Secondly, Radical candidates were unable to halt the rise of socialism in Provence. Their retreat was almost a rout in Var; in one election, that of 1898, they lost seats to socialists in Toulon I and Draguignan.

This decline within the space of two elections had as its most immediate cause the breakdown of Radical organization, the proliferation of Radical candidates, and the bitter infighting which made cooperation extremely difficult and sometimes impossible. The most notorious example was the 1893 plot against Clemenceau at Draguignan. All of his enemies, and he made many among Radicals, united to defeat him. Jourdan, the winner, was a weak deputy, hardly a Radical; he was easily defeated in 1898 by an aggressive socialist. These internal fights destroyed the departmental organization which had been one of the strongest since mid-century. A notable loss was the city of Toulon where Jean Baptiste Abel went down before a socialist. Neither Jourdan nor Abel, both anti-Dreyfusards, could use the affair effectively against their socialist opponents, though they tried. And their tactics and their moderate goals had the effect of driving many Radical voters toward the socialists.

In Bouches-du-Rhône, the Radical loss of its former strongholds in Marseille was a more gradual process. First came the by-election to replace Peytral (Marseille I) and then the betrayal of Bouge (Marseille II) who joined the *progressistes,* was denounced by his former mentor, C. Pelletan and lost to a socialist. The electoral victory of "false" Radicals, actively supported by the local organization and its press, was not uncommon. In Montpellier, the deception possibly aided the election of a socialist in 1898, a result similar to that in Marseille II. Whatever the immediate cause of the changes, the consequences were the same; Radicalism was losing out in the larger cities as the turn of the century approached.

When it lost Nîmes I in a by-election in 1901, the tendency was confirmed.

At precisely this time, several prominent men who were not deputies took the initiative of founding a regular political party to replace the vaguely defined Radical group in the Chamber of Deputies. They convened a constituent assembly in Paris during June 1901, and with the somewhat hesitant concurrence of many deputies, established the "Parti républicain radical et radical-socialiste."[9] Southern deputies, particularly Lafferre, Doumergue, and Pelletan, were later to play directing roles in the new party. There was considerable enthusiasm about the prospects of the party among most old and new Mediterranean Radicals, at least their press welcomed the move and gave considerable space to it (see appendix V). They were in an increasingly difficult position because of some notable advances made by socialist candidates in 1898. A more effective political formation, they believed, and more generous funding of electoral campaigns, by a party treasury seemed a suitable means to overcome the stagnation which hindered their increase of followers since 1893.[10] Because the socialists were so divided among themselves, a unified Radical movement would be all the stronger.

Before going into a study of the fortunes of the new party, it will be instructive to look back over the twenty-odd years when Radicalism was simply a movement in the country and a group in the Chamber of Deputies, and to observe some of its general characteristics.

NOTES

1. See *L'Eclaireur,* 24 April, 1, 15 December 1888; A.D. P-O 2M 1-83, prefect report, 1 September 1889.
2. See reports in A.D. Hérault 39M 277-78, 291, 15M 40, police report 4 May 1889. Also *Petit méridional,* 24 June 1889.
3. See A.D. Gard 2M 84, report of 12 April 1889.
4. For varying points of view see *Le Démocrate* (Marseille), 14, 26 January, 18 September 1889; *Petit provençal,* August-September 1889; A.D., Bouches-du-Rhône. 2M 3-48, various reports.

5. A.D., Var 2M 3–35, police reports of September–October 1889. Vivien, the leading Radical, was backed by *Le Petit Var*. He was weakened by E. Magnier who retired for the run-off and Fabre, the republican mayor of La Seyne who ran in the run-off and his mere 676 votes deprived Vivien of the small number needed to win, the election was that close.

6. *Républicain des Pyrénées-Orientales*, 4 December 1897, 29 January 1898. Bourrat voted for the Mahy resolution urging the cabinet to put an end to attacks on the army (October, 1898). So did most Radicals.

7. 2 January 1895; 14–27 January, 30 October 1898.

8. *Petit méridional*, 5 December 1893.

9. See Jacques Kayser, *Les Grandes batailles du Radicalisme*, 290–310.

10. Radical deputies held seats in sixteen out of thirty-four circumscriptions.

CHAPTER EIGHT

CHARACTERISTICS OF THE RADICAL
MOVEMENT, 1881-1900

THE MEN

During its twenty-year period of primacy in the lower South the Radical movement acquired certain characteristics which became common there during and even after its decline. The Radical phase marked the South as indelibly as the South marked the Radicals.

First we may note the important role of personal popularity in several districts. To be sure, the Radicals won their most impressive victory under the *scrutin de liste* system when presumably impersonal forces came to play. But personal attraction played a role even under the list system. In Pyrénées-Orientales, for example, the personal popularity of Edouard Vilar and Charles Floquet in 1885 brought the highland cantons over to the Radical side. When Vilar was elected senator and Floquet moved elsewhere, these highland cantons returned to the moderate republicanism of the Arago tradition. In Aude, the popularity of Ferdinand Théron was an important force regardless of the electoral use. So it was with Adolphe Bosc in Uzès and with Auguste Maurel in Toulon II; after these men left, the chances of a Radical victory declined sharply. There were several circumscriptions which became personal bailiwicks: Perpignan II for Emile Brousse (won four elections), Carcassonne II for Ferdinand Théron (five elections), Limoux for Henri Dujardin-Beaumetz (six elections), Béziers I for Emile Vernhès (five elections), Alès I for Frederic Desmons (four elections), Aix I for Victor Leydet (four elections), and Aix II for Camille Pelletan (eight elections). Saint-Pons became the personal fief of the Razimbaud family, passing from father to son; similarly Marseille IV belonged to the Chevillon dynasty. Personal attractiveness, then, influenced elections in two ways. First, it could lead to Radical victories in highland cantons, but such victories were like plants without roots and lasted only a season. Second, it could decide on the style of Radicalism in a circumscription, from the moderation of Dujardin-Beaumetz to the socialist Radicalism of Pelletan.

Were more personal information available about Radical deputies the value of this study would be considerably enhanced. Unfortunately, neither the press nor local archives contain enough of this kind of data. Since the historian today is entirely dependent on written sources because all direct witnesses are dead, it is a difficult task to explain just why a particular man was popular. Camille Pelletan, for example, was a Parisian at heart and a near bohemian by temperament. Trained as a paleographer and archivist, he was really an artistic person, firm in his ideals, brutal and trenchant in his verbal attacks upon conservatives and moderates to whom he appeared a madman with wild eyes, unkempt beard, and long hair. If legend is truthful he was a devotee of beer, which he drank in big mugs, and sausages. Understandably there was general consternation in upper-class circles when he became minister of the navy under Emile Combes. But in 1881, twenty years before his appointment, he quit his comfortable Parisian constituency for the semirural one of Aix II and reigned there for thirty-two years! Among voters, most of whom were small landowners and modest tradesmen, Pelletan was indeed an oddity. Many of them never voted for him, others never voted; yet, he was their spokesman and the Radical program he proudly enunciated was intended to further their interests.

Close to Pelletan in ideology was his good friend Georges Clemenceau who also left a Parisian constituency, in 1885, to represent Draguignan (Var). Both men were nationally recognized leaders of the extreme left, and referred to themselves as Radical-Socialists. As directors of the Parisian daily, La Justice, they spent no more than a minimum of time among their respective voters. Clemenceau was also a true Parisian and an artist in politics, but colder, more brutal, and, with his balding head and cropped moustache, far more elegant than his hirsute comrade. Their political styles were comparable, but different. Pelletan attacked with the sabre, Clemenceau with the rapier.

More typical of the southern Radicals was Ferdinand Théron of Carcassonne. In 1885, when he began his long career as a deputy, he abandoned his previously moderate doctrines and set out to create a movement combining the Radical program with a kind of socialism. This was also the aim of Pelletan, Clemenceau, and the left-wing Radicals. But Théron, unlike most of his colleagues who were Parisians at heart, was a true *méridional*, a native of the lower Midi, who spent a great deal of time visiting his constituents, building up a clientele even in remote villages of the Minervois and the Corbières. Jovial and well-liked by the rural folk, whether workers or small owners, he embodied the extreme left and made it acceptable even in communes formerly under the thumb of conservatives. He was himself a *vigneron* and understood the problems of wine production in an area where it was a major crop, the Aude Valley, or an important cash crop, the highlands.

Equally typical was Emile Brousse of Perpignan II. Perhaps he was even more typical because he represented that middle group of Radicals who did not display strong socialist tendencies, but who had, rather, to overcome growing socialist dissension in the ranks of his followers. He held the loyalty of workers by playing a prominent role in mutual-aid societies and by authoring several bills on old-age pensions for wage-earners. He was an astute politician, knew well how to defend the wine interests of the Roussillon plain, but steadily lost support in the city of Perpignan. He therefore resigned in 1895 to accept a judgeship in Aix, only to discover later that from this "exile" there could be no return. He had, apparently, lost that personal touch, the intimacy between voters and deputy, that was a prerequisite in the Roussillon where there was remarkably little turnover among deputies.

More politically gifted was Frederic Desmons, a Protestant clergyman in the most militant Protestant zone of France, Alès I. He was the only clergyman among the anticlerical Radicals, most of whom were free-thinkers anyway. Yet Desmons was a power among them, entering the highest councils not only of Freemasonry but of the Radical party itself, and, indeed, presiding over them. A spare man, simple in his tastes, learned in Calvinist theology, he was nonetheless a consummate politician, Radical to the core, secularizer, yet gentle by nature and tolerant of all movements not violently and openly opposed to his beloved Republic. This combination of firmness in Radical principles and breadth of view endeared him to his Protestant voters who identified their religion with the extreme left.

Generally, the personal politics of an attractive candidate coincided with the political tendency of his circumscription. Exceptional were those Radicals, Vilar, Floquet, and Bosc, who could lead a majority of voters in a political direction which ran counter to tradition. Left-wing Radicalism won chiefly in circumscriptions where objective factors encouraged left-wing politics. The most persistent exception to this tendency was the vineyard area north of Perpignan *ville* where moderate republicans won victories comparable to those of left-wing Radicals in the town and in wine communes south and west of it. The canton of Saint-Gilles in Gard was also exceptional as regards socio-economic forces. Here Catholic conservatism, based on the old monastery of Saint-Gilles, continued to influence the vineyard workers regardless of inducements from the left.

Personal attractiveness had remarkably little to do with wealth. Rich men with political ambitions simply did not turn to Radicalism until Radicalism became respectable—around 1900 and after. The only person with considerable income and property who became a Radical was Jules Pams, and he ran as a moderate republican in Céret until 1898 when he joined the movement. Other men, classified as moderately wealthy, were as moderately Radical: Dujardin-Beaumetz, landowner and artist in Limoux; Ménard-Dorian, industrialist in Montpellier I, later in Lodève; and Razimbaud, landowner in Saint-Pons.

The average Radical deputy, in the South and in the nation, belonged to the middle professional classes. Between the 1876 and 1898 elections there were about fifty deputies of the lower Midi who were clearly affiliated with the Radical movement.[1] As might be expected, lawyers, fourteen in number, made up the largest single group. Next came the six medical doctors and five merchants. Three of these merchants were wine wholesalers. *Vignerons* were not generally well disposed toward wholesalers who bought their wine as cheaply as possible and were often accused of using spies to find *vignerons* without adequate storage space so as to buy their excess wine more cheaply. It was a mark of true popularity that these three were elected. There were also three professional journalists, though many other deputies wrote for newspapers and some, such as Doumergue, were frequent contributors. There were two industrialists and two teachers, a mechanical engineer, a locomotive engineer, a highway inspector, an artist, a Protestant clergyman, a mechanic, and a soldier. There were only five listed as agriculturalists, but a much larger number owned land, chiefly vineyards, which in most cases provided an important revenue. The lawyers and doctors, as well as the wine merchants, were heavy investors in vineyards and specialists in wine legislation. Land, then, was an important base of politics, even in highly urban districts.

This factor probably accounts for the demographic stability of Mediterranean Radicalism prior to 1902. Over three-fourths of the deputies were either born in the department they represented or had lived and worked there for some time before being elected and had earlier been engaged in local politics. Only about one-fourth of the deputies were outsiders brought in by local committees for a particular election. This latter policy was more acceptable east of the Rhône than west of it. The two departments of Var and Bouches-du-Rhône had a total of five outsiders, the four departments of Languedoc and Roussillon had five also. Var held the record with three. Gard, at the other extreme, had none and Pyrénées-Orientales only one: Floquet. Of course there were numerous outsiders who ran in elections, especially candidates of the extreme left. They were often called "candidats exotiques" by their opponents and rarely won elections. In Pyrénées-Orientales the three men of the extreme left who ran as "Radical-Socialistes" in 1885 against the "Radical" list of Brousse were called "enfants du pays" by their supporters because they had been born in the department. But they no longer lived there and were hardly known; as a result they received few votes. Of the three Radicals, Floquet was the only outsider, but had already succeeded in a by-election in 1882, with the backing of moderates, so he was familiar to most voters and highly popular. In Aude, the Alsacian and retired engineer, Emile Wickersheimer (a name difficult to pronounce in the local dialect) managed to win as part of a slate in 1885; but in 1889 he was defeated by Edouard Théron, an *enfant du pays*. At the opposite extreme was Camille Pelletan, a Parisian by temperament and choice, who was lucky in 1881; victorious in Paris and Aix II, he opted for the latter. The name Pelletan was well-known in Bouches-du-Rhône because of his father, Eugene. Once launched on his career, however, Camille's own prestige carried him to victory until he was elected to the Senate after 1910. That he spent a minimum of time in his district did not weaken his popularity in the slightest. It must be pointed out, however, that Pelletan's strength was located in Salon, a remakably active town, a center of commerce between Marseille and the remainder of the department, and quite cosmopolitan with a rapidly growing population. In general, however, an outsider had a short career as a deputy. Either he frustrated too many local ambitions, as in Georges Clemenceau's case in Draguignan (two elections) or he left for a more comfortable district, as in Floquet's case, or he suffered defeat in the next election. Of the ten outsiders only three enjoyed a long political career: Pelletan, who had connections through his father, Charles Dujardin-Beaumetz in Limoux, where he owned vineyards, and Louis Lafferre in Béziers I where he had numerous personal friends through his Masonic connections.

THE MOVEMENT

It can be cogently argued that republicans of all shades, and especially Radicals by the 1880s, were more effectively organized in their Masonic lodges than in their political group.[2] As Radicalism grew in the Midi its proponents came to play an important role in the lodges. Anticlericalism became the stock in trade of the Grand Orient; however, under the influence of left-wing Radicals, social and economic reforms were also stressed, a throwback on the Masonic movement in the Lyonnais during the Second Republic. Masons, like Radicals, preached fraternity, equality, and liberty. The extreme left carried out much of its propaganda activity through local lodges which became increasingly politicized. The left-wing press, the *Radical du Midi* of Carcassonne, *Petit méridional* of Montpellier, *Petit Var* of Toulon, to mention the most popular, were defenders of Masonry and directed by Masonic officials such as Jules Gariel, Omar Sarraut, and Pierre Massé. Between 1870 and 1914 southern departments were fairly well endowed with lodges. Pyrénées-Orientales had only two, but Aude acquired six, Hérault was well supplied with ten,

Gard had seven, Bouches-du-Rhône twelve, with seven of them in Marseille, and Var had four. As might be expected, most of the leading politicians were members: Emanual Arago when he was a Radical in Pyrénées-Orientales, the Sarrauts in Aude, Salis, Ménard-Dorian, L. Lafferre, and Rouvier in Hérault, Doumergue, Bosc, Favand, Desmons, Bouchet, and Senator Dide, plus some moderates in Gard, Camille Pelletan, E. Lockroy, Henri Michel, and A. Magnien in Bouches-du-Rhône. There were undoubtedly more, but their names have not come to light. Several Radicals rose to leadership in the Masonic hierarchy: Desmons was Grand Master five times, Lafferre twice, others were elected to councils. Lafferre was head when the scandal of the *fiches* broke out, which encouraged anti-Masonic outbursts.

There were some Radicals who felt it inexpedient to join the Masons: Leydet in Aix and Pezet in Montpellier I where in 1914 conservatives falsely accused him of being a Mason in the hope that he would not unseat Leroy-Beaulieu. Where Catholic forces were strong, anti-Masonic—which meant anti-Radical—organizations appeared. They were powerful and, as will be shown later, supported socialist candidates in 1910 in order to defeat Radicals.

Apart from their connections with Freemasonry, the Radicals also belonged to local committees for the purpose of designating candidates. The organization of the Radical movement, until 1901 when an official party came into being, was usually rather haphazard, spontaneous, and lacking in professionalism. And the founding of the party did not introduce serious improvements, because it could never overcome the strong attachment felt by most voters to their particular local interests. There never arose in the circumscriptions a demand for centralized control and financing. Practically no one paid party dues. There was no impulse toward centralization because the sentiment that favored local men in politics also favored local control. The national party was weak precisely because it was merely the extension of local organizations and, by the 1880s, these latter were self-sufficient enough to feel no need for a strong party.

As regards party organization before 1900, France was an underdeveloped country, and the Radical movement was almost primitive. On the other hand, Radicalism in such an environment had many positive features of a grass-roots movement. At the departmental level, men inclined toward Radicalism ordinarily began by creating a newspaper in oder to put forward programs and to publish editorials or "leaders" which elaborated Radical ideas and attacked opponents. Most of these journals were shortlived; their fortunes rose and ebbed with those of their political supporters. However, there were several which, beginning in the late 1870s or early 1880s, continued into the twentieth century: *Le Radical du Midi* (Carcassonne), *Le Petit méridional* (Montpellier), *L'Union républicaine* (Béziers), *Le National* (Aix), *Le Radical de Marseille* and *Le Petit provençal* (Marseille) which was left-wing Radical and socialist, *Région radicale* (Brignoles), *Le Petit Var* (Toulon) which evolved from moderate to Radical. West of the Rhône *La Dépêche de Toulouse* enjoyed considerable influence; it became the rival of *Le Petit méridional*. Both journals had numerous special editions for surrounding departments and the conflict between them was often a bitter one, and possibly weakened the Radical party after 1900. The local newspaper was an important center of organization; its offices served often times as party headquarters in larger towns; more often, however, "headquarters" was located in a cafe or simply in the coat pockets of a local militant. Several prominent men, usually mayors and general councilors, organized a central committee which awakened as election time approached. By means of the press it sent notice to sympathizers in each commune to set up a local group and to send delegates and their credentials to a congress in each circumscription for the purpose of choosing candidates. During this congress, hopefuls put forward their names and made speeches outlining their programs; they might or might not be chosen as candidates. Rarely was there effective machinery for controlling the credentials of delegates so enemies of particular men and even of the movement came simply to create disorder. At times there was a formal ballot, sometimes simply loud applause and shouting—reminiscent of the ancient custom of electing tribal rulers among the Gauls and Franks.

The local candidate proclaimed so happily at the congress was inevitably a man who had worked his way up the political ladder. He often began his public career as a municipal councilor and then advanced to the office of mayor or assistant-mayor. From this position he built up his personal following; with numerous jobs to be filled he now saw the approach of new office seekers who joined those who had earlier sensed his destiny. If a candidate was not himself a mayor he had to have the backing of numerous small-town mayors, the notables who exercised remarkable influence in both legislative and senatorial elections. The successful candidate usually also had to pass through the general council of his department and prove that his influence extended throughout a canton which he represented in the general council. Finally he had to impress other councilors who would then swing their cantonal clientele to his side. Of course, the local politician who held office both in a town and in the departmental council was further strengthened as a candidate by the fact that he could hold two or more elected offices at once and need not give up his local seats after his election to the Chamber of Deputies. Radicals campaigned against this practice known as *cumul,* but none of them attempted seriously to abolish it once in office. On the contrary, those with long careers in the Chamber or in the Senate were precisely the ones who profited from it. The attack upon *cumul* and the demand for the *mandat impératif* (recall) were part of campaign oratory intended to create the image of a grass-roots movement, not really to be made the law of the land.

Once in office, few Radicals withdrew voluntarily before they had reached an age suitable for retirement. Emile Brousse of Perpignan II retired in 1895 because of quarrels with local notables, but he was exceptional. More traditional was the practice whereby aging Radicals either died in office or won a seat in the Senate; in fact, the Senate served at times as an escape door for getting rid of deputies whose longevity threatened to frustrate ambitious younger men nearing the end of their apprenticeship in local politics. To be sure, senatorial elections were not, given the importance of rural notables in the voting system, so easily manipulated. Entrance into the Senate marked the high point of most political careers.

National politics offered local Radicals a means of upward mobility not readily available in other professions. Unfortunately, there exists in the archives insufficient data about the finances and prospects of Radical deputies to allow of valid generalization about their social advancement. Men such as Jules Pams and, to a lesser extent, Ménard-Dorian were well off in their own right. Most Radicals, however, were small-town professionals for whom politics opened horizons and financial prospects not at all available in their local spheres of influence. For a teacher such as Louis Lafferre of Béziers to attain high position in government, in the party hierarchy, and in Freemasonry, was indeed upward mobility. So it was also for another teacher, Mas, who entered the executive committee of the Radical party, for the Protestant pastor, Desmons, a major power in Freemasonry and the party, for the local lawyers and doctors whose only other means of ascent apart from politics was viticulture. Of course some lawyers, after their careers as deputies, became judges, but in France, where judgeships were too numerous to bring notable prestige or extensive monetary rewards, politics was far more preferable to a man bent on making his way up in society. Politics, then, was more than a way of life, it was the opportunity of a lifetime for the petty and middling bourgeoisie out of which came most Radicals.

Given this situation as well as the looseness of Radical organization, it is quite amazing that there was not more infighting for the candidacies. Until the late 1890s, there was generally one recognized Radical candidate for each circumscription. There were, however, sufficiently numerous exceptions to cause one to pause over the validity of this generalization. In particular, Var, during the 1889 and 1893 elections, was the center of some ferocious infighting. Traditionally, communal and cantonal delegates met at Le Luc in their congress, often a boisterous, ebullient gathering, to hear and select candidates. But even when a candidate received official backing he could expect competition during the election from one or two other men who ran as "independent" Radicals. In Draguignan in 1893, there were five Radical candidates, Toulon I in 1889 had four, and in Draguignan and Brignoles there were two. In Bouches-du-Rhône during 1881 Clemenceau and Granet in Arles and Lockroy and Victor Leydey in Aix I fought each other. Similar infighting occurred during 1881 in Béziers II between Vernière and Sigismond Lacroix from Paris, during 1898 in Béziers I between Mas and Louis Lafferre, during 1889 in Carcassonne II between Théron and Wickersheimer, in Perpignan I where three Radicals entered the campaign, and in Perpignan II between Emile Brousse and Eli Alavaill.

Many of the unofficial candidates were moderates who appropriated the title of Radical simply because it was so popular; but rarely did they win an election. This in itself would indicate that backing by the local cadres was of major importance. An outside candidate never won if he did not have official local support organized in a congress and access to the local press. When dissidents invited him, his only hope was right-wing backing and he then served as the tool of the conservatives to attack the Republic. This awkward position made him even more obnoxious to local Radicals.

The label "Radical," however, had become so popular by 1885 that outsiders often took it up and even moderates used it. Moderates referred to their slate as "Radical Progressiste" in Aude, "Union Radicale" in Gard, "Alliance Républicaine Radicale" in Bouches-du-Rhône, and "Républicaine Radical" in Var.

This popularity of the title is not amazing, at least for the area under study. By 1881 the Radicals constituted the largest single political movement in the Mediterranean region, and party evolution there did not follow the national pattern. Nearly all the cabinets from 1876 to 1900 contained a strong majority of center-oriented politicians grouped under various labels: *opportunistes* in the 1880s and *progressistes* in the 1890s. During this period Radicals, chiefly moderate ones, participated in only five ministries: those of Brisson (1885 and 1898), of Floquet (1888–89) which were pro-Radical or, as the French say, *Radicalisant*; that of Leon Bourgeois (1895–96) which was chiefly Radical, and that of Waldeck-Rousseau (1899–1902) which was a grouping of anticlerical republicans known as *Le Bloc des Gauches*. Save for these rare and short-lived cabinets, most Radicals were in opposition to political leaders who were mainly concerned with preserving the Constitution of 1875, extending political and civil liberties, democratising the educational system, removing churchmen and religion from public affairs, and conquering a foreign empire in Indo-China and North Africa.

CHARACTER AND DOCTRINES

The distinction between national weakness and local strength further emphasizes the importance of local issues in the political life of France. We have already underlined the southern voters' emphasis upon the local origins of his candidate, but this was not an attitude exclusively *méridional*. In region after region a large part of the electorate was convinced that only local men were fully competent to advance local interests, and there are enough local and regional studies to show that local concerns enjoyed a major role in electoral battles. If we consider only agriculture, the North had its sugar interests, most of the Center its cereal and cattle interests, the Southwest its wine and lumber interests, and the lower South its wine interests. Viticulture, of course, was an important force in several regions of France: the Southwest, the Loire Valley, Burgundy, Champagne, the Rhône Valley, and the Mediterranean coast. But only in the first and last was it sufficiently predominant to overshadow public life in a continuous way over numerous generations and therefore to influence politics deeply, especially after the phylloxera. By 1900 no other region in France was so heavily dependent upon wine for its livelihood as the lower Midi. Inevitably politics turned around wine issues, whatever other issues entered in. And the most successful politicians were often those who were local men and usually owners of vineyards. This does not mean that viticulture excluded all other issues; it simply means that it brought winemen prominently into politics and that it distinguished southern politics from the national norm. The Radical movement rose early to predominance there (most wine districts of the Mediterranean coast were ruled by the extreme left when a major part of France was still under opportunist control) and it declined at precisely the time when so much of France turned massively toward Radicalism, as Table 24 makes clear.

TABLE 24: PERCENTAGE OF RADICAL DEPUTIES IN RELATION TO ALL CONSTITUENCIES[3] IN FRANCE AND LOWER SOUTH

	1876	1881	1885	1889	1893	1898	1902	1906	1910	1914
All France	11	14	20	16	20	25	33	41	43	40
Lower South	37	58	76	50	50	47	50	50	42	33

By 1914 it was a commonplace among political observers to affirm that all of France was Radical.

Does all this mean, then, that the southern Radicals were merely a pressure group for the wine industry? The answer to this pertinent question must be an embarrasing yes and no. The answer is affirmative in the sense that any electorate highly dependent on a single economic resource would see most problems colored by the needs of that resource. And to the fulltime *vigneron* of France, regardless of his region, wine was not merely an economic factor, it was a cultural one also; indeed, it got worked into the very basis of western civilizaion. This *idée fixe* even made it possible to rationalize that adulterated wine might be sold to compensate for short supply after the phylloxera, and later that adultera-ted wine was a sin against mankind when wine was in abundant supply after 1893. No ambitious politician in his right mind would have denied this axiomatic basis of a whole way of life. Southern politicians on the whole were not particularly heroic types, although they were not with-out their heroic moments. And they usually did not go against the prejudices of their constituents. In the Chamber they formed an impor-tant part of the wine defense committee which became the most powerful voice of the wine lobby. This wine defense group, incidentally, was not exclusively Radical; it cut across party lines and included deputies and senators who were moderate republicans, some who were royalists, and, after 1900, some socialists. Until the twentieth century, however, constituencies which produced cheap table wine and low grade alcohol, such as those of the Midi, were not as effectively organized as they would become after the wine crisis of 1907. Therefore, the individual deputy rather than the professional organization created for lobbying was the chief defender of wine interests. Naturally, then, he had to recognize his role and capitalize upon it during electoral campaigns and Radicals were remarkably good at this.

But to what extent did the Radical deputy, after having won the election, aspire to represent broad national as distinct from purely local interests? Each politician must defend the economic interests of his constituents, but if we are to judge the true stature of the man, we must ask what else he does besides defending pocketbooks.

Southern Radicals passed though their heroic period. They helped to found the Republic in the 1870s and were as active in this task as their Parisian counterparts. They also sought to give the Republic a more reformist role; although ever mindful of local interests their leaders and a majority of the rank-and-file deputies adhered to a program elaborated for the purpose of guiding the Republic along reformist lines. By 1881 southern Radicals were conspicuous among the left-wing supporters of

Clemenceau and Pelletan, which explains why these two Parisians moved into southern constituencies. The program, it was claimed, had originated in the egalitarian ideals of Robespierre's Declaration of the Rights of Man (1793), had been brought up to date in 1848–51, and was now fully developed for the elections of 1881 and 1885. This program specifically formulated an ideal of both political and social democracy. Unlike most republicans, Radicals insisted that political freedom, that is, the right of all adult males to elect deputies and senators, was an insufficient basis of citizenship, because the form of government could frustrate the voters' rights. They acrimoniously condemned the Constitution of 1875 because it provided for a strong executive not elected by all adult males and a Senate elected chiefly by small town and village notables, most of whom were opposed to economic and social reform. They wanted a government directly responsible to the people and solicitous of the needs of the lower classes.

Central in their program was constitutional revision to abolish the Senate and the Presidency. Radicals, at this time, wanted a unicameral legislature with a cabinet entirely responsible to it. Some of them, in addition, demanded the voters' right to recall their deputies and political and administrative decentralization. All of them wanted the basic civil liberties guaranteed by a constitution to be voted on by adult males. Radicals never called for female suffrage because they feared the conservative influence of clergymen over women. In consequence they vigorously called for the separation of church and state. They were at one with the opportunists in their desire to secularize society and to democratize education by making it free, secular, and obligatory at the primary level. They were well in advance of them, however, with their demand that judges be elected, that women be given legal, if not political, equality, and that the death penalty be abolished. Further, they demanded that military service be reduced to three years and that the regular army be replaced by a militia of citizens.

Their economic platform consisted of demands intended to justify the word "socialist" in their title and therefore was more characteristic of their left than of their moderate wing. Of course, even the moderate Leon Bourgeois called for a graduated income tax and some nationalization, of railroads, for example. His more advanced colleagues, however, expanded the call for state ownership to include mines, large insurance companies, and banks, really all economic activity of a monopolistic nature. They vigorously defended trade unions and, aiming at the eventual creation of a welfare state, called for public regulation of hours and working conditions and an extensive system of social security, partially financed by the state. They demanded cheaper credit to help small farmers buy land and to encourage worker's cooperatives. Finally they condemned the invasion of Indo-China because it absorbed funds needed for social reform. The extreme left of the early Republic, especially the Radical-Socialists, would have taken France far in the direction of social democracy and they recognized that the way to this goal was not in the wine defense committee but in their party as a national movement transcending particular interests.

In fact, the programs drawn up in Paris contained little about agriculture and the peasants. However, in the lower Midi, especially west of the Rhône, proposals to aid farmers of all sorts and *vignerons* in particular always took a leading place in the platforms of each candidate. No politician could hope to win if he did not condemn the taxes on alcohol and on land, high railroad rates, the absence of good roads and irrigation canals, and the *octrois*. For the elections of 1881 and 1885 the lower South was still suffering from the results of the phylloxera and voted accordingly.

Undoubtedly, economic and social grievances influenced the voter; however, Radicalism, in its rebirth under the Third Republic, enjoyed already a traditional attachment in the areas it had penetrated during the Second Republic. Its initial thrust as an opposition movement, therefore, came from Paris and the Seine department, the Mediterranean South, the Rhône and Saône valleys and the Center. Until 1889 the Parisian basin furnished the largest contingent of Radical deputies, most of the newspapers and intellectual leadership. The lower Midi followed close behind and even attracted two members of the Paris "brain-trust," Camille Pelletan (1881) and Clemenceau (1885). After 1889 and until the early twentieth century the Mediterranean South usually held the lead, and its lead is even stronger if Vaucluse is included. With the turn of the century, however, its position began to weaken, and after 1906 it gave way to the new left of socialism. It was, alas, the victim of a new wine crisis.

TABLE 25:   NUMERICAL STRENGTH OF RADICAL DEPUTIES BY REGION
IN RELATION TO ALL RADICAL DEPUTIES*

Region	1876	1881	1885	1889	1893	1898	1914
Seine	24.4%	25.3%	26.2%	14.1%	10.0%	6.7%	1.1%
Paris		4.8	8.1	5.4	8.4	8.7	7.7
West	1.7	2.4	0.8		1.6	3.3	7.0
East		2.4	0.8	4.3	1.6	3.3	2.2
Southwest	1.7	3.6			4.2	4.0	12.6
Burgundy	7.0	8.5	9.8	8.6	11.7	14.1	5.0
Center	5.4	6.0	13.8	16.2	10.0	14.1	11.5
Mediterranean South	35.0	21.9	24.6	21.7	18.7	13.4	8.4

*Kayser, pp. 372–74. In the Mediterranean South, Kayser includes Vaucluse which was pro-Radical, and Basses Alpes and Alpes-Maritimes which were not. Vaucluse raises the percentage by one or two points. The figure of 35 percent for the Mediterranean South in 1876 is of doubtful value; it certainly requires a very broad definition of the term Radical during a period when the extreme left was still most vague in its aspirations.

NOTES

1. There were several deputies whom the press referred to as Radicals, but all of my indications connect them to the moderate republican group. In particular, their voting records on social legislation underlined their moderation. They were E. Déandreis, J. Roche, E. Jamais, J. Jourdan, and P. L. Peytral. I have included Dujardin-Beaumetz and Mas despite their weak voting records, chiefly because they consciously identified themselves with the Radical party even if they did not always vote with it. By 1885 Peytral and Déandreis also identified with the Radicals and ran on their lists, without improving their voting records.

2. Most of my information comes from the *Bulletin du Grand Orient de France* (1880–1900) (Title varies); Bibliothèque Nationale, Salle des Manuscrits, *Fonds Franc-Maçonnerie; Revue maçonique de Lyon et du Midi* (1838–52); Jules Gariel, *Discours . . . à la fête d'adoption maçonique célébrée par la loge Egalité-Travail de Montpellier* (Montpellier, 1900); Mildred Headings, *French Free Masonry* (Baltimore, 1948); Albert Lantoine, *La Franc-Maçonnerie dans l'Etat* (Paris, 1935). Fragments of information appeared also in the local press, and in police reports.

3. Jacques Kayser, *Les Grandes batailles du Radicalisme* (Paris, 1962), 366–67; Peter Campbell, *French Electoral Systems and Elections, 1789–1957* (London, 1958), 69–80. The figures for 1876 are of doubtful value. For 1914 Kayser gives 29 percent, obviously too low, and Campbell gives 40 percent which seems to me closer to the truth, perhaps not as regards dues-paying membership in the party, but as regards adherence to Radicalism as a style of politics and petty-middle-class frame of mind. After all, Clemenceau was never a member of the party, yet he was the embodiment of the Radical view of life.

CHAPTER NINE

WINE CRISIS AGAIN, 1901-1907

The Radical party in the lower South entered its period of decline at the same time that the national Radical party became the ruling party in the Chamber of Deputies and based itself increasingly on the provinces. Since 1889 Radical power in Paris had fallen sharply. Consequently, it relied more heavily on its followers in the Midi, the Rhône and Saône valleys, which were old bastions, and the Southwest, a recent conquest.

The changes taking place in the Radical movement were part of a general realignment of political forces around 1900. Monarchists declined sharply, and on the far right appeared a fanatical nationalist movement, small in numbers but loud and activist. Conservative voters during the 1890s had turned to right of center republicans of a new generation, who called themselves *progressistes,* and who emerged as defenders of private property and religion now threatened by the rising socialist movement. Moderate republicans split between this new conservatism and the older opportunism with its anticlerical tradition. The latter forces, after the Dreyfus case, allied with the Radicals and most socialists to form the *Bloc,* a coalition whose goal was to separate church and state and to eliminate royalist officers from the army. Under Radical domination the *Bloc* ended the Concordat of 1801, curtailed the number of Catholic religious orders, and practically forced the resignation or retirement of army officers implicated in anti-Dreyfusard movements. In these endeavors it was assisted by Freemasonry to such an extent that the Radical party and the Grand Orient were considered interchangeable parts.

Both were regarded with especial horror by the right and not without cause. Information was leaked to the public that Radicals and Freemasons kept dossiers (*fiches*) on the army officer corps and that officers openly hostile to the Republic were either to be retired or denied promotion. This, of course, was what the Catholic and royalist high command had done in the past. Now that the tables were turned, a loud cry of protest went up from the right. Much of the protest was also directed against the Law of Associations (1901), which enabled the *Bloc* to cut down the number of Catholic teaching orders, and the Law of Separation (1905), which ended the Concordat of 1801 by cutting off subsidies to all churches.

VITICULTURE AND SOCIAL STRUCTURE

While the government in Paris was acting so vigorously, the seven-year period following the turn of the century witnessed economic and social changes with a far greater impact on southern politics than either the Boulanger crisis or the Dreyfus case. Purely political crises emanating from Paris did not have a measurable influence on the lower Midi save as they filtered through the mesh of economic and social conditions. Therefore not even the conflict over church-state relations, so intense in other parts of France, changed appreciably the political situation of the south until the mass of peasants were gravely affected by a new wine crisis, until public opinion became excited again over a local issue.

In order to understand the political import of the new wine crisis, it is necessary to look more closely at the social and economic changes which had been taking place during the 1880s and 1890s.

Social structure passed through another phase. The numerous medium and small owners ruined by the phylloxera either emigrated or became full-time workers on larger domains where the struggle against the malady and the replanting process were carried out with greatest intensity. For a while there occurred a tendency toward greater centralization of ownership and proletarianization of small and even some medium peasant owners. However, this process in its most intense form was not universal; it was a dominant factor chiefly in the plains of Roussillon, the Narbonnais, and Hérault, the costière of Gard (the vineyard area south and east of Nîmes), and in the Toulonnais, and littoral of Var.

The tendency toward the creation of a true rural proletariat was checked, however, even in the Narbonnais and Hérault where it was most pronounced, by several counter forces. One was psychological: the intense desire of most peasants to own land. Undoubtedly many of them conceived of ownership as a form of upward mobility; such a conception was clearly expressed in their land purchases during the prephylloxera period. Undoubtedly most of them bought land as a conditioned reflex. Land purchase on a wide scale, which began during the 1890s, was more seriously pursued than in the 1860s, less accompanied by the gaudy side effects of the "good old days"; it was the accomplishment of a new generation somewhat more cautious, yet still given to speculation, not in land as such, but in the expansion of vineyard acreage to profit from high prices for wine. When the *vigneron* bought land he wanted it for himself, not to sell it at inflated prices. And the *vigneron* who sold land, usually sold only a small part of his plot because he needed cash, or because his plot was too large for his family to cultivate but not large enough to justify a full time *journalier*.

Another counter force was economic opportunity. As income from wine sales rose because of shortages, wages increased and this enabled many workers to purchase small, usually scattered plots. Those owner-workers who had held their little holdings during the crisis and worked part time were in a particularly advantageous position with rising income being derived from their wine and their labor. Many became full-time owners as they bought bits and pieces from large and medium owners. Medium owners had been hard hit: their costs of production were the highest of all wine producers and they invested heavily in viticultural equipment so that their debt burdens, added to their tax and mortgage burdens, were insurmountable in many cases. They therefore were compelled to sell parts of their holdings, with the result that small ownership rose at the expense of medium. Of course, many large estates, located in the low hills, were broken up and sold because the owners moved to the sandy soils of the coastal flats to escape the phylloxera.

Unlike the modernization of industry which created a full-time, dependent working class, capitalist viticulture engendered, along with a true working class, a class of full and half owners who worked part time on larger domains and were independent in their own minds and individualistic in their politics. However, like all vintners, they became increasingly interventionist as regards state control of the wine market. In consequence they found Radicalism particularly attractive with its emphasis on a balance between personal freedom and solidarity. On the other hand, the renewed fragmentation of property, combined with a reluctance to organize cooperatives, created a situation of near anarchy in the production of wine which would make it extremely difficult—if not impossible—for the state to intervene effectively to control the market. Individualism in production on the one hand and control in marketing on the other proved an unworkable combination that contributed to the intensity of the wine crisis after 1900.

This crisis was the inevitable result of the return to monoculture by most vintners west of the Rhône after the phylloxera. They were convinced that wine was the only profitable commodity available to them. Their problem in the 1880s was to produce enough of it to take advantage of high prices. They now demanded of the government, in addition to subsidies, cheap credit, low taxes, and various aids in transportation, a relaxation of regulations concerning wine making. Radical deputies played an important role in achieving this relaxation of pure food practices. In addition to making a second and even a third wine from local grapes, a false wine could be made by the use of imported raisins and the addition of sugar and water. To these so-called wines were often added various chemicals to prevent spoilage or to disguise the taste. That some of these chemicals had a deleterious effect on the intestines or kidneys was not of great concern to the wine men—nor to the government.

But this began to change as early as 1889. Indeed, vintners were less concerned with Boulanger than with the new situation in the wine market. Adulterated and false wines, combined with a notable increase in the volume of natural wine and the continued importation of Spanish and Italian wines, made for a supply quite adequate for the market. The quantity of natural wine was considerably augmented. Despite the decline in acreage since the 1870s, wine production was improved in quantity by more efficient techniques on the larger estates, by the greater use of chemical fertilizers, by sulphuring, by planting in drier, sandy soils, and by the use of the high-yield Aramon grape.

Productivity per acre went up; in some cases it doubled the prephylloxera yield.

As supply began to equal demand, Midi vintners grew concerned about two factors: the importation of foreign wine (including Algerian wine) which they hoped to curb, and the volume of false wine which now began to benefit the wine merchant rather than the wine producer. Their first step was to get a legal definition of fermented liquids which could be sold under the title of wine, thus excluding false wines, and to provide the consumer with information about the contents of the bottle, thus excluding adulterated wines. These two aims formed the substance of the Griffe law, named after its sponsor, a republican senator of Hérault. It was guided through the Chamber by Brousse and Vilar of Pyrénées-Orientales and passed into law during August 1889.[1]   Henceforth only liquids naturally fermented from unpreserved grapes could be sold as wine. This law, of course, was only the first step in a long battle to increase the police powers of the state in the field of food regulation. In quick succession an amiable and complacent governmental apparatus passed a series of laws prohibiting the watering and chemical adulteration of wine.[2]

The passage of these laws, pushed through by southern senators and deputies, was hastened by a brief crisis in 1893 resulting from an excess amount of wine on the market. This recession occurred after the general elections and therefore did not influence them. But now the lower Midi appeared excitable, beset by a persecution complex, by a keen sense of victimization, especially at the hands of the northern sugar interests who profited from sales of sugar for making second wines, and by the conviction that fraud must be stopped by the most stringent legislation.[3]   The practitioner of fraud, once Everyman, now became the enemy of the people, and the more volatile vintners were already prepared for some witch hunting. This mentality was not common to all wine producers in the rest of France where quality wines commanded high prices, nor even in Provence where monoculture was less characteristic. Many wine merchants were hostile to extensive government regulations because they felt compelled, during the process of blending, to add sugar or alcohol or various chemicals, presumably to improve the quality of Languedocian wines. They also recognized that between producer and consumer wine passed through many hands. To supervise and test it at every exchange would have required an enormous police apparatus, and the *Moniteur vinicole,* the review of the merchants, constantly warned against an inquisitorial state. This opposition did not discourage many vintners nor lessen the promises of their deputies.

The deputies further antagonized merchants by abandoning their traditional tariff policy; their shift from free trade to tariff protection came rather suddenly. Midi Radicals during 1885 expressed mixed feelings about taxing imports, especially cereals and meat which would adversely affect their urban constituents. By 1889, however, no southern candidate advocating free trade could win an election—save in Marseille. In return for tariffs on Italian and Spanish wine, vintners and most southern Radicals and republicans were willing to favor protection for other foodstuffs. With the Jules Méline program, taxes on imported wine rose to 55 percent or more.[4] This turn to restrictions on imports marked an important step of Radicals away from their urban constituents and toward predominantly agricultural interests. On other issues dealing with fiscal policy, transport, and credit, the Radicals changed little, hardly at all. Their fiscal demands would soak the rich, their transport policies would lower the cost of food in cities, and their credit policies would help small self-employed men in town and countryside.

Experience proved, however, that they were much better at formulating programs than at carrying them out. This weakness became apparent with the creation of a predominantly Radical cabinet (1895–1896), headed by the philosopher of *solidarité,* Leon Bourgeois, and the first legally constituted left-wing government in French history since 1793–1794. Its major program consisted of a moderately progressive income tax bill, which it failed to get through the Senate, thereby setting the pattern of low accomplishment for future Radical cabinets. There was considerable disappointment, even disgust, with the pusillanimous Bourgeois.[5]   There is some reason to believe that this failure of the Radicals to pass into law the very foundation of their entire reform structure disillusioned the left wing population of Provence, especially of Var, who now turned to socialism. The disenchantment became profound when most Radicals either abandoned or toned down their traditional demand to suppress the Senate, that graveyard of serious reform bills. After all, each senatorial election opened the door of that body wider to Radicals who had served their time in the Chamber, and with the steady rise of socialism, the moderates among them came to see in it an important bulwark against collectivist measures. But in reality the Senate blocked Radical economic and social measures, and when Clemenceau from 1906 to 1909 failed to get his reform program approved by it, Radicalism was practically swept out of the Midi.

There were, of course, pressures more potent than doctrinal concerns among the voters which led them in 1898 and after to begin electing socialists in place of Radicals. One of these appeared in 1901 and is usually called the *mévente,* i.e., a drastic decline of sales and prices of wine. In fact, the first decade of the twentieth century witnessed a series of dramatic events which brought about changes in political loyalties. Each one, taken alone, did not produce a measurable, immediate effect; rather, they must be viewed as part of a general crisis the totality of which led to notable changes. Each can be noted briefly, after which their total result can be examined.

In 1901 the French wine market became satiated and prices and profits dropped precipitously. Increased production is noted in Table 26.

TABLE 26:   LOWER MIDI WINE PRODUCTION

Department	Vineyard area (hectares)	Mean production 1890–1900 (hectolitres)	Production in 1899	Production in 1900
Pyrénées-Orientales	63,449	1,705,717	2,915,403	2,891,878
Aude	133,568	3,627,598	5,330,781	6,313,101
Hérault	191,352	7,521,051	12,360,400	11,493,728
Gard	74,133	2,006,494	3,656,363	3,794,796
Bouches-du-Rhône	28,888	1,073,201	1,324,403	1,720,010
Var	45,341	686,916	1,234,968	1,729,358
Total	536,731	16,620,977	26,822,318	27,942,871
France	1,730,451	35,965,000	47,907,680	68,352,661

Source: *Annuaire statistique.* These are the official statistics of legally produced wine and do not include false wine.

As a result, vineyard employers reduced wages, a decision in which workers acquiesced. Vintners at all levels suffered a setback; so did the artisans and merchants who were their local provisioners. However, in

1903 there came a marked improvement in prices; as a result, workers, many of whom had recently established trade unions, demanded better wages. When employers refused after the fall harvest, strikes broke out in several communes of Hérault during December, followed by a general wave of strikes during January-February 1904. This was the worst time for laborers to stop work; winter was the dead season! Yet, they had a strong sense of grievance, and the unorganized rapidly created unions or joined those set up earlier. They were aided and encouraged by craftsmen and agents of the *bourses du travail* (trade unions headquarters) which existed in the larger coastal towns. The rural strike movement, whatever its immediate results, was important in that it gave syndicalists, many of whom were revolutionary, an opportunity to spread their ideas among vineyard workers. This was an important step in the socializing of a rural class that had been a main bulwark of the Radical movement. The extent of the unions' influence can be recognized by the large dimensions of the work stoppages: they occurred in about half the predominantly wine communes of Hérault, most of the coastal communes of Aude, and many in the lower Aude Valley, and about half the communes of Perpignan-*Est* and Rivesaltes cantons. In Gard only three communes were involved: Saint Gilles, Fourques, and Beaucaire; in Provence, only the vast commune of Arles.[6]

Ill-timing notwithstanding, a strike movement began which continued into 1904, with sporadic work stoppages continuing into the next year. In Roussillon and lower Languedoc, 123 communes experienced strikes between November 1903 and December 1905. In all there were 32,701 strikers out of 33,154 workers, that is, participation achieved the remarkable level of 92 percent. This is unprecedented for agricultural workers spread over so large an area. Such unity of purpose was highly significant for politics. A tendency toward extremism was probably checked by the brevity and success of the stoppages. The mean duration was 4.6 days and over 90 percent were successful as regards wage demands (the mean raise was 38.9 centimes per day) and reduction of hours (usually from 8 to 7 or 7.5). That workers were organized in 106 communes out of 123 indicated the widespread gains of syndicalism. Also, local workers settled most of the strikes by direct bargaining with employers (24 percent), while a smaller number were settled by local officials (15 percent) or by departmental administrators (11 percent). Since these gains soon spread to nonstriking communes, satisfaction was widespread in the spring of 1904. This successful strike movement was in marked contrast to the unsuccessful general strike among miners in France two years earlier. Its success also popularized the idea and practice of unionism, at least into the next year. It seemed that quite a large number of workers were turning to syndicalism rather than politics to accomplish their goals, but this tendency, whatever it signified in 1904, was not to become characteristic of the lower Midi. If the figures in the *Annuaire des syndicats* are more or less accurate, labor forces in Var seemed determined to use syndicalism to solve their problems as early as 1898; but they soon turned to political socialism and the syndicalist movement did not gain wide acceptance outside of the southwest industrial corner. So it was in most of the lower Midi, in particular among vineyard workers who were confronted with an economic malaise whose cure was beyond trade union power.

POLITICAL RESULTS OF THE CRISIS.

A renewal of the wine crisis that began in 1904 plunged the lower Midi into the gravest crisis it had faced since the phylloxera. The emergence of class feeling now practically ceased to be of significance. The crisis threw together nearly all elements involved in the production of wine, from the richest owners to the lowest laborers. The weapon they all seized was politics, and when they organized, they created political pressure groups cutting across class lines. The irony of this was that the socialists profited in the next elections.

The vintners west of the Rhône became more interventionist because they were convinced that the French market was glutted with false and adulterated wine. Here was their idée fixe. It is of no immediate concern to the historian whether their claim was accurate or not; they acted on their conviction and their action determined the course of politics in the South—and perhaps in the rest of France. Since the commencement of the crisis in 1901, peasants had an ambivalent view toward the *Bloc*, the left-wing coalition governing France. On the one hand they favored its reformist policies; on the other they condemned fiscal authorities for expropriating the land of tax delinquents. Where local officials were zealous, Jacqueries broke out, as in Béziers *arrondissement* in 1901. Curiously enough, the population of Narbonne, the scene of later violence, was relatively quiet at this time and Ferroul sought to restrain his followers. The subprefect there warned his superiors to moderate tax collections since there was widespread suffering.[7] The ministry was not insensitive; it was however, concerned about income. A year earlier it had suppressed taxes on wine save for the circulation tax fixed at 1 franc 50 per hectolitre. When the crisis worsened in 1904, the hard-pressed southerners wanted an end to land taxes, at least on small holdings. Most Radical deputies had been calling for an income tax to replace wholly or partially the land tax. They were also vociferous in defending their bills to curb the sale of fraudulent wine, hence their wide popularity in the 1902 and 1906 elections; where they were not sufficiently vociferous to satisfy local vintners, they saw their many voters turn to socialists.

But it was neither a socialist nor a Radical who rose to leadership among vintners; it was a simple peasant, a moderate republican from Argeliers (Aude), Marcellin Albert. Argeliers was located in the canton of Ginestas where *progressistes* had wide support. No strike broke out there in 1903–4; the inhabitants were nearly all small and medium owners threatened with extinction because they suffered from falling revenues in a time of rising production costs. Albert came to symbolize the sense of grievance so widespread in the Midi precisely at the time that Clemenceau, senator from Var, became prime minister. By October 1906 the situation in Aude was especially tense. Peasants were again aroused because treasury officials were seizing land for tax arrears. This time the prefect warned the government that the department's economy was in a shambles: cereals in the uplands were ruined by bad weather; small vintners, to clear their vats for the new wine harvest, had to sell last year's wine at a terrible loss.[8] There was a growing anti-northern feeling, especially since a bill backed by Doumergue of Gard and Maurice Sarraut and Aldy of Aude, to prohibit the sale of northern beet sugar to vintners for adulterating wine, had been defeated in June 1905. All efforts since then to strengthen legal prohibitions against fraud had also failed. In consequence, local leaders and peasant masses had turned to large-scale demonstrations to pressure the government in their favor. The first such demonstration took place in the late spring of 1906 at Narbonne where Albert and his fellow leaders, known as the committee of Argeliers or the "comité des gueux," steadily expanded their influence, especially after Ferroul joined forces with them.

Pressure of this sort was precisely what the new premier, Clemenceau, distrusted, although he was, of course, sympathetic to the Midi. His cabinet was heavily southern in its composition and he, himself, was a senator of Var, elected in 1902 . He curtailed expropriations, made available sums to prime the pumps of local credit bureaux, and created a parliamentary committee to study the wine crisis. Yet, he did not act with dispatch, although his prefects and southern Radical deputies warned him that the situation was extremely tense. To find a comparable confrontation one must go back to March 1871 when Thiers, then head of the executive power, faced a Paris held by determined men of the extreme left. In May-June 1907 Clemenceau displayed toward the Midi an attitude quite like that of Thiers toward Paris; the Midi must be patient and its problems will be solved.

But the Midi in 1907 was no more patient than Paris in 1871. Almost a year after the Narbonne meeting came one at Béziers which according to reports, attracted over 100,000 demonstrators.[9]   This time there was violence and property damage. Radicals accused royalists of instigating it and royalists turned the accusation against them. Fearful, Radicals of the Midi, Lafferre at their head, urged Clemenceau to push along a bill to put a surtax on sugar; this gesture, they argued, would appease most southerners. But Clemenceau, still smarting from the postal workers strike and the violent diatribes against him by the CGT, hesitated as though he were trying to ride out the storm. Probably believing that it would soon abate, he even allowed local officials to provide free railway transport to the public demonstrations that became larger: Perpignan (172,000 people), Carcassonne, where violence again erupted (200,000), Nîmes (150,000) and Montpellier on 9 June (500,000). Everywhere Marcelin Albert was idolized. No one paid taxes any more and no fiscal agent dared try to collect lest he be lynched.

Then emerged a tactic once advocated during the brief 1893 wine crisis: mass resignations of local elected officials in order to bring all public life to a halt. Clemenceau, refusing to accept them, decided to arrest the most notorious leaders, Ferroul, mayor of Narbonne, and all the committee of Argeliers. It took an army unit to get the impassioned doctor out of Narbonne. On 19–20 June the city was in a condition bordering on rebellion; police agents were openly attacked and beaten, troops were stoned, the subprefect and two generals were almost lynched, the town hall was attacked and one part of it set on fire. Not since its brief experience with a communard insurrection in 1871 had this ancient city been the scene of so much violence. The climax came when troops fired on a crowd angrily pursuing two policemen; several persons were killed and others wounded. By this time nearly all southern politicians had broken with Clemenceau and denounced his tactics, especially his absurd decision to use the Seventeenth Line Regiment to quell disorder. Most of these soldiers were Languedocian and they mutinied rather than use force against friends and relatives. They were subsequently shipped to North Africa.

Meanwhile, the law of 29 June placed a limit of twenty-five kilograms on the amount of sugar that could be used for making wine without a special permit. Other hastily passed measures provided the government with more controls over the grape crop and information about the quantity of wine owned by buyers of sugar. But what really brought to an end the violent phase of the wine movement was Marcelin Albert's secret trip to Paris, his surrender and abject posture before Clemenceau, and his return to the Midi a defeated man. Intransigent vintners, many of whom were fearful of how far they had gone toward open rebellion, now turned to passive resistance. Many were strongly attached to the Republic and more and more republicans, both moderates and Radicals, grew fearful that reactionary forces would profit from the crisis. Radicals again accused royalists of instigating violence and Ferroul of being their dupe. They did not, however, entirely disassociate themselves from the demonstrations; on the contrary, these, they claimed, had been necessary to get the government to act.[10] They undoubtedly hoped to acquire enhanced prestige by a vigorous championing of wine interests. Since numerous cantonal and departmental wine defense committees had grown up, Lafferre called on them to keep wine off the markets when prices dropped. This tactic, he argued, would be more effective than mass meetings, resignations, and tax strikes. In reality Lafferre and most Radicals consciously set out to politicize the movement. They attacked big landowners for underselling little owners.[11] They also set out to create democratically oriented wine groups as a counterforce to the newly organized Confédération Générale des Vignerons.

The CGV was the creation of large-scale producers, men who had been traditionally in control of departmental wine committees.[12]   However, it came to include extreme left-wing forces hostile to Radicalism. Created in Narbonne during August 1907, it fell under the influence of Ferroul. His organ, *La République sociale,* called on workers to join the CGV. He identified Clemenceau with the Radicals and warned that the cabinet was seeking to divide owners and workers in order to weaken wine interests. He assured them that only through the CGV would they obtain arrears in wages.[13] His call for the unity of wine interests over and above class interest, a curious position for a member of the new socialist party, (SFIO), was echoed by the conservative *Courrier de l'Aude.*[14] But in truth the CGV became the instrument of large owners hostile to the Radicals. As such it was not necessarily conservative in politics, and Ferroul sought to use it, as will be shown, in the 1910 elections. As a menace to Radicals, however, its influence did not spread far beyond the Narbonnais and the Bitterois.[15]

The viticultural movement declined in scope and intensity as it spread eastward of Hérault, the geographic limit which had also characterized the 1904 strike wave. Despite the sizable meeting in Nîmes, the people of Gard reserved their passions more for religious issues created by separation; at any rate they did not reveal the same intensity of feeling as their Languedocian neighbors to the west. Even more remarkable was the lack of commitment displayed in Provence. In 1905 there had been a wine congress in Var; adulteration was condemned and the government called on to act.[16] In May 1907 some vintners of Le Beausset canton took up the movement. A well-attended meeting was held in the commune of Carnoules, followed by a few resignations of local officials. But Var was Clemenceau's department, despite its abandonment of Radicalism since the 1898 and 1902 elections, and no serious wine manifestations took place. There was in Provence a certain distrust of fanatical winemen which penetrated much of the leftwing there. Somewhat self-righteously, journalists accused large owners in Languedoc of making an excess of wine and of false wine which they dumped on the market. They were then said to have used the resulting panic to attack the Republic; the mass meetings merely strengthened their hand. The crisis, moreover, was the vintners' own fault; they should never have abandoned the old polyculture to which Provence held firm.[17]

These views did not lead most of the extreme left to defend the Tiger. On the contrary, he was as vehemently attacked by the socialists as he was by conservatives of every variety. Leftwing opposition to him really did not originate in the wine crisis but in his rough handling of striking postmen and the CGT. Well before the wine demonstrations even began Jean Jaurès and the SFIO had voted against him on several occasions in the Chamber. They were joined by only a few dissident Radicals: Bourrat (Pyrénées-Orientales), Razimbaud (Hérault), Michel and Pelletan (Bouches-du-Rhône), Louis Martin and Abel (Var), that is, mainly from Provence where Radicals were pressured by the SFIO. But in a vote of confidence following the violence in Narbonne, the count was 328 for, 227 against his policies. This time, the minority contained all the Midi deputies save Dujardin-Beaumetz (Aude), Doumergue and Poisson (Gard), and three independent socialists of Bouches-du-Rhône. Among the Radicals only Doumergue represented a predominantly wine area, but he was preparing himself for the Senate. Most southern Radicals were clearly trying to disassociate themselves from Clemenceau; they were embarrassed, however, in that the old man's chief backers were the great hoard of Radicals from other areas of France who had won in the 1906 election. The fortunes of these Midi deputies, therefore, were tied to the positions taken by their party. Since 1901 they represented voters most of whom were fully devoted to wine, were discouraged and excited at the same time, and were converted to a form of sectionalism which viewed politics as a conflict between wine and sugar, and therefore between South and North. Ferroul and conservative folklorists sought to remind them that they were the descendants of the Albigensians, also victims of the North, and that they possessed a great past and a noble language of their own.[18] What, then, were the electoral fortunes of Radicals in this climate of opinion?

NOTES

1. See the debates in *Journal officiel, Chambre des Députés*, 15 August 1889; Warner p. 39.
2. For these laws see *La Bataille républicaine* (Carcassonne), 19 October 1906.
3. On 1893 crisis see A.D. Hérault, M12 unclassified reports on conditions and prices; A.D. P-O 3M 1-163, prefect reports of 1893–94: *Conférence interdépartementale sur la mévente des vins* (Paris 1894), 9 ff; *La Démocratie* (P-O), November 1893-March 1894, *passim; Petit méridional* 12 December 1893, 28 March 1894.
4. Paul Degrully, *Essai historique et économique sur la production...du vin* (Paris, 1910), 326-27; *Suffrage universel* (Montpellier) 12 February 1888; *Région radicale* (Draguignan), 7 February 1884; *Ligue démocratique* (Brignoles), 1889 and *passim;* A.D. Gard, 2M 84; A.D. P-O 2M 1-85, 3M 1-163. Silk interests in Gard and Var were also protectionist as were cereal producers and coal interests.
5. See *Petit méridional*, 18-20 April 1896.
6. France. Direction du travail, *Annuaire des syndicats* (1904-5). France. Direction du Travail, *Statistiques des grèves, année* 1904 (Paris, 1905).
7. A.D. Aude 13M 86, report of 4 November 1901. In a report of October 1906 the prefect reiterated his warning.
8. A.D. Aude 5M 66, report of 9 October 1906.
9. For these demonstrations see *Petit méridional* May-June 1907; *Républicain du Gard,* June-August 1907; A.D. Hérault, 39M 281; A.D. Aude, 5M 66 and 71; Le Blond, *Crise du Midi,* 13 and *passim.*
10. *Républicain du Gard* (Nîmes), 9 July 1907.
11. See *Petit méridional*, 18 July 1907.
12. For the CGV see Maurice Coupert, *Essai sur la CGV* (Montpellier, 1921). Partisan but good.
13. 5 September 1907.
14. 12 September 1907.
15. On the situation in the upper Aude Valley see A.D. Aude, 5M 66, reports of subprefect of Limoux.
16. A.D. Var, 14M 29-2.
17. *Avant Garde* (Aix), 15 June 1907; *Dépeche radicale* (Brignoles), 18 October 1907.
18. *Justice sociale*, 1, 2 September, 14 November 1908.

CHAPTER TEN

RADICALISM VERSUS SOCIALISM
1902 - 1914

RISE OF SOUTHERN SOCIALISM

The years between the 1902 and 1906 elections brought not only a serious wine crisis but a novel, perturbing element into the politics of lower Languedoc: aggressive socialism. The ideal of social reform, of modifying existing social structure in the interests of greater equality, had become an integral part of politics there since the 1880s. For two decades the Radicals had implanted the idea of social and economic justice. They naturally identified themselves with these ideals and the more left wing had added the term socialist to their party label of Radical in order to further emphasize their commitment to social reform. Of course, their identification with reform had not gone unchallenged; socialist candidates had run in elections during the entire period, and there had been extreme left Radicals who occasionally challenged the more moderate ones. But until 1898 the socialist challenge had not been a successful one, and socialist voters had usually rallied to the support of Radicals in run-off elections. Cooperation between these two major components of the political left continued during the period of the *Bloc*. The change which occurred lay rather in the intensity and greater success of the socialist challenge to Radical leadership, and this chapter discusses the rise of socialism at the expense of Radicalism after 1898.

Save in Aude and Hérault, displacement by socialists was not checked seriously by the formation of the Radical and Radical-Socialist party of 1901. Radical federations were formed in all six departments and several politicians, Lafferre, Doumergue, and Pelletan, held important

196

TABLE 27:   RADICAL/TOTAL AND SOCIALIST SEATS BY DEPARTMENT

Department	1902		1906		1910		1914	
	Rad./Tot.	Soc.	Rad./Tot.	Soc.	Rad./Tot.	Soc.	Rad./Tot.	Soc.
Pyrénées-Orientales	2/4	0	2/4	0	3/4	0	1/4	1
Aude	4/6	1	5/6	1	5/6	1	4/5	1
Hérault	6/7	1	5/7	1	3/7	3	3/7	3
Gard	2/6	3	2/6	3	1/6	4	1/6	5
Bouches-du-Rhône	3/9	4	3/9	5	2/9	4	2/9	5
Var	1/4	3	1/4	3	1/4	3	1/5	4
Total	18/36	12	18/36	13	15/36	15	12/36	19

posts in the party's national organization. However, politiking remained a highly personal undertaking combining individual initiative and skill, local financing, good relations with the departmental press, a strong personal following, and a program emphasizing local economic and political issues.

In the Midi for the 1902 and 1906 elections there were a combination of local and national factors which influenced the results. Locally there was the wine crisis the solution of which clearly held first place in all programs. It was this economic debacle that helped socialists to win a position of strength in the lower South which they could never attain on the national scene. Then there was the right-wing nationalist revival, and the simultaneous formation of the republican, Radical, and socialist *Bloc des Gauches* to defend the Republic from the nationalists and to separate church and state. Separation played a relatively minor role during elections in the lower South, partly because antirepublican forces were so weak, partly because dechristianization had greatly moderated religion as a vital force, save in the highlands and in the traditionally conservative towns such as Montpellier and Nîmes. Far more important was the dramatic formation in 1905 of the SFIO or Unified Socialist Party. Its central officers withdrew from the *Bloc* and set out to make collectivism a force of its own. In the South, independent and unified socialists sought for issues with which to win mass support. And fickle nature provided them with one. The first decade and a half following 1900 reminds one of the fifteen or so years following the outbreak of phylloxera. These were crisis years and such a period was conducive to a change of loyalties in *arrondissements* where wine prices were studied as a matter of life or death.

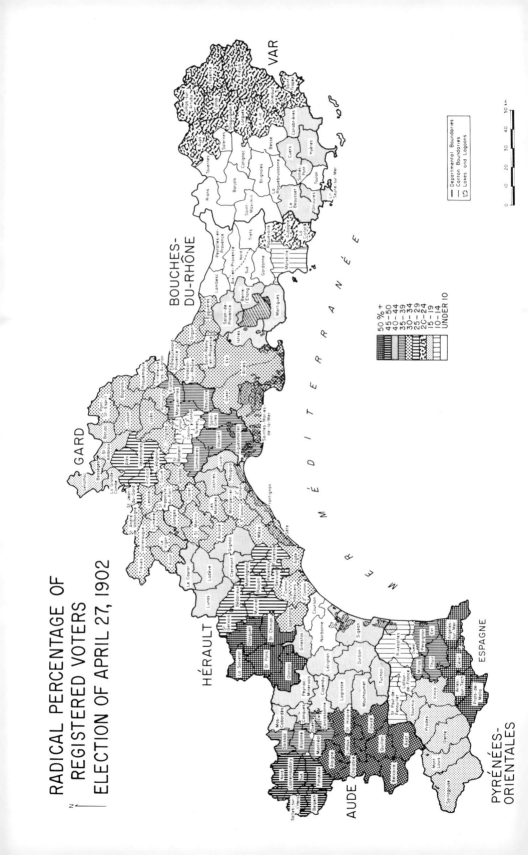

RADICAL PERCENTAGE OF
REGISTERED VOTERS
ELECTION OF APRIL 27, 1902

While the *Bloc* existed, however, there was relatively little change; in the 1902 and 1906 elections the mass of voters remained loyal to Radicals and looked to them to end the *mévente*. And yet, political evolution was underway and a study of several circumscriptions will help us to understand the forces behind it.

The initial decline of the Radical movement began in the 1890s and in circumscriptions where, with one exception, wine was not an important factor. Most notable was the gradual Radical demise in Gard and Provence, and to understand the collective behavior of voters in this area the historian must penetrate their psyche rather than their pocketbooks.

As a political phenomenon in Gard the Radical movement had never dominated public life to the extent that it had in Hérault or in Provence before 1900. In 1898 it was reduced to Nîmes *arrondissement,* the chief wine-producing area of Gard, and it lost the city of Nîmes to a socialist in a by-election during 1901. In this latter year, Gaston Doumergue, Pierre Poisson, Dr. Crouzet, and Beauregard of Nîmes founded the Radical-Socialist federation. They also created in January 1906 the *Républican du Gard,* the first pro-Radical paper to enjoy a long life in the department. It was a tragic irony that with the appearance of a Radical press the Radical movement was well on the way to extinction. Apart from the wine crisis which certainly weakened its hold in the coastal plain, there were psychological factors which influenced the voters' collective behavior. Most notable was the decision of numerous Protestants to terminate their old marriage with the Radical left. This divorce explains the death of Radicalism in the city of Nîmes where it had never been strong and also in Alès I where it had predominated since mid-century.[1]

In Alès I the lure of the new extreme left, socialism, proved irresistible to Protestants and to the numerous freethinkers of Protestant families. Freemasonry, spread by Desmons who had been an active leader of it, lived side by side with Protestantism and so tended to identify itself with the extreme left, once Radical, now socialist. From 1898 until 1914 the independent socialist Paul Devèze won most of the Protestant vote. Curiously, he was not a Protestant and some Catholics supported him for this reason. A Protestant pastor, running as a Radical in 1902, tried to become the belated successor of Desmons but ran third in a four man contest. Religion as such, therefore, was not the important factor; it was religion as a political temperament, the imperative need to be on the extreme left. In a by-election in 1894, Protestants had chosen a moderate of their religion but could not abide him longer than three years. This need to be on the left was not new with southern Protestants, albeit there were moderate ones in Lédignan and Vézenobres. The novelty was for a fair number of Catholics to vote for the extreme left. Here was the supreme irony. Most Protestants voted for the extreme left as an atavistic protest against Catholic persecution in past centuries. And they were certainly voting for separation in 1902 and the defense of it in 1906. Some Catholics, on the other hand, now voted for the same candidates of the extreme left, to oppose the *Bloc!* And there were also some Catholics who argued that Devèze was not sufficiently leftwing, that he was really a *blocard,* and that Catholics should vote for the revolutionary candidate, Hubert Rouger! But only a handful followed this advice. Apparently Catholics were more squeamish about the extreme left now than later. And Devèze profited from this balance of forces until 1914.

Religion as a political factor also played a role in Le Vigan *arrondissement.* A moderate who ran as a Radical, Frederic Gaussorgues, had won there in 1889 and 1893. In the heat generated by the Dreyfus case, a socialist, Ulysse Pastre, who claimed to be a collectivist, and who also had patriotic leanings, was elected in 1898. He won again in 1902 and 1906. Now there was less of a socialist tradition in Le Vigan than there was in Alès I and practically no real working class save in some silk textile centers, such as the towns of Le Vigan and Sumène where, in 1902, Pastre ran behind the Radical candidate, A. Deshons. Given the fact that Protestant conservatives were strong here, Deshons must have won some of their votes, despite his claim that he was a disciple of the advocate of a progressive income tax, Leon Bourgeois.[2] But the Catholic conservative vote, especially in 1902, as well as much of the Radical vote, went to the socialist, and undoubtedly for the same reasons as those which prevailed in Alès I. Pastre won major victories in the Catholic conservative cantons of Trèves, Alzon, and Valleraugue. He won a more decisive victory in 1906, which was curious, for according to the subprefect's estimates, there were in the *arrondissement* only 1,800 socialists, 6,400

Radicals, and 5,000 "réactionnaires." Even allowing for errors in this estimate, it is evident that advanced Radicals joined with socialists to support Pastre in order to resist efforts by moderate Radicals to give the *Bloc* a rightward orientation.

Pastre, in conjunction with Devèze, remained faithful to the *Bloc*, and they refused to remain in the SFIO with its revolutionary, anti-patriotic wing. Since Fournier equally refused to enter the SFIO, socialism in Gard was independent or republican, which meant quite simply that it was hardly a step removed from the advanced Radicalism of Desmons and Doumergue. In 1906 all the socialist candidates in the highlands were more definitely dependent on the Radical vote. Radicals in the highlands, who could not bring themselves to vote for a candidate of their color, seemed almost the victims of a political death wish, a determination to commit political suicide. This was a curious, psychological factor, as true of many moderate republicans as of Radicals. For mainly psychological reasons, republicans of nearly all shades decided that they must be represented by an extreme leftist or at least by one claiming to represent this end of the political spectrum. To be represented by someone not as vehemently committed seemed demeaning. Left-wing Radicals were particularly distrustful of "anticollectivist" Radicals who represented an effort to turn Radicalism from its commitment to the left toward a compromise with the center. There was no logical argument around this position. But the tendency toward the left which became a political characteristic in Gard and Provence possibly was a reaction to the tendency of urban Radical organizations to drift toward the center and moderation.

The situation in Bouches-du-Rhône resembled that in Gard; there was a steady decline of the Radical party. From five deputies out of eight in 1893 it fell to three in 1898, and to two out of nine in 1910. Its centers of strength were primarily outside of the city of Marseille.

In Marseille the newly organized Radical federation was taken over by the "comité" Martino, so called because it met in the Cafe Martino. Its official name was Comité d'Union Républicaine Radical et Socialiste. Its head, Nicolas Vassal, a big soap manufacturer, was an anticollectivist Radical, hostile toward the socialists and more friendly toward the *progressistes*. In Marseille there was no longer the bond between

Radicalism and socialism which had produced deputies such as Clovis Hugues and F. V. Raspail and even Paul Petral who, although a moderate, enjoyed socialist support. In Bouches-du-Rhône, as elsewhere, socialism had made considerable headway in organization and electioneering and had set out to replace Radicals. The Vassal group represented a tendency, well established before the SFIO was founded in 1905, to sever ties with the extreme left in favor of ties with moderate republicans.[3] But this group had relatively few followers in the port city and Vassal himself could not win a majority in his own district, Marseille I, which fell to a socialist in 1898. Marseille II, after re-electing the turncoat Bouge in 1893, also went socialist in 1898. By 1902 Radicalism had ceased to be an important force in politics in Marseille.

Elsewhere it held out and the socialist opposition was not serious— save in Aix I. When the intransigent Leydet was elected senator in 1897, there followed a period of confusion because the Radical group had become so narrowly based on him that it could not find a suitable replacement. At first it turned to a local notable, Gabriel Baron, mayor of Aix, who was considered "Radical et socialiste." He won in a by-election in 1897 but lost in the general election of 1898 because of a split between Radicals and socialists. Baron now became an out-and-out socialist, or so he claimed. By 1902 the political situation in Aix I was quite confused. Some Radicals, headed by Pelletan, disliked Baron, not really for doctrinal but for personal reasons; he had quit Freemasonry and courted Catholic support. To oppose Baron, they did not look for another Radical but for a moderate socialist. They hit upon A. Lefèvre, editor of *La Petite république* of Paris. Although officially a socialist, Lefèvre resembled Pelletan: he believed that Radicalism and socialism were blood brothers.[4] To confuse the issue even more, a moderate who had won in 1898 thanks to the split between Radicals and socialists, now in 1902 decided to run as an "independent" Radical. Baron had the endorsement of most socialists and of a good many Radicals who resented Lefèvre as an outsider, as a menace to left wing unity, and as a former Boulangist.[5] Naturally the pro–Lefèvre faction, which included many Radical notables, accused Baron of anti-Semitism and of right-wing support.[6] This last charge, made when the campaign became filled with personal invective, was contrary to the facts. Baron won in the run-off, and his votes came predominantly from communes which had been pro-Leydet in 1889 and 1893. Quite clearly, most Radical voters chose Baron. Those who had voted for Lefèvre in the first election turned to the moderate for the run-off.

By 1906 these animosities had ended and Baron easily defeated a moderate, his only opponent. By this time he was quite acceptable to most Radicals, for he had refused to join the SFIO and sided with the independent socialists, who were hardly different from left-wing Radicals. However, he did not join the Radical party either, and Radicalism as a distinct political organization practically disintegrated. The local popularity of Baron discouraged party organization for a decade, and the moderate socialism of Aix I took root in the predominantly rural, wine-producing communes north and east of the town of Aix, once the bastions of Leydet.

The department of Var followed a somewhat different pattern. There socialism permanently replaced Radicalism chiefly in the more rural circumscription of Draguignan in 1898 and in Brignoles in 1902. Unlike their counterparts in Bouches-du-Rhône, Radicals in Var turned to the socialists in the semi-urban cantons more consistently than in the more fully urbanized ones of the Toulonnais. In Draguignan and Brignoles, the socialist candidates took up the defense of local interests, chiefly wine, and satisfied the needs of most peasants. Octave Vigne in Brignoles identified both with Radicals and socialists and was supported by Pelletan, Doumergue, even by Leon Bourgeois, against a revolutionary.[7] He joined the SFIO right wing in 1905 and held the circumscription until the war. Quite different was the situation in Draguignan. Clemenceau's defeat and the incumbency of Jourdan had turned many voters away from Radicalism. In 1898 rather, they not only took up socialism to express their disapproval, they turned to a revolutionary, Maurice Allard, who later attacked the *Bloc*. Clearly the political issue of church and state did not interest these free-thinkers enough to determine their vote. Radical notables, as well as the *Petit provençal* and *Petit Var,* supported a moderate socialist but to no avail. Allard's victory against a Radical in 1906 was even more decisive, 10,097 to 4,218.

The wine crisis can explain this phenomenon in part. Allard's support

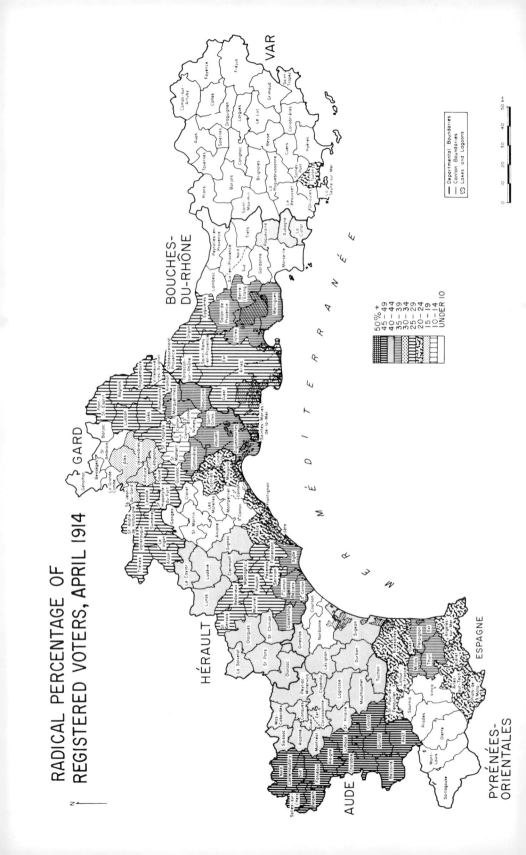

RADICAL PERCENTAGE OF
REGISTERED VOTERS, APRIL 1914

GARD

HÉRAULT

AUDE

PYRÉNÉES-
ORIENTALES

ESPAGNE

BOUCHES-
DU-RHÔNE

VAR

MER MÉDITERRANÉE

50% +
45 — 49
40 — 44
35 — 39
30 — 34
25 — 29
20 — 24
15 — 19
10 — 14
UNDER 10

Departmental Boundaries
Canton Boundaries
Lakes and Lagoons

0 10 20 30 40 50 km

came largely from wine-producing communes which responded to his active support of bills to prevent fraud. The socialist Vigne in Brignoles and the Radical Louis Martin in Toulon II, also running in areas affected by the wine crisis, stood on a program emphasizing legislation to aid vintners, and both repeated in 1906 their victories of 1902.[8] Undoubtedly the wine crisis was a major catastrophe in Toulon II, in southern Brignoles, and the coastal areas of Draguignan. Yet, there was an additional psychological element or drive that cannot be ignored. Voting for the extreme left was now an old tradition taken up by each succeeding generation and simply irresistible in most of Provence. To be red here was the equivalent of being white in the Vendée. And this reflex, conditioned by historical memories, was probably more deeply rooted in the rural than in the everchanging urban population. It was a "gut" reaction of the horde of small landowners, the majority of the population outside of Toulon, and of many naturalized Italians, who could never be convinced that socialism, even revolutionary socialism, was the enemy of the small owner. Of course, one looks in vain for truly collectivist planks in the plaforms of successful socialist candidates, especially in rural areas. These same socialists proudly announced to their electors that they supported bills to suppress fraud, to encourage distilling of wine to lessen the supply, to build irrigation canals to help small owners diversify crops, and to implement the rest of the old Radical program.

The city of Toulon enclosed an environment more constantly changing, more dynamic, more diversified. Radicals held it until 1898 when a moderate socialist, Prosper Ferrero, emerged victorious and remained so until 1910. It then returned to a very moderate Radical, Jean-Baptiste Abel, a lawyer and scion of an old left-wing family. But the voters were highly divided and elections were close. Radicalism in Toulon, like that in Marseille and Montpellier became more and more moderate, responding to the needs of middle class voters, and losing to the SFIO much of its support among the working class.

Republican discipline in the run-off election tended to favor socialist candidates in three out of four circumscriptions, and the formation of the SFIO did not prevent in 1906 the withdrawal of the minority candidate in the run-off election. The departmental federation criticized local socialists in Toulon II for supporting Martin and refused to condone their action. However, it did not run a candidate against him. Socialists in Toulon II remained quite independent of the SFIO and many voted for another Radical in 1909 to replace Martin when he was elected to the Senate.

Socialism in its rise to power was able to exploit a certain malaise, a disenchantment among many Radical voters in several areas. The Radical movement to which they had turned in mid-century no longer fulfilled either their social aspirations, their economic grievances, or their psychological leanings. And the latter was by no means the least important of these factors. However, psychic need, this leftism of the mind, retreats to a secondary role in the evolutionary process of most of the lower Midi after 1900.

TRIUMPH OF SOCIALISM

The elections of 1910 and 1914 brought to a close the period of Radical domination in the lower Midi. And the Radical movement which survived shifted its locus from the central area consisting of Bouches-du-Rhône, Gard, and Hérault, to the western sector consisting of Hérault, Aude, and Pyrénées-Orientales.

How is one to explain this decline of Radicalism and the rise of socialism which replaced it? The trend, it is obvious, preceded 1910 and in Var was nearly complete by 1902. One must go back in time in order to generalize and then return to 1910 to observe the final death struggle. Earlier chapters of this book emphasized that the left wing usually profited from crises: the big agricultural crisis of 1847–49, accompanied by the Roman expedition and the Falloux law of 1849, provided a background in which the Mountain could win numerous converts. The coup d'état of 1851 brought this crisis to a close and with it the initial phase of Radical growth. Next came the phylloxera. However catastrophic it was to the Midi it was an important boon to the Radicals. It gave to the leaders and cadre of the left the leverage to shift the republican movement, already growing since 1871, toward Radical control. Where the phylloxera had least effect, the extreme left was slow to grow. During the 1890s replanting was nearly complete and Radicalism now seemed the normal political form in most circum-scriptions where vineyards were important.

Until 1898 there was no serious inclination to go beyond the programs of Clemenceau and Pelletan. Where socialist victories occurred, they were the result of a leftward impulse among voters normally in the Jacobin tradition. In fact, these early changes followed a pattern. They occurred earliest where the incumbent was an old timer who had struggled to found and then maintain the Republic during the 1870s. First he held local office and then he was a deputy during the 1880s and 1890s. He then died, at which time his funeral became a great occasion for a civil burial, or he entered the Senate, the body he had promised to abolish. Now it was at times difficult to find a Radical candidate with enough prestige to replace him. Lucky it was when he left an heir apparant: Bourrat who followed Brousse and who was in turn followed by Dalbiez in Perpignan II; Lafferre who followed Verhnès and Mas in Béziers I, Paul Pujade who succeeded Pams in Céret, Augé who took over from Vernière in Béziers II, Leydet who came after Lockroy in Aix I, Michel who succeeded Lagnel in Arles, August Girard who inherited the well-worn seat of Pelletan in Aix II, Jean Bonnail who won the equally worn seat of Dujardin-Beaumetz in Limoux, Malavialle who followed Théron in Carcassonne II. Of these nine seats, only four eventually fell to socialist candidates: Aix I in 1902, Béziers II and Arles in 1910, and Céret in 1915. And Baron in Aix I and Rameil in Céret were more Radical than socialist. Succession therefore usually took place in Radical strongholds. There were two circumscriptions in which succession was actually based on blood ties: the Razimbaud in Saint-Pons and the Chevillons in Marseille IV.

On the other hand, where local Radical groups could not find a suit-able candidate, many of their members showed a marked distrust of the men who came forward to claim the seat of the grand old ex-incumbent, and willingly or not, they turned to a socialist candidate. Somehow the socialist seemed more pure, more committed to the social and economic reforms to which all true Radicals clung, and most of which had not been enacted into law.

The earliest socialist victories resulted from this left-wing mentality, as fixed as the North Star. Up to 1906 socialists had won nine seats with the aid of a majority of Radical voters: Toulon II (1888), Marseille I (1894), Nîmes I, Le Vigan, Alès I, Toulon I, Draguignan (1898), Aix I and Brignoles (1902). In six of these nine seats, the Radical incumbent died or became a senator. In only three did the socialist defeat a Radical victorious in the previous election: Toulon I, Draguignan, and Le Vigan. In the last two districts the incumbents were borderline Radicals, really moderates who never won the approval of left-wing Radicals. These latter therefore more willingly turned to a socialist, if only to relieve their deep frustrations.

Of course, these frustrations were really thwarted ambitions in many cases, especially among newer Radicals who were an out-group unable to replace the in-group of the older generation. By 1902 they became dissident or independent Radicals. Although members of the federation they saw little chance for advance through regular channels, the congresses where candidates were chosen. They referred to the in-group as "la petite chapelle," with its structure of clients who dominated cantonal committees and therefore the congresses. Between 1906 and 1910 this internal struggle became quite bitter. Sometimes it was a conflict between moderate and pro-Pelletan Radicals, sometimes a conflict of personalities and ambitions. Since few of the dissidents could win elections, their candidates divided Radical voters, and for the run-off they might either support the party candidate or oppose him with the socialist. Dissidence of this type helped socialists defeat three official candidates after 1906; Augé in Béziers II and Michel in Arles (1910) and Coreil in Toulon II (1914). Lafferre was nearly toppled by the dissident mayor of Béziers in 1910 but survived. Clemenceau's defeat in 1893 was the most famous and the forerunner of this tactic.

These internal conflicts contributed to the disruption of the old alliance between Radicals and socialists during the 1910 and 1914 elections. Socialists found themselves in an especially advantageous position; not only might independents support them, so did many right wing clericals who were determined to destroy the champions of separation and secular education. In 1910 four Radical seats were won by SFIO candidates aided by clericals, and two of these four were further weakened by dissidents. That many right-wing nationalists held their

Gallic noses in order to vote for members of a party with a program calling for international socialist unity is indicative of the high intensity of partisan passion. That most socialist candidates willingly accepted clerical support is an additional indication. Several of these candidates sought actively to win this support by mentioning, when campaigning in conservative strongholds, the possibility of modifying the 1901 law on associations as it affected religious teaching orders; that is, these orders might be given more freedom to teach. But this was an individual's policy and did not affect the SFIO if he belonged to it. Clericals and socialists had only one party policy in common and that was proportional representation. Few Radicals favored it since their party was the dominant one by 1910 when it served as a rallying point for their right and left wing opponents.

The 1910 election is worth more investigation. Clerical voters supported socialists running against Radical incumbents in at least eight circumscriptions: Perpignan II, Castelnaudary, Narbonne II, Béziers I and II, Montpellier III, Uzès, and Arles. As noted above, socialists were successful in four. Save Castelnaudary, all of these districts were in the wine belt. Clemenceau's policies in 1907, therefore, must have weakened the Radical party there. But more important was the general economic malaise which wine laws did not dissipate, the delayed impact of the separation law of 1905, and of the SFIO's policy to break with the *Bloc* which also had a delayed impact in the Midi. In 1906 not many socialists were seriously prepared to ally with the right against the Radicals. Not even Jean Molle in Montpellier III, who hated Salis, turned openly to the right for support.

The importance of Clemenceau's oppressive policies, not only in the Midi but throughout France, lay in the fact that they aroused many socialists to the point where they were willing to accept right-wing support. And in Arles, Languedoc, and Roussillon, where the *mévente* was a major catastrophe, resentment against Clemenceau was most bitter and it was here in 1910 that the extremes of right and left joined against the Radicals.

In Perpignan II, for the runoff, many socialists, *progressistes,* and royalists lined up behind an obscure socialist, Pierre Rameil, who failed to defeat the Radical, Victor Dalbiez, by only 250 odd votes. In 1914

Rameil moved to Céret and in a similar situation won the seat from a Radical; this time he got Radical support in the second election and emerged victorious because two socialists split the extreme left-wing vote. Having learned a lesson he became a Radical-Socialist. In Perpignan I, the moderate Radical Frederic Manaut and the socialist candidate opposed each other in the runoff despite the menace of a royalist victory. But here, conservative voters remained faithful to the royalist, and Manaut won. This same situation came about in 1914 and a conservative republican won in the run-off because of the split left-wing majority.

In Pyrénées-Orientales the Radicals' shift toward the center was pronounced, save for the followers of Bourrat. *Le Radical des Pyrénés-Orientales,* founded in 1907, and the local correspondent of the *Dépêche de Toulouse* sided with Clemenceau during the wine crisis. A strong element in the departmental federation became anticollectivist, a sure sign that they had become moderate. The disappearance of Bourrat weakened the intransigents so that the drift to the center continued under his successor Dalbiez in Perpigan II. He, too, had to defend himself against a socialist-conservative coalition.

The Radical movement won a far more solid victory in Aude. In fact, Aude became the Radical stronghold in lower Midi as most Radicals showed signs of weakening elsewhere. In 1898 the formerly dominant *progressistes* had begun to lose followers in wine areas of the department; 1902 brought their downfall. The Radicals became organized and united; a departmental federation was created, with an annual congress, to replace the loose congress system of former times. Undoubtedly electoral success would have come even without the federation and it has been impossible to determine whether that body made a significant contribution. Certainly the value of the candidates, set against the background of the wine crisis and population shifts, was of major importance. An economic catastrophe was an objective condition the use of which depended on the particular skills of each candidate. The phylloxera did not bring the Radical movement to full fruition in Aude during the 1880s. On the other hand, the *mévente* provided a relatively new generation of Radicals with the opportunity to identify themselves more successfully with the dominant wine interests.

Of course there was an overlap of generations. Dujardin-Beaumetz, who joined the party in 1901, remained solidly ensconced in Limoux. Even more solidly ensconced was Théron in Carcassonne II which lay east of the town. Identified as a "radical et socialiste," he too joined the Radical party in 1906. He was a true disciple of Omar Sarraut and the *Radical du Midi* in his long-time belief of a blood tie between Radicalism and socialism. He was an astute politician, with a clientele of teachers, forest guards, numerous mayors, and Masonic brothers; he naturally took care of local interests. His major centers of strength were the Carcassonnais, the Aude Valley, and the Corbières.

Not until 1902 did the Carcassonnais produce another notable comparable to Théron. Jules Sauzède was mayor of Carcassonne and active in local politics before he became the deputy of Carcassonne I. His program constituted a revival of the 1885 platform of the Clemenceau Radicals.[10] More definitely than Théron he was a true Radical, without socialist pretensions. His chief enemies were urban-based socialists and the struggle between them for Carcassonne town was an old and bitter one. As left-wing candidate his task was particularly difficult; there was no large wine-producing population to rely on outside of the cantons of Carcassonne and Montreal, and in the latter conservatives enjoyed a wide following. On the other hand, depopulation had so reduced the number of voters in rural communes, where his opponents' strength lay, that he won in the first round by carrying large majorities (40 percent) in the canton of Carcassonne *Ouest,* which, containing the town, had more voters than all the other cantons combined. Since vineyards began at the town's border, he was the candidate of wine interests; indeed, he was himself a large vineyard owner and understood the problem of fraud. And if that were not enough to endear him, he was the grandnephew of Armand Barbès, patron saint of the left in the Carcassonnais. He ran successfully in three elections until he won a Senate seat in 1912.

Another important achievement was the work of a newcomer, Albert Sarraut: he conquered and held Narbonne II, the old stronghold of Adolph Turrel, *progressiste* of note and minister. Turrel's victory had been annuled in 1898 because of fraud, so he shifted over to Narbonne I for 1902. Sarraut carried the prestige of his father, Omar, and the backing of the *Dépêche de Toulouse,* widely read in Aude. He, Théron, Massé, editor of *Radical du Midi,* and Senator Barbaza have been credited with creating the new Radical federation of Aude department.[11] With the backing of most socialists he just barely won in the first election in 1902. Turrel's former voters did not support him; rather Sarraut, with party backing, ran as the only left-wing candidate and therefore received votes formerly scattered over several competitors claiming to represent the left and voters who had previously abstained and who were now drawn into politics by the *mévente*.

Turrel ran against the socialist Felix Aldy in Narbonne I. Aldy won because he carried Narbonne town, not the important wine communes. Not until the 1906 elections and the worsening wine crisis did Narbonne I give more enthusiastic support to Aldy, and the riots of 1907 drove it violently into the socialist camp.

The Radical federation did not attempt to profit at the expense of the socialist. On the contrary, it backed him and continued to look upon him as a brother. And he reciprocated, as did most socialists,[12] at least those outside of Carcassonne. The formation of the SFIO did not bring any change in Aude as regards unity of the left. Cooperation continued and it was the Radical party which expanded, not into Narbonne, but westward into the hitherto forbidden *arrondissement* of Castelnaudary.

Jean Durand, a medical doctor, won here by campaigning as a defender of peasants. He organized a Groupe Républicaine de Défense Paysanne, consisting of petty owners, tenants, and sharecroppers. He finally convinced them that an income tax would lead to a reduction of their land tax, that they would be spared large sums which they could use to purchase land, and that they would be included in new pension bills sponsored by the Radicals. Durand was an imaginative man and a hard-headed politician who, as a doctor, was close to the peasants and understood their needs. Like them he was a fervent protectionist and patriot, and patriotism bordering on nationalism was strong in the highlands. Durand, however, profited more decisively from the decline of population in the countryside. The bulk of his support came from the towns of Castelnaudary and Fanjeaux, somewhat less from Belpech and Salles sur l'Hers which lay in the heartland of deep southern conservatism. Radicalism was still rather weak in many rural communes, and even to appeal to the townsmen it had to be identi-

fied with a candidate who was a moderate enjoying the strong support of
the subprefect who was working, as he put it , to liberate peasant workers from the control of their employers.[13]   He might also have added
from their priests.

The law of separation did not arouse keen antagonism. The coast
was remarkably dechristianized and practically immune; even in Castelnaudary there was no immediate reaction. People were "beaucoup
plus attachés aux pratiques religieuses qu'aux croyances dogmatiques."[14]
The subprefect of Limoux also insisted that there was little opposition to
separation, and that the local priests chose to cooperate with the government. It was, rather, the wine crisis that attracted public attention.[15]
Moderate and conservative candidates did not even choose to raise the
religious issue; they ran, rather, on the wine issue and accused the *Bloc*
of having caused the crisis.[16] But the wine crisis, in a formerly *progressiste*
department, encouraged a political shift to the left. The Radicals profited,
not the moderates, nor the socialists save in Narbonne I.

In Aude, therefore, the electoral situation did not change after 1906.
The only serious challenge from the socialists came in Narbonne II where
the infuriated Ferroul, now president of the CGV, bitterly fought Albert
Sarraut. Ferroul, in cooperation with deeply antirepublican elements,
politicized the CGV and used it in his effort to unseat Sarraut whom he
hated for once having served in Clemenceau's government.[17]   He used
dubious tactics. He set out to arouse antagonism between the North and
South, which he identified with sugar and wine, and he accused the
Radicals of favoring northern interests. Sarraut won by only 200 ballots
out of over 15,000. He really emerged victorious because of his strong
backing in Lézignan town. Ferroul picked up about 2,000 conservative
ballots, but he could not penetrate the bastion of Radical power: the
stretch of land from the Aude River, through the lower Corbières and
Sigean down to the sea. This was a region of middle-sized vineyards
where people lived in large scattered villages or small towns. They had
voted for moderate republicans before 1900 and for moderate Radicals
afterward. Sarraut's strong victory in 1914, after the right abandoned
Ferroul, was evidence of his popularity. By 1914 even Ginestas canton,
home of the *comité des gueux* and Marcellin Albert, had become Radical.

In 1910 the right also decided to back a revolutionary socialist to defeat Durand in Castelnaudary; for the first time in its history the royalist canton of Belpech gave a majority to the extreme socialist left, and Salles sur l'Hers nearly did so. Durand won, 42 percent to 35 percent, thanks to his Radical followers in Castelnaudary.

Radical forces emerged stronger from the wine crisis in Aude, in part because die-hard conservatism had been too weakened in the wine areas to bring enough strength to the extreme left, in part because republican evolution in Aude had only recently moved into the Radical phase and was not yet prepared to move beyond. The skill of Sarraut in political maneuvering between 1907 and 1910 must be taken into account. He had been in a most difficult position. He was undersecretary in the Interior Ministry when Clemenceau decided to use force in Narbonne. He immediately resigned, but there was already intense animosity toward him. Ferroul, Aldy, Bourrat, and Pelletan led the chorus of anti-Clemencist oratory, which was widely popular in Languedoc and Roussillon. During the heat of the crisis few vintners heeded the warnings of Pierre Massé and Sarraut that wine prices would not rise as a result of violence and of massive resignations by local officials.[18] They warned that conservatives and revolutionaries were using the crisis in an effort to destroy the parliamentary regime. Sarraut continued these arguments and in preparation for the election of 1910, added to them. The Republic, in his version—which was remarkably accurate—was the friend of wine and had been since the 1880s. It had passed stringent wine laws, and by 1909 prices had improved. Clemenceau was not a villain, he was a reconciler trying vainly to reason with Marcellin Albert and Ferroul. The latter was the villain: personally ambitious, he used the crisis for his own ends and then heartlessly dropped Marcellin Albert whose simple, good mind was not enlightened until his interview with Clemenceau in Paris.[19] After 1906 Sarraut led the attack on Bourratists and Pelletanists, as well as on the SFIO, the CGT, and CGV. In Aude and elsewhere, efforts were made to organize vintners in republican-oriented agricultural committees, with greater success in the Aude Valley than along the coast.

Conservative support for socialists was more effective in Hérault, largely because socialism had already, in 1902 and especially in 1906, made notable advances in organization and recruitment. The coastal cantons had early passed into the Radical phase of their evolution and the wine crisis of 1901 and the strike wave of 1903–4 were preparing the way for a new shift toward the extreme left.

The decision of many conservatives to rally to the socialist candidate, however, was undoubtedly a result of the law of separation. Prior to 1905, when the law passed, large numbers of them, in company with moderates, were thoroughly frightened by the strike wave of the previous year and also by the rise of revolutionary syndicalism. Radical candidates, in a wide sampling of wine communes, picked up 26 percent of their 1906 votes in moderate and conservative communes where strikes had broken out. This gain more than compensated for the socialists' gain of 15 percent in strike-bound Radical communes (see Appendix III). The law of separation had the effect of replacing some of this fear with a keen hatred of Radicals. But it was mainly the right-wing extremists who decided to vote for socialists in order to avenge themselves on the Radical party. Many moderate republicans, believing themselves more clever, decided to take over the party, to bore from within.

The Radical federation had already crumbled in Montpellier, for the same reason that it had in Marseille: it was taken over by moderate men who lost mass support without winning the conservative middle class.[20] Salis, in Montpellier III, was an astute politician; however, by 1910 he too lost much of his backing in Sète and became dependent on Frontignan. Sète, however, had more registered voters than Frontignan and Mèze cantons combined. Therefore the socialist mayor of Sète came out ahead in the first election and Salis retired. The race was extremely close and the socialist, without conservative backing, would have probably lost. Moreover, Salis was further weakened by the appearance of a dissident Radical who took away some of his votes. In the run-off, most of Salis's votes went to the dissident, save in Sète. Now the dissident was really a former *progressiste,* and the willingness of many Radicals to vote for him indicates that the old motto, "No enemies to the left," no longer held their allegiance. That the socialist won again in 1914 without conservative votes indicates that his power now rested more on the working classes of Sète and of the vineyards and on left-wing Radicals who abandoned their party.

Right-wing support of the socialist left was more in evidence in Béziers

II; however, here too socialism had made gains over a period of several years, especially along the coast. Radicalism, formerly paramount in the lowlands, had become increasingly dependent on the highland cantons of Bédarieux and Saint Gervais, as well as the middle cantons of Pezenas and Roujan: all in the Radical square save Saint Gervais. Since 1902 Augé was faced with serious opposition ; there were dissident Radicals backed by conservatives in 1902 and by the SFIO in 1906. The latter force steadily advanced in Pezenas and Florensac so that by 1910 Augé was heavily dependent for support on Roujan and Sainst Gervais; but since both had been losing population, his base had fritted away. When the right wing came to the aid of the SFIO in 1910, he was doomed. In both Montpellier III and Béziers II, the wine crisis which reached its peak in 1907 influenced politics; but it did not truly change the direction of but rather hastened the evolution of political changes already underway.

The situation in Béziers I resembled that of Montpellier III more than that of Béziers II. Lafferre's circumscription was a coastal one, with a sizable city, and fully devoted to wine production. The city of Béziers had really become the center of the Languedocian Radical movement since the swing toward the right of the first district of Montpellier and toward the extreme left of its second. Unlike Augé and Salis, Lafferre had certain advantages. He had prestige since his election as president of the executive committee of the Radical party in 1908. This meant that he had power in the Chamber.[21]   And he had used that power, in conjunction with Sarraut and Doumergue, to defend wine and to push the acceptance of anti-fraud legislation. On the other hand he had earlier supported Clemenceau during the postal strikes and was critical of the CGT. During the demonstrations of the summer of 1907 he had disapproved of violence and of Ferroul, but also of military force and of Clemenceau. Afterward he used his influence to obtain amnesties for Ferroul and other vintners accused of disorder. He was also active in organizing and guiding a Comité de Défense Viticole to limit the power of the CGV, to control the production of wine, and to encourage the formation of producer's and distributor's cooperatives.[22]   Equally important was Lafferre's influence in Freemasonry. He was a high official and Béziers had many Masons. According to the police reports already cited, he had a clientele of nearly a thousand persons both in the city and in rural communes.

Yet, Béziers had an affinity for Narbonne. Its citizens not only sympathized with the Narbonnais, they were infuriated at the treatment of southern soldiers who had mutinied in 1907. In 1910 its mayor, Henri Pech, ran as a dissident Radical, which seriously weakened Lafferre's standing in the city. Worse, all the clericals immediately rallied to Pech out of hatred for freemasonry. Many property owners, with dwellings in both Béziers I and II, now shifted their voter registration to the city in order to oppose Lafferre.[23]

His centers of strength, therefore, shifted to the communes east and south of the city where property was important. He relied heavily on smaller and medium vintners with five to thirty hectares of vines. These men had been active in the demonstrations; they were entirely dependent on wine sales and put all of their southern passions into the defense of wine and their way of life. They were relative newcomers to Radicalism. They had rallied to Lafferre in 1906, seeing in him a reasonable defender against striking workers and revolutionary syndicalism. In addition, Lafferre won the votes of numerous small owners and the large working class in Nissan and Agde communes. Agde was no longer the center of conservatism it had once been, and the conservatives there probably did not vote for the official Radical but for the dissident. In the first election, Lafferre had a lead of only 797 over the dissident and his majority of 424 in Agde made it possible for him to stand in the run-off with hope of success. Agde partly replaced Béziers, which he lost in the first election and which he won by only 166 votes in the run-off. Like nearly all southern Radicals, after 1900, he was highly dependent on rural communes for electoral strength. With their aid he achieved a better victory in 1914.

There is hardly need to enter into a detailed account of losses in other departments since the pattern was similar to that of Hérault. During 1910 in Gard the party socialist Compère-Morel won Uzès with the aid of the right; and in Arles, Sixte-Quenin of the same party defeated Michel, also with right-wing support, added to which were dissident Radicals. Quite different was the victory of the party socialist, Hubert Rouger, who replaced Doumergue in Nimes II. This was a case in which

Radicals turned to socialism for want of an attractive candidate from their own ranks. After the election of Doumergue to the Senate even the official Radicals had turned to a moderate socialist for the by-election, but Rouger won it as a native son and he won the legislative elections of 1910 and 1914 largely for the same reasons.

NEW GEOGRAPHY OF RADICALISM

A striking feature of the last years of Radicalism was its decline in coastal areas and its rise in the hills and mountains of Languedoc and Roussillon. In Pyrénées-Orientales it gained strongholds in the Val-lespir and in the Fenouillèdes while socialism made headway in Argelès and the Salanque just north of Perpignan. In Aude it expanded into the northwest corner, that is, the lower Lauragais and Cabardès, and held out in the Corbières. It expanded its following in the Minervois and had deep roots in Saint-Pons where an orthodox party member, Charles Caffort, in the highland cantons of La Salvetat and Olonzac, achieved an outstanding success by unseating Razimbaud the younger in 1914. It remained strong in the Lodevois despite the defeat of Pelisse in 1914 by a dissident. In Gard, a party member, Louis Mourier recovered Alès I in 1914. Other upland districts, Le Vigan and Uzès, were not recovered. In Provence, it was limited to the northern hilly country of Aix II.

Although once a coastal phenomenon, the Radical movement by 1910–14 held only "fortified points" in the plain: Perpignan II, canton of Sigean, Béziers I, and the third canton of Montpellier lying west of the city. In Provence, it was limited to the low hilly country of Marseille IV and to the city of Toulon.

From the above list it is evident that the movement had lost out in dense-ly populated areas and, in consequence, had become more representative of rural than of urban voters. This change was in line with the general evolution of the party in the rest of France. As the national party con-centrated its forces in the economically backward southwest, Roussillon and western Languedoc became its Mediterranean frontier. In most large towns and cities it ran a losing race, so that by 1910–14 it was fairly secure in only three: Perpignan (chiefly the eastern canton), Béziers which Lafferre recovered in 1914 and, further inland, Carcassonne. These were towns with a strong Radical tradition since mid-nineteenth century.

Toulon, also with a long Radical tradition, became socialist from 1898, but then, in 1910 and 1914, elected Abel, a moderate Radical who turned the tables on the socialists by winning conservative support against them. In Toulon, in Marseille, Nîmes, Montpellier, and Narbonne, there were Radical organizations, and Radicals published their most important party newspapers in these urban centers. But the party organizations became increasingly conservative, took up the epithet of "anticollectivist" in the hope of rallying moderate and conservative opinion in their struggle against dominant socialist forces, and put aside the old mystique of no enemies to the left. Of course the now dominant moderate Radical was perfectly prepared to side with the moderate or republican socialist. But the separation widened because the socialism that won out in the lower Midi, by 1910–14, was that of the SFIO which preached revolution and collectivism, albeit only in the interval between electoral campaigns.

The ideal of socialist reform became equally popular in smaller cities and medium-sized towns; Radicalism gave way to the extreme left in Sète, Arles, Aix, La Ciotat, Hyères, Brignoles, and Draguignan, and in the smaller towns of Lunel, Pezenas, Lodève, Rivesaltes, Collioure, and Banyuls. To be sure, Radicals did not lose out entirely in small municipalities. Along the coast they continued to receive majorites in Argelès, Port Vendres, Elne, and Thuir in Pyrénées-Orientales, Lézignan and Coursan in Aude, Agde, Mèze, and Frontignan in Hérault, and Martigues in Bouches-du-Rhône. These were important wine centers. Inland towns were Céret, Castelnaudary, Limoux, Saint-Pons, Aniane, Clermond l'Hérault, west of the Rhône and Salon, Aubagne, Tarascon, and Châteaurenard, east of the Rhône. In the last two named, Radicals were intensely divided and the dissidents voted for the SFIO to weaken the party.

These retentions not withstanding, Radicalism was doomed in the lower Midi precisely because it lost support in the coastal urban areas to which the population was moving. As Radicals settled into the uplands the more dynamic, forward-looking members of the population there were pulling out, and once settled in the coast they turned to socialism for the same reason their fathers and grandfathers had turned to Radicalism. Inevitably, then, the age of the average Radical voter went up and so did the age of the average Radicsl deputy in the deep South.

But, in the long run, even the age factor was not favorable to the Radicals, save in Aude. After World War I, older people, including older highland people, moved steadily toward socialism, and by the 1930s there were upland districts more red than those in the lowlands.

Before and after the war change continued. Along the coast where there were vineyards, where there were ports, and river mouths, new generations of agricultural workers and small owners, of stevedores, of coopers, artisans of all specialties adopted socialism to express their demands. A long psychological conditioning created a mentality of protest, of excitement against the government. The mass meetings and the riots of 1907 did not create this mentality, rather a whole way of life, in which wine was either a predominant or important factor, was behind it. Clerical support of the extreme left in 1910 did not initiate the left-wing orientation of this mentality; but it did hasten the next step toward socialism. Clericals gave their followers a taste of danger, with the result that voting for the left, even the extreme left, became habitual, even in former Catholic areas. By 1910 religion as a political issue, so important to Radicals, lost its former power: the Mediterranean coast had become highly dechristianized even before it became socialist. Henceforth red and white existed chiefly in wines; in politics most of the lower South became red or, more accurately, rosé.

The impulse to the left resulted, in part, from the movement of numerous workers away from Radicalism to the new extreme left. In areas near large towns, industrial workers led the way. Numerous artisans still served as cadre for reform movements as they had in 1848. Since the 1890s they were active in labor centers called Bourse du Travail where they picked up revolutionary or simply reformist ideas. In Montpellier, for example, numerous meetings were organized, and propagandists came to speak.[24]   Most of the prominent socialist leaders, from Jean Jaurès to Gustave Hervé, made lecture tours which were well attended. Their work was continued by socialist municipal councilors as they became more numerous after 1900. The young workers, the new generation, were increasingly attracted. After these meetings they sang the "Internationale" and danced the carmagnol, as their fathers and grandfathers had sung the "Marseillaise" and danced the farandole during the Radical period.

It was with indignation that Radical leaders, who had often been instrumental in founding the *Bourses,* began to complain that the labor leaders using them carried on propaganda for socialist candidates. Radicals, who continued to meet in cafes, insisted that the *Bourses* must remain neutral in politics. Their protest was in vain.

With the *Bourses*, trade unions began to appear. It is impossible to discover how many or how large they were.[25]   Outside of the larger towns they hardly existed and in some of the socialist centers, such as Draguignan, their membership was infinitesimal. In the rural districts of a department such as Var there was clearly no meaningful correlation between syndicalism and socialism or between social structure and socialism. The same can be written of agricultural laborers. There were few of them in Provence and these were hardly organized. In Languedoc, where socialism came later, both industrial and vineyard workers, the latter far more numerous than in Provence, tended to organize more extensively. The wave of strikes in the vineyards in 1904 encouraged the formation of unions among workers and worker-owners, but apparently most of them were shortlived. What evidence is available seems to indicate that numerous small farmers and vintners turned to socialism as an alternative to syndicalism, as in Var, or as a result of the inefficacy and brief existence of unions, as in Languedoc and Roussillon. Undoubtedly the formation of the CGV retarded unionism in some coastal areas, particularly so because some important socialist politicians used it to attack Radicals in Aude and Hérault and encouraged workers to join it during 1910–14. Particularly active were Ferroul in Narbonne, Barth in Béziers II, L. Molle in Montpellier III, Bénezech and his successor Camille Reboul in Montpellier II. Their tactics, carried out in conjunction with the extreme right represented by Pierre Leroy-Beaulieu and Rodez-Bénavent of an old noble family, were a complete electoral success.[26]   The vineyard workers, however, acquired neither class consciousness nor improved conditions as a result of it.

But the triumph of socialism has causes more profound than electoral tactics. The CGV and the CGT were institutions utilizing, creating, and channeling popular discontent; their success as instruments of political change resulted from the combination of traditional attitudes toward life and newer views on economic organization.

To understand the style of life of the lower Midi, one must consider several factors. The typical southern outlook was a combination of joyous hope in a better life to come and bitter frustration upon failing to realize it. The southerner's horizon was broad, stretching over vast vineyards green in their season and over the flat blue sea. There was a sense of contentment that lured the highlanders, eager to leave the confinement and stern ways of their ancestors. Wine production or commerce offered rich rewards and hope when prices were high, but they brought ruin and frustration when prices fell. There was doggedness in the southerner, and there was quick anger when nature thwarted his efforts. The instability characteristic of a monoculture raised men and it dashed them down. Easy social mobility was a promise; it could also be the opposite.

The social structure of wine regions was curious. Since the rebuilding of the 1880s it had assumed a misshapen form, sharply pointed at top, flattened at bottom. At the top peak were the old aristocracy of big owners and capitalist investors in vineyards, most of whom were of middle-class financial and professional origin. Toward the center were various groups of medium owners whose numbers were diminishing because their costs of production were too high in relation to income. There were numerous professional men here too, owners of vines who exercised their professions in a nearby town. Below them came a host of petty owners who were self-employed, and then came the owner-workers and full time native laborers skilled in handling vines. These latter did not form the true base of the diamond; below them in the flattened but still pointed base were the immigrants, chiefly Spaniards west of the Rhône, chiefly Italians east of it.

The *mévente* seriously upset the ranks of this structure, as had the phylloxera in the previous generation. Men who had rebuilt their vineyards and those who had been laboriously purchasing land and enjoying the upward mobility that came with land and high wine prices were now actually pushed down by loss of land or threatened with downgrading. The southern vintner as well as the cereal grower were accustomed to change, and for about three generations they had supported political groups favorable to change: at first moderate republicans, then Radicals, and finally socialists. Each shift to the left was made to obtain new advantages and, at the same time, new safeguards lest change become retrogression rather than progress. These two counter directions were widely judged in in terms of the availability of land ownership on the one hand; agricultural, especially wine prices, on the other. State intervention during the Radical period was useful, but it could not solve the problems of excess harvests and low prices. Moreover Radicalist intervention proved to be limited in usefulness. It coincided with the period of individualism among vintners, when they demanded state intervention to aid each individual or grower, when they ignored or resisted cooperative organization.

Socialism emerged in part because many voters sought to express their discontent, not with private property but with the individualistic system of wine production, indeed with the anarchy of production and distribution which encouraged fraud. From their extreme individualism, hordes of vintners became proponents of cooperative enterprise. There was practically no call for collective ownership of land, and no successful socialists demanded an end of small private holdings. More cleverly they identified themselves with the form of cooperation whereby each individual belonged to an enterprise that collected his grapes, made and marketed the wine, and provided him with a pro rata income. Radicals, of course, had always preached the benefits of cooperatives, but failed to emphasize their identification with or to implement coops. Rather, they emphasized an easy credit system to aid the individual producer. Southerners therefore looked to socialists as true cooperativists, and socialists were active in the cooperative movement.[27]

The Radical party's loss of identification with effective governmental intervention and a more collective economy was undoubtedly the result of the increasing conservatism of the party after 1906. It was difficult to convince left-wing voters that the party was still left wing. It now defended the Senate and had a hierarchy dominated by aging moderate politicians against whom the old Pelletan raged, in chorus with younger militants whose influence was limited to annual congresses where historic reform programs were drawn up, adopted, and then forgotten. Radical federations in the lower Midi, among the oldest in France, took the lead in turning the party toward the center. Most of the Radicals who survived their party's decline after 1906 were moderates: Malavialle, Albert Sarraut, Jean Durand, Jean Bonnail (Aude), Pezet, Lafferre,

Charles Caffort (Hérault), Louis Mourier (Gard), Frederic Chevillon (Bouches-du-Rhône), and Abel (Var). The heroic age of Radicalism had come to an end in France and in the Midi.

This decline was of course both absolute, as Table 28 reveals, and relative. It can be argued that the absolute decline was not catastrophic. From twenty-four seats in 1885—really an average of seventeen from 1876 to 1898—the Radicals fell to twelve in 1914, or 33 percent of all seats compared to the socialists' 53 percent.

TABLE 28 : PERCENTAGE OF RADICAL AND SOCIALIST DEPUTIES

	1902		1906		1910		1914	
	Rad.	Soc.	R	S	R	S	R	S
Lower South	50	33	50	36	42	42	33	53
France	33	8	48	12	43	17	40	22

An adequate response to this charge is that a 20 percent decline in relation to socialism is serious enough. Moreover, this percentage represented a 50 percent decline from their 1885 high, and a 17.3 percent decline from their pre-1900 average. The situation looks serious, indeed, if one observes that in 1906 the Radicals held 50 percent of the seats, in 1910 only 42 percent, and in 1914 only 33 percent, in 1924 still 33 percent, in 1928 up to 35 percent, in 1932 down to 16 percent, and in 1936 merely 27 percent.

But, in truth, these percentages reveal only a numerical decline, not marked change in the meaning of southern Radicalism. Nor, for that matter, do they indicate the meaning of southern socialism. To get at the meaning of the transition, it is useful to study the topographical pettern of Radical strength (see Table 29.) It is evident that the Radical party, once a coastal phenomenon, retreated or held out chiefly in the highlands, or in certain coastal districts where it retained the loyalty of numerous landowners, owner-workers, and the petty middle class in viticultural towns, that is, social types who clung to personal ties with their deputies and to their classic individualism. They saw in Radical success a defense against reaction and revolution. Radicalism, when all the old rhetoric was cleared away, represented moderation without the glorification of it.

TABLE 29: TOPOGRAPHY OF RADICAL PARTY, 1910–1914

	Highland 1910	1914	Coast and Highland 1910	1914	Coast 1910	1914
Department						
Pyrénées-Orientales			Céret Perpignan I	[Céret]c	Perpignan II	Perpignan II
Aude	Carcassonne I	Carcassonne			Narbonne II	Narbonne II
	Carcassonne II Castelnaudary Limoux	Castelnaudary Limoux				
Hérault	Lodève Saint-Pons	[Lodève]a Saint-Pons			Béziers I	Béziers I [Montpellier I]d
Gard	Le Vigan	[Alès I]b				
Bouches-du Rhône	Aix II	Aix II	Marseille IV	Marseille IV		
Var					Toulon I	Toulon I

a. Radicals remained strong and recovered after 1918
b. Radicals weak, lucky victory
c. Socialist deputy became a Radical
d. Radicals weak, lucky victory

Did this mean that voters for socialists were inclined toward revolution? That is highly doubtful. The rise of southern socialism presents the historian with the same problem of party identification that he encountered with southern Radicalism in its early phase. Trying to decide whether Mas, or Déandreis, Frederic Gaussorgues, Jamais, Peytral, and Chevillon were truly Radicals leaves a keen sense of inadequate terminology. Among their voters were numerous moderates, and the triumph of Radicalism was, in a certain sense, the triumph of moderation, quite early in practical politics, eventually in political ideology. Now when it is necessary to state that socialism won out in a given district because the successful candidate was a socialist, the historian experiences sometimes the same feeling of doubt about the validity of his statement. Some of the "independent" socialists were to the SFIO what "independent" Radicals were to the official party. One could validly argue that the triumph of these moderate socialists was, in reality, merely the continuation of the Radicalism of the heroic period. Therefore it can be asserted that, despite the percentages above, the Radical "phenomenon," if not the party, survived the party's decline. This assertion seems particularly valid for the circumscriptions of Céret, Montpellier III, Nîmes I, Aix I, and Brignoles.

Radicalism as a party, by 1910–14, was confined to the territory stretching from the Bitterois, through the Minervois, up the Aude Valley to Carcassonne and Castelnaudary, down to Limoux, through the Corbières and the southern part of the plain of Roussillon. Here it enjoyed both geographic cohesiveness and the domination of a block of territory. Elsewhere it held out only in isolated outposts: Aix, the northeastern sector of Marseille, and Toulon town (see Table 30). Radicalism had a solid minority of followers in the remainder of Lanquedoc

TABLE 30: CIRCUMSCRIPTIONS OF RADICAL VICTORY, 1914

(35 percent of Registered Voters or Equivalent)

Circumscription	% for Radicals	Observations
Perpignan II	37	
Narbonne II	41	
Carcassonne	44	Abstention 37%
Limoux	46	
Castelnaudary	47	
Saint-Pons	42	
Béziers I	36	
Aix II	38	
Marseille IV	43	Chevillon was an "independent" Radical
Toulon I	21	Equivalent over 35 percent of registered voters because abstention came to 48 percent.
Montpellier I	37	Lucky victory, Radicalism weak
Alès I	19	Lucky victory, Radicalism weak

and Roussillon, save in the upper reaches of Prades *arrondissement* where no candidate ran in 1914. In the remainder of Provence, the Radical party had practically ceased to function on the eve of World War I and even earlier in rural Var and the city of Marseille (see Table 31).

TABLE 31: CIRCUMSCRIPTIONS OF RADICAL STRENGTH, 1914

(20–35 percent of Registered Voters)

Circumscription	% for Radicals	Observations
Perpignan I	21	Strongest in highlands
Céret	20	Abstention 42 percent. Strongest in towns of Argelès, Céret, and Arles-sur-Tech.
Béziers II	27	Strongest in highlands
Lodève	36	Strong in Clermont and Gignac only
Montpellier II	24	Strong in city and Mauguio
Montpellier III	23	Strong in Mèze and Frontignan
Nîmes II	37	SFIO won in run-off
Le Vigan	25	Strongest in moderate and conservative cantons.
Uzès	29	Radicals strong in Bagnols and St. Chaptres
Arles	27	Abstention 40 percent. Radical dissident weakened the official candidate who was strongest in Tarascon, Arles, and Eyguières.

The transition to socialism was more complete east of the Rhône than west of it. In Provence, the mentality of urban workers and peasants tended to be left wing by tradition and followed a distinct path from republicanism to Radicalism to moderate socialism. West of the Rhône, there was a similar mentality, but it was slower to appear and uneven in its evolution to the left. A sharper quantitative decline of the Radical party came in the 1930s, after another major wine crisis resulting from overproduction and a general world depression. But by this time southern Radical-socialists, like most of their fellow members, were no longer part of the left; they were a center group, defenders of the status quo and, as the old saying goes, "neither radical nor socialist."

CONCLUSION

The demise of the Radical party as a significant political force in the Mediterranean South was the result of several factors. Uppermost was the wine crisis and the inability of cabinets dominated by Radicals to prevent and then end it. Of course, it is true that the appeal of the Radicals had begun a slight decline before the crisis but hardly at all in wine cantons. Unfortunately for them the crisis lasted too long, nearly eight years, and reached its peak in 1907 when the failures of party politicians seriously undermined their party's ability to win the mass of voters. West and east of the Rhône economic and social factors carried great weight. Wine production, both as a rural industry and as a marketable commodity, determined the standard of living of a majority of the working population in areas of Radical strength. The tragic drop of their income, the loss of land and status, drove many vintners to accept extremist views and also to accept new forms of economic organization and government intervention which seemed more compatible with socialist ideals than with those of the Radicals.

But economic conditions were as much the result as the cause of human motives. The two, economic factors and men's motivation, were contrapuntal. Excess production of wine, however much it was encouraged by nature, resulted from the decision of viticulturalists to specialize in wine. And their all-too-human reaction to the *mévente* was their conviction that the legislature should intervene to maintain wine prices at a profitable level. After 1903 they became equally convinced that Radical cabinets, particularly that of Clemenceau, were reluctant to help them and worse, were too friendly to northern sugar interests, the enemies of wine producers. Whatever doubts wine producers still entertained on this view were quickly dispelled by the violent events of 1907.

Economic conditions created tensions and prepared the way for change. Had the Radical ministers dealt effectively with the crisis they could have saved their party by dispelling the need or desire for violence. It was the failure of wisdom on the part of politicians and self-control on the part of winemen that provoked violence. A large number of voters later expressed their resentment and frustration by turning to the extreme left. Certainly a great many vintners assumed that there was a solution to the periodic crises which afflicted their industry. *Vignerons* were aggressive, nervous types in the otherwise rather lethargic agricultural population of 1907. They were among the first ruralists to seek organization on a massive scale and to bring pressure to bear on the Chamber of Deputies. They were, perhaps, the true forerunners of the "rural revolution," to use Gordon Wright's apt phrase.[28]

Given the long list of laws passed to aid them, they could also be called, as Charles Warner has put it, the "spoilt children" of the peasantry. Certainly their problems were manifold. Their legislative needs changed with market conditions and they strongly supported those politicians who promised them laws to meet these changing conditions. Radicalism rose to prominence on the waves of crisis and popular frustration because conservative and moderate republican government, most winemen believed, did not act to satisfy their needs. This was the situation in 1849–51, and after 1876. A notable exception was the *oïdium* crisis of the 1850s, but the local population was not free to express its political views under the authoritarian Second Empire. Now, after 1901, the Radicals were no longer in the advantageous position of being the opposition and therefore able to profit from the mistakes of the ruling party. They were the ruling party and their leaders made mistakes. They were also unlucky. They came to power when France was undergoing major transformations in economic development and social structure, when older political objectives having to do with forms of government were giving way to new problems involving the role of government in society. Probably their errors were similar to those of the opportunists and had more to do with their public image in the southern mind than their policies for solving the *mévente*. Whatever the case Clemenceau became the most hated man among wine producers and, in the popular mind, the head of the Radical party—which he was not.

Now for Clemenceau as for his predecessors, Emile Combes and Jean Sarrien, the wine crisis was merely one among others. Even before the crisis reached its acute stage cabinets had already confronted severe diplomatic crises as well as domestic ones involving church-state relations and social conflicts. Clemenceau, in particular, was unlucky. From an old defender of the working class he became, in many workers' eyes, their most hated enemy. He was partly responsible for this change, but so were events: the revolutionary intransigence of the CGT, an increase of strikes among workers, the end of the *Bloc*, the founding of the SFIO as a would-be revolutionary party no longer willing to work with the Radical party, and the strikes of postmen and some other government employees, who demanded the right to join the CGT.

Now all these inflamatory events and issues, to which can be added the equally inflamatory law on associations (1901) and the separation of church and state, injected national factors into the intense southern arena of politics. But none of these events had exercised a significant influence locally until the wine crisis of 1907, and to the caustic premier it was simply one more nuisance detracting from his efforts to get reform bills passed in the conservative Senate. Had another Radical, more attuned to the electoral needs of the party, been in office, southern deputies may have been more successful in getting the regulatory laws demanded by their constituents. But the premier was not a member of the party. And he was equally contemptuous of the SFIO. A "loner" since his defeat in 1893, he proved a bane to the Radicals of the Midi. However the historian may judge his policies, Clemenceau caused hordes of southerners to abandon their Radical affiliation and enough of them turned to socialists to weaken seriously the electoral position of the Radicals.

Was southern politics, then, merely a matter of economic interests? Did the humanistic ideals of the nineteeth-century left become mere verbiage behind which lay concealed purely material concerns? Charles Péguy used to state that everything began as ideals and ended as politics. In a sense he was right, at least as regards the lower South. The major political changes which took place there, when the voter was free to choose, followed predominantly economic crises. In the midst of such a volatile population, economic discontent was politicized with remarkable rapidity.

On the other hand, the changes that came after 1871 were not intellectually aimless. Rather they went in the direction pointed out by left wing ideals since 1789: greater political democracy, social and legal equality, and the brotherhood of all men—except sugar interests. All the detailed programs of left-wing candidates since the 1870s, indeed, since 1848, had these ideals in mind. They accorded with the aspirations, both economic and intellectual, of the mass of peasants, artisans, and petty middle class who dominated politics in the lower Midi, and in most of France. By the turn of the century the older watchwords, so dear to Radicals, were taken over by socialists and reinterpreted.

Freedom meant freedom from the crises which beset *vignerons* of all levels; equality meant more than easy access to landownership, it meant better methods to control production so as to avoid excess in a limited market, hence the desire for cooperatives. Similar to Radicalism in the 1880s, socialism in the 1900s brought an ideology which meshed with the economic needs of winemen, silk producers, truck gardeners, and woodsmen, as well as with those of workers in industry and commerce.

Just as important, socialist politics now attracted the more aggressive and younger local men, whose programs, mannerism, and vocabulary were more attractive to the left wing temperament of many southerners. This left wing inclination, which manifested itself earlier east of Aix than in Languedoc and Roussillon, would perhaps have favored the triumph of socialism even without the crisis of 1907. There were other areas of France which held promise for socialist expansion and given the leftward leaning of the deep South, it might have followed. In fact, much of Provence had become socialist before the crisis, and the explanation of this early evolution is partly a psychological one having to do with tradition and regional temperament as well as with problems of viticulture before 1907. The rapid turn of many Languedocian *vignerons* to socialism had both economic and psychological causes. That so many *vignerons* were quick to politicize their economic grievances was a mental trait characteristic of the Mediterranean voter as a political type. Once he turned leftward, the SFIO acquired one of its chief strongholds in the South.

The decline of the Radical party, then, resulted from the interplay of economic and psychological factors. Economic discontent aroused the desire for change, and this desire led voters to follow a new image of reform which accorded with their leftist propensity. This does not mean that a majority of southerners became collectivists. Workers in some of the larger cities undoubtedly became revolutionaries; but the mass of peasants, whatever party label they placed in the ballot box, remained attached to the fundamentals of the old Radical movement. The Radical party died; the Radical phenomenon lived on.

Whether the persistence of the Radical phenomenon under another name was a benefit for the lower South is a matter of debate. A majority of voters there deliberately turned away from the ruling party in order to elect deputies with less influence in the Chamber, with practically none in the Senate, and with no likelihood of entering a ministry because of the SFIO's self-denying ordinance which forbade party deputies from sitting in any nonsocialist government. But this was a decision comparable to that made in the 1880s when southerners elected a majority of Radicals most of whom were outside of official circles. But inside or outside, the representatives of wine interests, whatever their political coloring, were remarkably successful in getting laws favorable to the economic interests of their voters.

The Radical party was more adversely affected by the change than the southern voters, for the party lost its major left wing and progressive constituency. The lower South, as regards its ideology, and its willingness to innovate, was a dynamic area of France. For two political generations it had infused the national Radical group with a sense of movement and with a keen notion of technological, organizational, and social change. Its wine economy combined large-scale production and an artisanal, almost domestic, system.

Large-scale producers carried out technological improvement; small wine makers were saved from stagnation by new forms of production. The expansion of agricultural cooperatives among small producers brought another forward step in economic organization, a thrust ahead along the road of modernization. The party, however, reflected its loss of their support. From a reforming, progressive movement it rapidly became the hardheaded defender of traditionalist-minded economic and social types, that is, voters who resisted or were indifferent to innovation. As the party found its majorities in the stagnant southwest, and as it lost its former labor support and relied more heavily on the small-town middle class fearful of modernization, it naturally changed its character. Even where it retained its hold in the lower Midi, its voters were traditionally moderate and attached to the status quo. What the party lost was a balance between retarded and active constituencies, for other dynamic areas followed the same path leftward as the Mediterranean South. There remained, of course, a left wing in the party, but only a few of its members came from the Midi after World War I. On the contrary, Radicals in Aude, which remained their stronghold, and those in the other circumscriptions they retained, were among the more conservative members of the party. Gone were the days when the party could respond to the fiery radical oratory of a Camille Pelletan, a Victor Leydet, a Frederic Desmons, a Jacques Salis or a Justin Augé. The only prewar leader of the left who lived into the postwar decades, Gaston Doumergue, became a moderate. In this he summed up the later history of Radicalism.

NOTES

1. On politics see A.D. Gard, 2M 292, 298.
2. *Radical des Cévennes*, 12 April 1902.
3. For the Vassal group see *Radical de Marseille* March-April 1902; A.D. B-du-R, 2M 3-53 a-b, police and administrative reports, March-April 1902.
4. For the campaign see A.D. B-du-R, 2M 3-53a-b, 53g, reports of subprefect for March 1902.
5. *La Bataille* [Aix], 6 April 1902.
6. Pelletan in *Le National* [Aix], March-April 1902. *Le Franc-parleur* [Paris], 26 April 1902.
7. *Petit provencal*, 10 May 1902.
8. *Cri du Var* [Toulon], 25 April, 4 May, 1906.
9. *Ibid.*, 15 April 1906
10. See *Radical du Midi*, April-May 1902; A.D. Aude 2M 71.
11. *Bataille républicaine* [Carcassonne], 26 February 1910.
12. *Radical du Midi*, 15 January, 2 June, 3 July 1905.
13. A.D. Aude 5M 66, report of 22 September 1906.
14. *Ibid.*
15. *Ibid*, reports of 24 September and 26 November 1906.
16. See *Le Réveil de l'Aude*, 18 April 1906.
17. See *Justice sociale* [Narbonne], 27 April 1910; *Radical-Socialiste* [Narbonne], 1 May 1910.
18. *Radical du Midi*, May-November 1907.
19. *Ibid.*, May and Sept. 1909; *Radical-Socialiste*, 13 May 1909. See 25 March 1909 for adverse criticism of Pelletan. *Bataille républicaine* [Carcassonne], 1909 *passim* for reorientation of Radicalism away from the extreme left and toward the left center. This was Sauzède's journal.
20. See police reports in A.D. Hérault, 15M 55, 60; *Petit méridional*, April-May 1910.
21. A.D. Hérault, 15M 60, subprefect report, 13 November 1909.
22. *Petit méridional*, 18 July 1907; 22 April 1910.
23. A.D. Hérault, 15M 55, various reports.
24. See police reports in A.D. Hérault, 39M 283.
25. France. Direction du Travail. *Annuaire des syndicats* (Paris) 1889–1914. This publication lists only the *syndicats ouvriers* organized in compliance with the 1884 trade union law. There were certainly unions which did not comply with it and yet met in the *Bourses*.

26. For socialists and the CGV see *L'Eclair,* 17 April 1914. Programs of the socialists were based on wine interests, not much different from old Radical programs; see A.D. Hérault, 15M 65.

27. Before 1914 there were merely 27 wine-making cooperatives, the first dating from 1901, in lower Languedoc and Roussillon; 180 were founded between 1919 and 1929, and 229 between 1930 and 1939, during a serious *mévente*. See G. Galtier, *Le Vignoble du Languedoc méditerranéen et du Roussillon* (Montpellier, 1960), I, 341–49. Socialism and cooperatives, then, tended to grow up together west of the Rhône especially after 1906. East of the Rhône the situation was similar. In Bouches-du-Rhône, outside of Marseille, producers' cooperatives and socialism were slow to develop; in Var, on the other hand, both took root shortly after 1900 in wine-producing communes. See *B-du-R, encyclo. dépar'le,* X, 507–9, and C. Silvestre, *Annuaire de l'agriculture et des associations agricoles* (Paris, 1903–14).

28. G. Wright, *Rural Revolution in France* (Stanford, 1964).

APPENDICES

One can make a good case for the statement that Radical victory in Hérault resulted more from demographic than social structure; that is, that population size was more decisive than the labor vote. The following frequency table offers some support for this view, but clearly, the Radicals carried most of the large communes which had a sizable labor force (those in italics).

Communes grouped by population	*Communes grouped by type*								
	Patronal		*Mixed Patronal*		*Mixed*		*Mixed Worker*		*Worker*	
	R	C	R	C	R	C	R	C	R	C
0 – 499	25	45	7	20	7	12	2	8	3	7
500 – 999	18	16	4	8	11	12	5	7	2	5
1000 – 1499	5	3	2	1	6	6				
1500 – 2000			4		5⎫10	1⎫4	2⎫9	3⎫4	2⎫7	1⎫2
2000 and over	1	2	1	4	5⎭	3⎭	7⎭	1⎭	5⎭	1⎭

The worker communes won by conservatives were small, often isolated and therefore, more easily dominated by a handful of notables and priests.

APPENDIX II

DEPARTMENT OF HERAULT. SOCIAL STRUCTURE BY ARRONDISSLMENTS. 1890–91

Agriculture

Arrondissement	Professional Group	Employers (Chefs) by ages			Workers by ages		
		6–20	20–60	60+	6–20	20–60	60+
Montpellier	Proprietors	87	4611	1695	1167	6196	1279
	Tenants, Share Croppers	44	555	104	200	1229	202
	Truck Gardeners	4	220	71	86	256	41
	Woodsmen		220	51	34	97	21
Béziers	Idem.	351	7886	1308	2315	7916	1415
		13	431	250	12	1514	372
		22	1203	346	191	2138	424
		27	298	96	25	311	195
Lodève	Idem.	124	2653	1027	957	1626	446
			421	109	113	525	147
			negligible				
Saint-Pons	Idem.	53	1805	850	895	1525	580
		7	1150	432	203	1130	242
			negligible				
Department	Idem.	615	16955	4880	5334	17261	3720
		64	2557	905	528	4338	963
		26	1475	420	284	2422	475
		28	549	151	63	412	235

APPENDIX III

PERCENTAGE($\pm$) CHANGE FROM 1902 to 1906 (N=281)

Political Majority based on 1902 election	Radical change	Socialist change	Republican change
Radical communes with strikes	–11	15	– 2
Radical communes without strikes	– .3	7	.7
Socialist communes with strikes	– 2	– 9	9
Socialist communes without strikes	2	7	– 7
Republican communes with strikes	– 5	14	–12
Republican communes without strikes	8	6	–11
Conservative communes with strikes	26	6	7
Conservative communes without strikes	16	7	17

Note. Excluded from these calculations are 35 communes with strikes in the circumscriptions of Carcassonne II and Narbonne II, both predominantly Radical areas. I do not have their communal electoral returns for 1906. No socialist ran in Carcassonne II, and the socialist pitted against Sarraut in Narbonne II won only 603 votes. Clearly the strike movement in the Aude Valley did not change the political balance there.

APPENDIX IV

AUDE: DIVISION OF VINEYARDS BY ARRONDISSEMENTS (1912)

	Number of viticulters				Areas Planted				Output			
	Carcassonne	Castelnaudary	Limoux	Narbonne	Carcassonne Hectares	Castelnaudary Hectares	Limoux Hectares	Narbonne Hectares	Carcassonne Hectolitres	Castelnaudary Hectolitres	Limoux Hectolitres	Narbonne Hectolitres
less than 1 hectare	4,045	2,864	4,727	4,252	2,122	1,279	1,617	2,429	100,833	37,062	48,921	131,727
1 to 5 hectares	5,389	372	2,768	5,631	12,709	607	5,663	12,673	606,577	20,421	230,581	659,767
5 to 10 "	994	36	292	1,344	6,726	234	2,047	9,097	386,424	8,316	103,855	523,047
10 to 20 "	451	28	127	714	6,136	398	1,597	9,579	362,810	12,859	86,295	535,541
20 to 30 "	146	10	32	255	3,572	233	753	5,952	190,263	8,554	37,961	368,738
30 to 40 "	73		12	101	2,480		399	3,441	147,216		20,275	221,750
40 to 50 "	51	2	9	70	2,248	87	394	3,175	123,789	4,125	19,860	198,661
50 to 60 "	33	1	5	35	1,780	50	217	1,910	119,830	4,400	14,900	123,210
60 to 70 "	20			24	1,242			1,548	69,455			102,140
70 to 80 "	14		1	25	1,014	70	75	1,850	51,430	7,500	5,200	126,925
80 to 100 "	19			27	1,667			2,395	100,923			156,195
over 100 "	15			23	2,572			4,593	138,611			293,989
Total	11,250	3,314	5,973	12,510	43,698	2,658	12,762	58,642	2,398,161	101,237	567,848	3,441,690

Source: Barbut, *Vignoble de l'Aude*, 1912, 65.

APPENDIX V

Circumscription	*Deputies adhering to party, 1901*
Ceret	Jules Pams
[Perpignan II]	Jean Bourrat
Limoux	Eugene Dujardin-Beaumetz
Castelnaudary	Louis Saba
[Béziers I]	Louis Lafferre
Béziers II	Justin Augé
[Montpellier II]	Jacques Salis
Saint-Pons	J. A. Razimbaud
Nîmes II	Gaston Doumergue
Arles	Henri Michel
Aix II	Camille Pelletan
[Marseilles IV]	Joseph Chevillon
Brignoles	Charles Rousse
[Toulon II]	Louis Martin

Circumscription	*Deputies vague about party in 1901*
Carcassonne	Edouard Théron (later joined)
Narbonne II	Paul Narbonne (did not run in 1902)
Lodève	Paul Vigné d'Octon (later joined, and expelled)

(Urban or chiefly urban circumscriptions are in brackets.)

APPENDIX VI

POPULATION OF COASTAL CANTONS, 1846–1911

CHIEFLY VITICULTURAL, WITHOUT A LARGE CITY.

Population peaks are in bold type.

Arrondissement	Canton	1846	1876	1881	1886	1891	1896	1901	1906	1911	% increase or decrease 1846–1911
Céret	Argelès	14,964	17,810	20,213	20,663	**21,051**	20,548	20,256	20,169	20,370	+36
Perpignan	Rivesaltes	17,712	25,318	**28,092**	27,025	25,489	24,861	24,675	24,107	23,582	+33
Narbonne	Sigean	11,109	15,018	**17,926**	17,377	16,121	15,366	15,149	14,091	12,521	+12
	Coursan	9,339	11,465	13,418	14,565	**15,153**	14,248	14,185	13,519	12,907	+38
Béziers	Agde	16,599	16,872	16,980	17,247	17,148	17,789	**19,629**	18,102	18,997	+14
	Florensac	6,507	**7,462**	6,641	6,557	7,022	6,892	7,162	7,062	7,130	+9
Montpellier	Mèze	13,770	**17,493**	14,534	14,418	15,898	16,129	16,627	16,321	15,457	+12
	Frontignan	4,725	6,940	6,192	6,860	7,296	8,075	9,252	9,496	**10,028**	+112
	Mauguio	4,677	**5,042**	4,263	4,755	5,338	5,843	6,170	6,099	6,002	+28
	Lunel	13,833	**15,701**	13,559	13,520	14,162	14,853	15,578	15,381	15,458	+11
Nîmes	Aiguesmortes	5,691	5,843	6,357	6,863	7,148	7,224	**8,100**	7,449	7,227	+26
	St-Gilles	7,762	**8,509**	7,082	7,351	7,930	8,055	8,461	8,412	8,292	+6
Arles	Stes-Marie	669	**926**	910	1,159	1,025	1,446	**1,531**	1,439	1,413	+111
Toulon	Ollioules	**18,125**	8,722	8,325	8,635	8,729	8,837	9,419	9,615	9,974	–44
	Le Beausset	**10,786**	10,007	8,258	7,893	7,833	8,167	8,360	8,137	8,240	–23
	Hyères	10,116	15,034	16,740	16,532	18,010	22,382	25,714	25,928	29,084	+187
Draguignan	Saint-Tropez	5,332	5,387	5,529	5,838	5,562	5,684	6,178	6,256	6,489	+21
	Grimaud	7,727	**8,191**	8,065	7,978	7,297	7,091	7,112	7,348	7,454	–3
	Fréjus	9,929	11,918	12,569	13,762	13,985	14,719	16,333	16,501	16,788	+69

APPENDIX VII

RADICAL LISTS OF 1885 ELECTIONS

Pyrénées-Orientales

Edouard Vilar	Radical
Charles Floquet	moderate Radical
Emile Brousse	Radical

Aude

Camille Pelletan	Radical-Socialst
Emile Wickersheimer	" "
Eugène Ferroul	Socialist
Fernand Digeon	"
Ferdinand Théron	moderate Radical

Hérault

Jacques Salis	Radical-Socialist
Emile Vernhès	" "
Michel Vernière	Radical
A. J. Razinbaud	"
Paul Ménard-Dorian	"
Auguste Galtier	Moderate Radical
Elisée Déandreis	" "

Gard

Frédéric Desmon	Radical-Socialist
Fernand Crémieux	" "
Emile Penchinat	" "
Alfred Madier de Montjau	" "
Edouard Gaussorgues	" "
Numa Gilly	" "

Bouches-du-Rhône

C. Pelletan	Radical-Socialist
Victor Leydet	" "
Clovis Hugues	" "
Félix Granet	Radical
Joseph Chevillon	"
Paul Peytral	Republican
J. B. Pally	"
Antide Boyer	Laborite

Var

G. Clemenceau	Radical-Socialist
C. Raspail	" "
Honoré Daumas	" "
Auguste Maurel	" "

APPENDIX VIII*

RESISTERS IN DECEMBER 1851, BY TOTALS, AGES, AND MARITAL STATUS

Department	Total of arrested	Percentage of national total	Ages						Marital Status	
			−20	21–30	31–40	41–50	51–60	60+	Married	Single
Pyrénées Orientales	692	2.6	21	184	272	151	50	14	495	197
Aude	251	.9	3	49	136	46	16	1	133	121
Hérault	2840	10.6	152	1020	955	523	162	28	1707	1133
Gard	380	1.4	8	134	131	75	27	5	255	125
Bouches du Rhône	777	2.9	23	243	339	152	42	5	379	391
Var	3147	11.7	155	1157	970	554	222	49	2015	1132
Regional Tota	8087	33	362	2787	2803	1501	519	102	4984	3099

*A.N. BB[30] 424, "Statistiques de l'insurrection de 1851." The totals in this dossier do not always accord with those in departmental archives. In the latter there are some individual files which lack necessary data so I have used the A.N. global data for the above table. These figures do not always add up to the exact totals given, but come close enough for our purposes.

APPENDIX VIII cont.

RESISTERS IN DECEMBER 1851, BY PROFESSIONS

Department	Professional and Rentiers	Textile workers	Artisans	"Ouvriers" or "journaliers"*	"Cultivateurs"
Pyrénées-Orientales	150	11	163	221	147
Aude	68	2	145	5	29
Hérault	367	280	1557	55	955
Gard	133	3	139	13	92
Bouches-du-Rhône	221		379	56	121
Var	261		1539	113	1228
	1200	296	3922	463	2572

* This column is of doubtful value. Many "journaliers' were listed as "cultivateurs."

APPENDIX IX

RADICAL STRENGTH AND WINE PRODUCTION, 1881–1898

Type of cantons	N.	Radical Domination %	Radical Strength %
Primary Income from wine	42	47	38
Secondary income from wine	32	34	41
Supplementary income from wine	24	.4	4.5
No significant income from wine	72	.4	2

BIBLIOGRAPHY

UNPUBLISHED ARCHIVAL SOURCES:
ARCHIVES NATIONALES PARIS

The information in this book was derived largely from departmental archives; however, numerous documents in the Archives Nationales made it possible to supplement local sources, and, occasionally, to verify them. Only the most important are listed here.

BB^{18} series, Ministère de Justice, "Rapports politiques."

BB^{18} 1443B, 1468, 1469-70, 1471-73, 1474A, 1474B, 1786, 1789, 1790, 1795. For the period of the Second Republic and Second Empire.

BB^{30} series, *ibid.*, "Rapports des procureurs-généraux". BB^{30} 370, dr. 8167a, cour d'Aix, 1849-68. Includes Bouches-du-Rhône and Var.

BB^{30} 389, 390, 391, 392a, 394, cours d'Aix, Nîmes, and Montpellier, 1868-1870.

C series, "L'Enquête du Comité du Travail de l'Assemblée Constituante, 1848, sur le travail agricole et industriel."

C 946-947, 953, 954, and 967. None for Pyrénées-Orientales.

C 3021, "L'Enquête parlementaire de 1872-76 sur la condition des ouvriers en France," région du Sud-Est.

C 3337-3338, 3345-3346, 3349, 3370, "Enquête sur la situation des ouvriers...en France, 1881-85." Unfortunately, numerous reports do not give the name of the commune and are useless for a detailed study in the 1880s.

F^{1}CIII series, "Rapports des préfects au Ministre de l'Intérieur, esprit public et élections," 1848-1870.

F^{1}CIII Aude 4^1 and 8, B-du-R 4 and 12-13, Gard 5, and 13-14, Hérault 4, and 14-15, P-O 3 and 8, Var 4 and 12.

F^7 series, "Police générale."

F^7 12681 to 12684, "Dépêches relatives au Seize-Mai 1877."

F^7 12710 to 12713, "Evénements de 1848 à 1851."

F^7 12773 to 12792, "Grèves."

F^7 12794, "Crise viticole dans le Midi, 1907-8." Highly useful.

F^{10} series, "Agriculture."

F^{10} 1610 to 1622, "Phylloxera."

AD XIX C43^3, "Enquête agricole départementale, 1866."

F^{11} series, same.

F^{11} 2697-2722, "Enquêtes agricoles décennales."

Chiefly for 1862 and 1882.

F^{12} series, "Commerce et industrie."

F¹² 4479–4550. "Situation industrielle des départements." Trimester reports, but incomplete. Comes to 1885-88. Useful were F¹² 4476A, 4476C, 4476F, 4530, 4543.

F¹⁸ series, "Imprimerie et librairie."

F¹⁸ 431 to 514, deals with departmental press, 1811 to 1881. See F¹⁸ 439 (Aude), 441A-E (B-du-R), 457A-B (Gard), 461A-D (Hérault), 492 (P-O), 507A-B (Var).

F¹⁸ 526 to 534, list of journals, 1872–1889, which sent two copies of each number to the prefecture, as required by law (dépôt légale).

F¹⁹ series, "Culte."

F¹⁹ 10031², "Culte Réformé. Statistiques sur la population Protestante, XIXe siècle." Very useful.

F¹⁹ 10031², "Cartes de la France et de l'Algérie Protestantes."

F²⁰ series, "Statistique."

For demography, sources in departmental archives are richer.

UNPUBLISHED ARCHIVAL SOURCES: DEPARTMENTS
PYRENEES-ORIENTALES

2M 1 series, "Elections législatives." Returns, often by commune, usually by canton. The election series in all the departmental archives also contain police and prefectural reports of varying quality, programs of some candidates, and official evaluations of each candidate, not all of which are accurate or impartial.

3M 1–81 to 89, "Condamnés politiques," For 1851 resistance to coup d'état.

3M 1–163 to 176, "Rapports mensuels des préfets et sous-préfets concernant la situation politique, administrative et économique." The quality of these reports varies considerably; most of them are useful but often repetitive.

None of the economic and demographic dossiers have yet been classified.

They are available, however, upon demand.

AUDE

2M series, "Elections législative." Some serious gaps, which must be compensated by returns in the press.

5M series, "Police général." Comparable to 3M 1 series of P-O.

11M, "Population." Huge losses. Particularly useful is 11M 35–36, Modèle

10, "Population classée par profession," 1886, and 11M 38–39, Modèle

11, same, 1891.

13M, "Agriculture." Most useful was 13M 306–307, which provides data on all important crops, by commune, for 1890, and 308–309 for 1892. 312 to 326 covers years 1905 to 1913. 13M 86 covers the viticole crisis, 1900–1906

HERAULT

12M series, "Plebiscites-referendums."

15M series, "Elections législatives," nearly complete returns.

39M series, "Rapports politiques," of prefects, subprefects, police and the military. Extremely valuable.

41M series, "Rapports de police." Chiefly 41M 95 to 147, cartons with some information on anarchists, Dreyfus case, and various political meetings.

114M series, "Dénombrements." In the process of classification. The censuses of 1851, 1876, and 1886 are particularly useful since they classify the population by profession at the communal or cantonal level.

None of the economic materials have been classified as of 1968; however, there is an abundance of data for agriculture and industry which can be consulted, as well as reports on strike activity.

GARD

In all the following series there are disastrous losses, especially in 2M and 10M and 13M.

2M series, "Elections législatives." Greatest losses are for mid-nineteenth century.

6M series, "Police et administration." Reports on local affairs, chiefly political. There is some useful data on the press.

10M series, "Population." Especially 10M 138 for 1851, and 10M 279 for 1886, the last census available listing professions of the population by commune.

12M series, "Statistique agricole." Removed from the 13M series. Especially useful is 12M 407, for 1910.

13M series, "Agriculture." Disappointing because of losses.

14M series, "Industrie et commerce." 14M 310, for 1883 is an industrial census by communes. 14M 444 to 454 has an abundance of material on strikes, chiefly in the coal basin.

15M series, "Rapports." Miscellaneous, ranging from information on anarchists and strikes to statistical data on agriculture and commerce for 1894–5 (15M 122 and 123).

15M 129 deals with Boulangism, and 130 with royalist propaganda in 1898–1901.

3U 5 to 13. Papers of the justice and legal administration. Important for resistance to the coup d'état of 1851.

4U 5–25. Of lesser importance.

BOUCHES-DU-RHONE

2M 1 series, "Plebiscites."

2M 3 series, "Elections législatives." Lacks several elections, notably those of 1848, 1849, 1881, and 1898 for Aix and Arles.

6M series, "Police et administration." A particularly rich series.

Combined with the numerous reports in the 2M series, the researcher will find highly detailed information on political forces and their activities.

10M 1 series, "Population." Rather thin as regards population classed by profession. Chiefly 10M 1–24 for 1851 and 10M 1–70 for 1881.

13M series, "Agriculture." Rather disappointing. Useful was 13M 153, "Statistique agricole décennal de 1892," which has detailed data on crops and on landholding, by communes. But it is not complete.

Similar is 248 for 1901 and 249 for 1902.

14M series, "Industrie." Also disappointing.

4U series, "Délits de presse." Numerous gaps.

12U series, "Rapports politiques addressés par le parquet au bureau général."

See 12U–1 for 1848 and 12U–2 for 1849. Monthly reports. Covers Var also.

17U 5 to 13, "Affaires de presse." For 1869 to 1879. Var included.

VAR

2M 1 series, "Plebiscites."

2M 3 series, "Elections législatives." Nearly complete, even or 1849.

4M series, "Police politique." Contains reports dealing often with public opinion, secret societies (during the Second Republic), and political activities of a subversive nature. Especially 4M 19 to 21 for resistance to the coup d'état of 1851. 4M 56 covers strikes.

11M 2 series, "Population." Especially 11M 2–7 for 1886, population classed by professions, and 11M 2–9 for 1891, same.

14M series, "Agriculture."

The 14M 4 series covered agricultural associations;

14M 7 series deals with agricultural cooperatives, 1900–1936;

14M 19 covers agricultural statistics;

14M 29 is useful for viticulture.

16M series, "Industrie." Rather slim, save for 1887 to 1894 period.

4J 78, electoral flyers and programs.

10T series, "Presse." Especially 10T 3–3 and 4, 1869 to 1914. In Var, as in other departments, archival sources on newspapers are skimpy.

3Z 2–5, legislative elections in Toulon *arrondissement*.

3Z 4–3, police reports regarding Toulon.

PRINTED STUDIES COVERING ALL OR PARTS OF THE LOWER MIDI

There are two periodicals, *Annales du Midi* specializing in the south-west and *Provence historique* in the south-east. Neither devotes much space to the post-1789 period, but both contain useful bibliographies. An important source of information is Michel Augé-Laribé, ed. *Répertoire bibliographique d'économie rurale* (Paysan du Midi, 1953.) When the place of publication is Paris, it is not listed.

Many of the works listed below have bibliographies, in addition to pertinent information:

Augé-Laribé, M. *Le Problème agraire du socialisme. La viticulture industrielle du Midi de la France.* V. Giard and E. Brière, 1907.

Avenel, Henri. *Comment vote la France. Dix-huit ans de suffrage universel, 1876–1893.* Librairies-Imprimeries Réunies, 1894.

Baudrillart, Henri. *Les Populations agricoles de la France.* Hachette, 1885–93. 3 vols.

Bouillon, Jacques. "Les Démocrates-socialistes aux élections de 1849," *Revue française de science politique,* 6 (1956), 70–95.

Bousquet, Raoul. *Histoire de Provence des origines à la Révolution française.* Monaco: Editions de l'Imprimerie Nationale, 1954.

Carrère, P. and R. Dugrand. *La Région méditerranéenne.* Presses Universitaires de France, 1960.

Caupert, Maurice. *Essai sur la C.G.V. Ses origines, son organisation, son oeuvre.* Montpellier: Imprimerie de "l'Economiste méridional," 1921.

Conférence interdépartementale sur la mévente des vins. Montpellier: Ricard frères, 1894.

Dugrand, Raymond. *La Garrigue montpelliéraine.* P.U.F., 1964.

———. *Villes et campagnes en bas-Languedoc.* P.U.F., 1963.

Dugrully, Paul. *Essai historique et économique sur la production et le marché des vins en France.* V. Giard and E. Brière, 1910.

Durliat, Marcel. *Histoire du Roussillon.* "Que sais-je?" no. 1020. P.U.F., 1962.

Fohlen, Claude. "En Languedoc. Vigne contre draperie," *Annales, économies, sociétés, civilisations,* 4 (1949), 290–97.

Galtier, Gaston. *Le Vignoble du Languedoc méditerranéen et du Roussillon.* Montpellier: Causse, Graille and Castelnau, 1960. 3 vols.

Genieys, Pierre. *La Crise viticole méridionale.* Toulouse: E. Privat, 1905.

France. Centre Régional de la Productivité et des Etudes Régionales. *Tableau démographique et économique du Languedoc-Roussillon.* Montpellier: Centre Régional de la Productivité ..., 1958.

France. Institut National d'Etudes Démographique. *Région Languedoc-Roussilon, économie et population.* "Travaux et documents," cahier no. 30. P.U.F., 1957.

Gide, Charles, "Bouilleurs de cru et viticulteurs," *La Revue politique et parlementaire,* (Aug. 1906), 227–46.

———. "La Crise du vin dans le Midi de la France," *Revue d'économie politique,* 21 (1907), 481–512.

Kayser, Jacques. *Les Grandes batailles du Radicalisme.* Marcel Rivière, 1962.

Le Blond, Maurice. *La Crise du Midi, étude historique.* Charpentier, 1907.

Le Roy Ladurie, Emmanuel. *Histoire du Languedoc* "Que sais-je?" no. 958. P.U.F., 1962.

Lorbert, A. *La France.* I: *La Provence, le Bas-Languedoc, le Roussillon, la Corse. Histoire et information politique ... économique.* Pierre Roger, 1928.

Marrès, P. *La Vigne et le vin en France.* A. Colin, 1950.

Muller, F. "L'Evolution du paysage rural languedocien," Etude de diplôme supérieur, University of Montpellier, 1952.

Nicolet, Claude, *Le Radicalisme* "Que sais-je?" no. 761. P.U.F., 1957.

Pressac, Pierre de. *Les Forces historiques de la France. La tradition dans l'orientation politique des provinces.* Hachette, 1928.

Sion, J. *La France méditerranéenne.* A. Colin, 1934.

Sorre, Max. "La Répartition des populations dans le bas-Languedoc," *Bulletin de la société languedocienne de géographie,* 29 (1906). 105–36, 237–78, 364–87.

Tenot, Eugene. *La Province en décembre* 1851. *Etude historique sur le coup d'état.* Le Chevalier, 1868.

Warner, Charles. *The Winegrowers of France and the Government since* 1875. New York: Columbia University Press, 1960.

Wolff, Philippe, ed. *Histoire du Languedoc.* Toulouse: Ed. Privat, 1967.

POLITICAL STUDIES, BY DEPARTMENT
PYRENEES-ORIENTALES

Vidal, Pierre and Joseph Calmette, eds. *Bibliographie Roussillonnaise.* Perpignan: C. Latrore, 1906.

Alart, M. Bernard. *Géographie historique des Pyrénées-Orientales.* Perpignan: J.-B. Alzine, 1859.

Brousse, Jean-Francois. "Trois siècles de presse Roussillonnaise," unpublished *Mémoire,* Institut Français de Presse, Université de Paris, 1963.

Carbonell, C.–O. "Les Députés des Pyrénées-Orientales de 1815 à 1870," *CERCA,* Nos. 13–14, (1961), 330–35, 356–57.

Chauvet, Horace. *Histoire du parti républicain dans les Pyrénées-Orientales de 1830 à 1877.* Perpignan: Imprimerie de l'*Indépendant,* 1909.

———. *La Politique Roussillonnaise de 1870 à nos jours.* Perpignan: Imprimerie de l'*Indépendant,* 1934.

Escanyé, F. "Le 4 septembre 1870 à Perpignan," *La Veu del Canigo,* September 5,1911.

Maudet, Félicien. *La Révolution de 1848 dans le département des Pyrénées-Orientales.* Perpignan: Imprimerie de l'*Indépendant,* 1929.

Robin, Marcel. "Contribution à l'histoire de la Révolution de 1848 dans les Pyrénées-Orientales," *Bulletin de la Société Agricole, Scientifique et Littéraire des Pyrénées-Orientales,* 51 (1910), 417–39.

AUDE

Carbonel, Paul. *Histoire de Narbonne.* Narbonne: P. Caillard [1956].

Feraud, Henri. *Histoire de la commune de Narbonne,* 1871. Châteauroux: Editions du 'Bazouka,' [1946].

Gastilleur, Victor. *Omer Sarraut. L'Homme, la vie, l'oeuvre.* Carcassonne: G. Servière, 1905.

Jeanjean, J.–F. *Armand Barbès,* 1809–70. Cornély, 1909.

———. *Le coup d'état du 2 décembre 1851 dans le département de l'Aude.* F. Rieder, 1924.

———. *Proclamation de la troisième République dans le département de l'Aude.* Carcassonne: Gabelle, 1920.

Raynier, Pierre. *Biographie des réprésentants du département de l'Aude de 1789 à 1900.* Toulouse: Passeman and Alquier, n.d.

HERAULT

Allaire, Roger. *Histoire de la ville de Bédarieux.* Bédarieux: Métry, 1911.

Appolis, Emile. "Un Démocrate social sous la seconde République, Marcel Atger," *Actes du 87e Congrès National des Sociétés Savantes.* 1962. "Section d'histoire moderne," pp. 363–75. Imprimerie Nationale, 1963.

———. "Les Catholiques sociaux dans l'Hérault sous la seconde République," *Actes du 85e Congrès National des Sociétés Savantes,* 1960. "Section d'histoire moderne," pp. 291–306. Imprimerie Nationale, 1961.

———. *Manuel des études Héraultaises.* Valence: Imprimeries Réunies, 1943.

———. "La Résistance au coup d'état du 2 décembre 1851 dans l'Hérault," *Actes du 77e Congrès National des Sociétés Savantes,* 1952 "Section d'histoire moderne," pp. 487–504. Imprimerie National, 1952.

Billange, A. *Mon village depuis 150 ans, Aiguesvives.* Service d'Etudes et de Documentation, Ministère de l'Agriculture, 1948.

Brieu, J. *Histoire du département de l'Hérault depuis les temps les plus reculés jusqu'a nos jours.* Lodève: A. Brieu, 1861.

Les Candidats à la députation nationale pour le département de l'Hérault. Montpellier: Gelly, [1848].

Clavier, Henri. "Le *Reveil d'une communauté protestante dans un village* [Pignan] du bas-Languedoc au début du XIXe siècles," *Actes du 86e Congrès National des Sociétés Savantes,* 1961, "Section d'histoire moderne," pp. 63–71. Imprimerie Nationale, 1962.

Gervais, Etienne. "La Révolution du 4 septembre [1870] à Montpellier," *Bulletin de l'Académie des Sciences et Lettres de Montpellier,* No. 60 (1930), 117–24.

Moulin, A.-E. *Un Républicain martyr, Casimir Peret; le coup d'état à Béziers, la déportation, la mort.* Montpellier: Cause, Graille, Castelnau, 1937.

Picheire, J. *Histoire d'Agde.* Lyon: Bissuel, [1906].

Premier Conseil de Guerre de la 10e Division Militaire. *Affaire de Bédarieux.* Montpellier: Malavialle and Grollier, 1852.

Puech, Louis. "Elections de 1851 et de 1852 dans l'Hérault," chapter II in *Essai sur la candidature officielle en France depuis* 1851. Mende: Chaptal, 1922.

Thomas, Louis. *Montpellier, ville inconnue.* Montpellier: A. Dubois, 1930.

———. *Montpellier en 1851. Le coup d'état du 2 décembre.* Montpellier: Imprimerie de la Charité, 1933.

Tudesq, A.-J. "L'Election du Président de la République en 1848 dans l'Hérault," *Annales du Midi,* 67 (1955), 331–42.

Vidal, André. *Histoire d'Agde.* Agde: J. Cros, 1938.

Diplômes d'Etudes Supérieures, University of Montpellier:

Arzalier, François. "Trois ans de journalisme d'opposition dans l'Hérault, 1869–71. Jules Guesde à Montpellier," 1962.

Bousquet, Alice. "1907, crise viticole dans l'Hérault, exploitation politique," 1958.

Chapal, François. "Opinion publique et les élections législatives de 1869 dans l'arrondissement de Montpellier," 1958.

Lignon, Mlle. "Comment l'Hérault est devenu républicain," 1959.

Martin, H. "Coup d'état dans l'Hérault, 1851," n.d.

Minet, André. "La Bourgeoisie Montpelliéraine et le second Empire," 1963.

GARD

Béraud, Abbé Pierre. *Histoire de la ville de Bagnols-sur-Cèze.* Nîmes: Maison Carrée, 1939.

Bruyère, Chanoine Marcel. *Alès, capitale des Cévennes.* Nîmes: H. Mauger, 1948.

Clement, Pierre. *Le Salavès, étude monographique du canton de Sauve (Gard).* Anduze: Languedoc Editions, [1953].

Gard. *Dictionnaire biographique et album.* E. Flammarion [1905?].

Goirand, J., ed. *Documents pour servir a l'histoire du département du Gard contre le coup d'état du 2 décembre* [1851]. Alès: Imprimerie de l'*Union républicaine,* 1883.

Gorlier, Pierre. *Le Vigan à travers les siècles.* Montpellier: La Licorne [1955].

Latzarus, Bernard. "Une Idylle électorale ou les élections à la constituante dans le Gard en 1848," *Nouvelle revue du Midi,* 2 (January 1925), 455–69.

Léonard, Emile G. *Un Village d'opiniâtres. Les Protestants d'Aubais (Gard), ...* 1685–1838. Musée du Désert, 1938.

Lompret [no first name given]. *Le Gard, son histoire.* Montpellier: La Licorne, 1956.

Nicolas, Abbé C. *Histoire de Génolhac.* Nîmes: F. Chastenier, 1896.

Pieyre, Adolphe. *Histoire de la ville de Nîmes depuis* 1830. Nîmes: Catelan, 1886–87. 3 vols.

Verne, Maurice. *Le Président Doumergue*. Berger-Levrault, 1925.

Mémoires de l'Académie de Nîmes:

Cabanès, Gustave. "Contribution à l'histoire économique de la ville de Nîmes," 48 (1928–30), 61–81.

Coste, Gustave. "L'Etat de l'agriculture dans le département du Gard vers 1835," 44 (1924–25).

Gallon, G. "Le Mouvement de la population dans le département du Gard ... 1821–1920," 48 (1928–30), 81–117.

Guérin, P. "Des Types de familles dans une commune rurale du Midi," 36 (1913), 63–75.

———. "Etude sur la population d'une commune rural," 37 (1914–15), 117–30.

BOUCHES-DU-RHONE

Aubray, Maxime and Sylla Michelesi. *Histoire des événements de Marseille du 4 septembre 1870 au 4 avril 1871.* Marseille: Samat, 1872.

Bellot, Etienne. *Marseille politique.* Marseille: Moullo, 1899.

Busquet, Raoul. *Histoire de Marseille.* R. Laffont, [1945].

Christofferson, Thomas R. "The Revolution of 1848 in Marseille," Ph.D. thesis, Tulane University, 1968.

Cours d'Assises de la Drôme. *Procès des accusés de juin* [1848] *de Marseille.* Marseille: Carnaud, 1849. 2 vols.

Dubosc, P. *Quatre mois de république à Marseille, 24 février - 24 juin* [*1848*]. Marseille: Sèves, 1848.

Linden, Jacques van der. *Alphonse Esquiros.* Nizet, 1948.

Marseille sous le second Empire. Plon, 1961.

Masson, Paul, ed. *Les Bouches-du-Rhône; encyclopédie départementale.* Marseille: Archives Départementales, 1913–1929. Vol. V for political history.

Naquet, Gustave. *Révélations sur l'état de siège à Marseille.* Bibliothèque Républicaine, 1875.

Olivesi, Antoine. *La Commune de 1871 à Marseille et ses origines.* Marcel Rivière, 1950.

———. "La Droite à Marseille en 1914; aspects de la géographie électorale...," *Provence historique,* 7 (1957), 175–99.

———. "Marseille," in *Les Elections de 1869,* ed. by Louis Girard. Marcel Rivière, 1960, pp. 77–123.

Ponteil, F. "Un Rapport de police sur l'état des esprits à Marseille, après les troubles de juin 1848," *Revue d'histoire moderne* 5 (1930), 412–18.

Revillon, Tony. *Camille Pelletan, 1846–1915.* Marcel Rivière, 1930.

Royannez, Adolphe. "*La Voix du peuple*" *et la démocratie marseillaise.* Marseille: Samat, 1868.

Tavernier, Felix, ed. *Marseille et la Provence, 1789–1851.* Marseille: Bibliothèque Municipale, n.d.

Diplômes d'Etudes Supérieures, University of Aix-Marseille:

Aune, Lucien. "Le Parti républicain à Marseille," 1963.

Combet, M. "Gambetta et Marseille," 1958.

Decanis, Suzanne. "Esprit public à Aix-en-Provence de 1830 à 1848," 1934.

Feraud, Eliane. "La Bourgeoisie Aixoise de 1830 à 1870," 1957.

France, R. "Esprit public de 1863 à 1870 dans les B-du-R d'après les rapports des pro-cureurs généraux et impériaux," n.d.

Pradeilles, René. "Bédarride et la Révolution de 1848 à Aix," 1951.

Rosaz, Marie-Jose. "La Presse républicaine à Marseille de 1870 à 1879," n.d.

Villiard, C. "L'Evolution politique dans les B-du-R à la fin du XIXe siècle: les théories et l'évolution des partis," 1948.

VAR

Alleaume, Charles. *La Terreur blanche dans le Var.* Draguignan: Olivier-Joulian, 1947.

Aulm, J.-J. *Le Conseil général du Var, étude historique.* Draguignan, 1877.

Blache, Noël. *Histoire de l'insurrection de Décembre 1851, Var.* A. Le Chevalier, 1869.

Campan, André. "Les Réfugiés politiques provençaux dans le Comté de Nice après le coup d'état du 2 décembre 1851," *Provence historique,* 7 (1957), 60–75.

Conseil-Général du Département du Var. *Procès-verbaux des déliberations,* 1838–89. 51 vols.

Dupont, Charles. *Les Républicains et les monarchistes dans le Var en décembre 1851.* G. Baillière, 1883.

Fournier, Victor. *Le coup d'état de 1851 dans le Var.* Draguignan: Olivier-Joulian, 1928.

Goirand, Yvonne. "Histoire politique et économique du Var de 1848 à 1870," *DES,* Aix-Marseille, 1955.

Letrait, J.-J. *Les Clubs démocratiques dans le Var, 1848–49.* Draguignan: Olivier-Joulian, 1950.

———. "La Presse dans le Var sous la monarchie parlementaire, 1815–48," *Provence historique,* 7 (1957), 286–93.

Parti Socialiste, SFIO. *Historique et vie de la Fédération du Var.* Toulon: Imprimerie du Sud-Est, 1936.

ECONOMIC AND SOCIAL STUDIES, BY DEPARTMENT

PYRENEES-ORIENTALES

Annuaire statistique et historique des Pyrénées-Orientales. Perpignan: Alzine, 1834–. Annual

Martimort, Jacques. "Rivesaltes, étude économique et urbaine." *DES,* University of Montpellier, 1964.

Rives, L. *L'Economie agricole des Pyrénées-Orientales.* Toulouse: Imprimerie du Sud-Ouest, 1942.

Roquette-Buisson, Comte. *Statistique de la propriété communale dans la zone montagneuse de l'Aude et des Pyrénées-Orientales.* Nancy: Berger-Levrault, 1909.

Vigo, André. *L'Evolution économique récente des Pyrénées-Orientales.* Montpellier: Imprimerie de la Presse, 1936.

AUDE

Annuaire statistique et administratif de l'Aude. Carcassonne, 1841–.

France. Ministère de l'Agriculture. *Agriculture française par MM. les Inspecteurs de l'Agriculture.... Département de l'Aude.* Imprimerie Royale, 1847.

Barbut, G. *Enquête sur la production du vin dans l'Aude en 1898.* Carcassonne: Gabelle, Bonnafous, n.d.

————. *Etude sur le vignoble de l'Aude et sa production, récolte de* 1912. Carcassonne: Pierre Polère, 1912.

————. *Historique de la culture des céréales dans l'Aude de* 1785 à 1900. Carcassonne: Gabelle, 1900.

Cros-Mayrevieille, Gabriel. "L'Evolution économique de Narbonne," *Bulletin de la Commission Archéologique de Narbonne,*17 (1926–27), 102–59.

Delmas, J. *Géographie de l'Aude.* Marseille: Arnaud, Cayer, 1867.

Khanzadian, Z. *Atlas de géographie économique du département de l'Aude.* Armenienne, 1928.

Pariset, F. *Economie rural, industrie, moeurs et usages de la Montagne Noire (Aude et Tarn).* J. Tremblay, 1882.

————. *Economie rurale, moeurs et usages du Lauragais (Aude et Haute-Garonne).* Bouchard and Huzard, 1867.

Passama, Paul. *La Condition des ouvriers viticoles dans le Minervois.* Giard and Brière, 1906.

Pellegrin, V. *Les Grandes étapes de l'agriculture dans l'Aude.* Carcassonne: Gabelle, 1937.

Plandé, Romain. *Géographie et histoire du département de l'Aude.* n.p.: Editions de la Nouvelle France, 1942.

Rivals, Jules. *L'Agriculture dans le département de l'Aude,* 1899–1900. H. Poirre, 1901.

Sentou, J. "Les Facteurs de la révolution agricole dans le Narbonnais," *Revue géographique des Pyrénées et du Sud-Ouest,* 18–19 (1947–48), 89–104.

HERAULT

Annuaire du département de l'Hérault. Montpellier: Ricard, Castel, Firmin et Cabiron, 1818–.

Appolis, Emile. *Lodève, étude de géographie urbaine.* Nîmes: Larguier, 1936.

Bertrand, René. "L'Evolution économique et sociale d'une commune viticole de l'Hérault (Adissan)." Law thesis, University of Montpellier, 1950.

Blanchard, Marcel. *Les Voies ferrées de l'Hérault…*1834–75. Montpellier: La Charité, 1922.

Callon, G. *Le Mouvement de la population dans le département de l'Hérault…*1821–1920. n.p.: Imprimerie Toulousaine, 1935.

Cazalet, Jean L. *Cette et son commerce des vins de* 1666 à 1920. Montpellier: Firmin et Montane, 1920.

Cholvy, Gérard. *Géographie religieuse de l'Hérault contemporain.* Presses Universitaires de France, 1968.

Combarnous, G. "Le Dévelopement topographique de Clermont l'Hérault," *Annales du Midi,* 72 (1960), 257–71.

Creuzé de Lasser, Hippolyte. *Statistique du département de l'Hérault.* Montpellier: A. Ricard, 1824.

Daruty, A. *Notice sur Cette.* Montpellier: Gelly, 1845.

Domenge-Dusfours, Y. "Contribution à l'étude de l'évolution démographique du département de l'Hérault," *DES,* University of Montpellier, 1958.

Joanne, Adolphe. *Géographie du département de l'Hérault.* 8th ed. Hachette, 1905.

Manuel, Frank. "Introduction des machines en France et les ouvriers: la grève des tisserands de Lodève," *Revue d'histoire moderne,* 4 (1935), 209–25, 352–72.

Marès, H. *Rapport sur l'état des vignobles de l'Hérault dans les années* 1885–1887. Montpellier: Imprimerie Centrale du Midi, 1888.

Marres, Paul. *L'Economie rurale d'une communauté méditerranéenne: Aniane.* Montpellier: Dehan, 1962.

――――. "L'Evolution de la viticulure dans le Bas-Languedoc," *Bulletin de la Société Languedocienne de Géographie,* 2nd ser., 4 (1935), 26–58.

Poulon, Auguste. *Etude sur le travail à domicile dans la bonneterie de sois des Cévennes (régions du Vigan et de Ganges).* Montpellier: Imprimerie de la Co-opérative Ouvrière, 1909.

Puaux, Yolaine. "Prolétariat et syndicalisme agricoles en Hérault, 1900–1940," *DES,* University of Montpellier, 1966.

Rigaud, J. "Etude économique et démographique du canton d'Agde" Law thesis, University of Montpellier, 1952.

Saintpierre, Camille. *L'Industrie dans le département de l'Hérault.* Montpellier: Gras, 1865.

Secondy, L. "Pignan au XIXe siècle," *DES,* Montpellier, 1964.

Teisserenc, Fulcran. *L'Industrie lainière dans l'Hérault.* A. Rousseau, 1908.

Tudez, M. *Le Développement de la vigne dans la région de Montpellier du XVIIe siècle à nos jours.* Montpellier: Imprimerie de la Presse, 1934.

Viala, L. *Le Vignoble de l'Hérault en 1900.* Montpellier: Imprimerie Serre et Roumégon, 1900.

GARD

Annuaire du département du Gard. Nîmes: Bell, 1810–.

Chabaud, Alfred. *Les Documents et la méthode pour l'étude de la structure et de l'économie agraire dans la France du Sud. Exemple de l'Uzège [Uzès] et du pays de Bagnols-sur-Cèze.* Uzès: H. Peladan, 1967. 2 vols.

Chauzit, M.B. "Monographie agricole du département du Gard," *Bulletin du Ministère de l'Agriculture* 7 (1898), 1529–89.

Dextremx de St. Christol, Leonce. *Agriculture méridionale, le Gard et l'Ardèche.* Maison Rustique, 1867.

Fraisse, R. "Historique de la sériciculture et de la filature dans la région d'Alès," *Revue du ver à soie,* 2 (1949), 46–75.

Joanne, Adolphe. *Géographie du département du Gard.* Hachette, 1896.

Laurent de l'Arbousset, A. *Les Grèves du bassin d'Alès et les collectivistes révolutionnaires.* Dentu, 1882.

――――. *Les Cévennes séricicoles.* Lyon: Moniteur des Soies, 1875.

Lombard, Henri. *Monoculture de la vigne et évolution rurale dans la vallée de la Cèze.* Montpellier: Causse, Graille, and Castelnau, 1951.

Malinowski, Jacques. *Essai historique sur l'origine et le développement progressif de l'exploitation du charbon de terre dans le bassin houillier du Gard.* 2nd ed. F. Lavy, 1869.

Perrot, Michelle. "Archives policiers et militants ouvriers sous la troisième République; un example, le Gard," *Revue d'histoire économique et sociale,* 37 (1959), 219–39.

Pin, Henri. *Les Mines de houille dans le Gard. La condition du mineur.* Montpellier; Imprimerie Générale du Midi, 1914.

Reboul, Henri. *L'Industrie nîmoise du tissage au XIXe siècle.* Montpellier: Firmin and Montane, 1914.

Rivoire, Hector, *Statistique du département du Gard.* Nîmes: Ballivet and Fabre, 1842. 2 vols.

Roussy, Michel. "Evolution démographique et économique des populations du Gard." Law thesis, Montpellier, 1949.

Tessier du Cros, Charles. *La Production de la soie dans les Cévennes.* Giard and Brière, 1903.

BOUCHES-DU-RHONE

Bousquet, Casimir and Tony Sapet. *Etudes sur la navigation, le commerce et l'industrie de Marseille,* ... 1850–54, Marseille: Camoin et Dutertre, 1857.

Chauvin, Fernaud, *Trets, Bouches-du-Rhône, et sa région.* Vaison: Macabet, 1958.

George, Pierre. *La Région du Bas-Rhône; étude de géographie régionale.* J.–B. Baillière, 1935.

Guiral, P. "Quelques notes sur la politique des milieux d'affaires marseillais de 1815 à 1870," *Provence historique,* 7 (1957), 155–74.

———. and L. Pierrein, *Les Bouches-du-Rhône, histoire et géographie du département.* Grenoble: Bordas, 1945.

———. Le Cas d'un grand port de commerce, Marseille," in *Aspects de la crise et de la dépression de l'économie française au milieu du dix-neuvième siècle,* ed. E. Labrousse. La Roche-sur-Yonne: Imprimerie centrale de l'Ouest, 1956, pp. 200–25.

Livet, R. "Quelques origines de l'habitat rural dispersé en Provence," *Annales, économies, sociétés, civilisations,* 9 (1954), 101–7.

Masson, P. ed. *Les Bouches-du-Rhône, encyclopédie départementale.* Marseille: Archives Départementales des B-du-R, 1913–1929. Volumes 6–10.

Vigouroux, Jean. *Essai sur le fonctionnement économique de quelques très grandes exploitations viticoles dans la Camargue et le bas-Languedoc.* Montpellier: Imprimerie Générale du Midi, 1906.

VAR

Agulhon, Maurice. *La République au village.* Plon, 1970.

———. *Une Ville ouvrières au temps du socialisme utopique.* Toulon de 1815 à 1851. Mouton, 1970.

Annuaire du Var [title varies]. Draguignan, 1851.–

Aubin, J.J. *Var. Dénombrement quinquinnaux de la population de 1856 à 1881. Etude statistique.* Draguignan: Latil, 1883.

Bernès, J. and S. Bernel. *Le Var agricole.* Draguignan: Négro, 1923.

Constant, E. "Les Conflits sociaux dans le département du Var sous le second Empire," *Actes du 83e Congrès National des Sociétés Savantes,* 1958. "Section d'histoire moderne," pp. 553–62. Imprimerie National, 1959.

Joanne, Adolphe. *Géographie du département du Var.* Hachette, 1894.

Noyon, [C.] N. *Statistique du département du Var.* Draguignan: H. Bernard, 1846.

Teissier, Octave. *Statistique du Var et résumés généraux de la statistique de l'Empire.* Draguignan: P. Garcin, 1855.

INDEX

256